THE ACTOR'S WAY

Erik Exe Christoffersen

Translated by
Richard Fowler

London and New York

First published 1993
by Routledge
11 New Fetter Lane, London EC4P 4EE

Simultaneously published in the USA and Canada
by Routledge
29 West 35th Street, New York, NY 10001

Routledge is an imprint of the Taylor & Francis Group

© 1989 Forlaget KLIM
Translation © 1993 Richard Fowler (translation of 'Training and
performance in relation to *Judith*', pp. 144–57, by Gordi Roberts)

Transferred to digital printing 2003

British Library Cataloguing in Publication Data
Christoffersen, Erik Exe
Actor's Way
I. Title II. Fowler, Richard
792

Library of Congress Cataloging in Publication Data
Christoffersen, Erik Exe.
[Skuespillerens vandring. English]
The actor's way / Erik Exe Christoffersen.
p.   cm.
Includes index
1. Odin teatret. 2. Experimental theater — Denmark.
I. Title. II. Series.
PN2746.H62029513 1993
792'.09489 — dc20 92-21086

ISBN 0-415-08795-3
0-415-08796-1 (pbk)

Printed and bound by Antony Rowe Ltd, Eastbourne

THE ACTOR'S WAY

In *The Actor's Way* four actors talk about the secrets and practical realities of over twenty-five years of theatre training with Odin Teatret. Under the unique direction of Eugenio Barba, director of Odin Teatret, they have explored issues such as the connections between physical and mental work on stage, how to gain and control the spectator's attention, and inter-cultural performance techniques.

In an interview with Erik Exe Christoffersen they provide the fullest account yet of Odin Teatret's ground-breaking combination of European and Asian Theatre which has put these actors at the forefront of a genuinely new kind of performance.

The Actor's Way is a fascinating account of personal and professional development in the threatre. It will be vital reading for drama students and actors, but enjoyable and illuminating for anyone interested in the craft of acting.

Erik Exe Christoffersen is Associate Professor at the Department of Dramaturgy, University of Aarhus and director of Theatre Akadenwa. He has worked closely with Eugenio Barba and the Odin Teatret for a number of years.

CONTENTS

ILLUSTRATIONS

ILLUSTRATIONS

PREFACE

Two men pass one another at an interval of about a hundred years. In 1864, Henrik Ibsen travelled from Norway to Italy. A hundred years later, Eugenio Barba made the same journey, but in the opposite direction. Separated by time and space, both men went into a kind of voluntary exile. Both were concerned with the individual who, in order to find himself, seeks out the foreign and the unknown. The two men are otherwise dissimilar.

To be a stranger in a foreign land, to travel out into the unknown, can be something one does out of desire or out of necessity.

Henrik Ibsen wrote *A Doll's House* in 1879, in his self-chosen exile in Italy. There, in the summer's burning heat, under the high blue sky, he wrote about the home in a Norwegian town which, in the dark wintertime just after Christmas, burst into flames and burnt to the ground. The difference between the two places is part of what creates the dramatic tension in Ibsen's drama. The distance is necessary for Ibsen's understanding of why Nora had to leave, why she had to give up her husband and children. She recognizes that they are strangers to her. In order to learn to know herself, she herself had to become a stranger.

Eugenio Barba travelled the opposite way. From Italy he went to Norway and later to Denmark. The central element in his artistic production is the individual who, like Nora, leaves home and becomes a stranger. In the same way, Odin Teatret has kept itself apart in a kind of self-chosen exile which is both geographical and mental. This situation, this 'not-belonging', demands a maximum presence. The actor must treat each and every performance as a last chance to speak. As a testament, says Barba in 'Letter to Actor D' (Barba, 1986a: 22), a parallel to Ibsen's perception of his authorship as a total Day of Judgement of himself.

A long series of authors, dramatists and actors have also 'betrayed' their original homelands to seek, just like Nora, their own identity in the unknown. It is paradoxical that it becomes necessary for some people to leave their homelands and choose an existence as strangers in order to find themselves, to be true to themselves having transformed their foreignness into artistic strength.

The same was true of another traveller, Marco Polo (1254–1324), when, after seventeen years as Kublai Khan's emissary, he had to describe the cities he had visited: unfamiliar as he was with the language, he expressed himself with signs, movements, props. The spectators had to decode the signs, and never knew if they expressed an experience or something he was told. Whatever they were, the signs had the power to become a part of the spectators' memory.

Marco Polo was the first European to explore East Asia. He travelled for twenty-five years.

Odin Teatret's dramaturgy is a break with psychological and social realism. It is not a form of dramaturgy which aims to organize reality according to clear polarities, meanings, or thematic oppositions. Its main characteristic is the very detailed study of extreme states of energy which are neither psychologically nor emotionally motivated but which contain their own contrasts. Barba works with montage technique, discontinuous jumps in action and thought, breaks between action and impulse. It is not a question of a linear, progressive time model or of a cause-and-effect logic, and therefore psychology and plot are no longer the dramatic foundation. The actors are not limited by their characters' psychological recognizability. They can jump between various characters and between various times and actions. They are not restricted by the immediate reality which they represent but can establish their own legitimacy. Many different actions can be executed together or against each other in a performance architecture which gives the spectators the opportunity to interpret the reality in which they find themselves and thereby become co-creators of the theatre.

The point of departure is not a completed dramatic text but the actor's ability to form his or her presence for the spectator in space and time. This presence is interwoven with textual material, a theme and the montage of stories and associations, and results in a 'performance text' which creates meaningful relationships in a simultaneous context.

When Marco Polo returned home to Italy and told of his experiences, he was called 'The Million', because everything he told was believed to be unreal: in a prison in Genoa he wrote his 'tall stories'.

THE PAST IS DANCING

Most of the theatre groups established in the 1960s are long gone. Many died, others split and broke up. Experience shows that these groups very often do not keep together for more than ten years. There is one exception in a small town in Denmark. For twenty-seven years Odin Teatret has worked in Holstebro with the same core of people. This is quite an event within theatrical history.

For twenty-eight years I have travelled with Odin Teatret in the world of theatre. To far-off countries and remote places, to cities, capitals and large towns. Where and when this journey will end I do not know, but I know that it started from a precise point, as does every adventure.

The adventure begins with a child who was lucky enough to know deep sorrow. At the age of 9 he lost his father. It was a fundamental experience for him to be present and to see the slow death of someone close to him, in the course of one night. This is an experience which every child should have: to be at the death of a loved one. I discovered what it meant to miss someone, to lose something essential. But at the same time I was liberated from a censor that restricted my freedom.

(From an interview with Eugenio Barba,
On the Way through Theatre, video, 1992)

Odin Teatret was established in 1964 in Oslo. The next year it moved to Holstebro after an invitation from the local government, which placed premises and an amount of money at the group's disposal. At that time, the European theatre was in the midst of an upheaval.

The ordinary and established theatres consisted of buildings where actors were employed and directed so that they could perform and fill a repertory of dramas. From the late 1950s to the early 1960s Grotowski's Theatre Laboratory in Poland and the Living Theater in the USA changed this conception of the theatre. They created theatre where the spectators and the actors actually met each other. Anytime and anywhere.

The theatre became a way of establishing social terms between the members of a group and in relation to spectators. This conception was adopted and developed by Odin Teatret. As Barba puts it, they were continuously pursuing new possibilities of creating these social relations: by means of the architecture of a performance (placing the spectators in a special way), or through a change from performing in closed rooms to being out in streets and squares where the situation is completely different. Or by performing in places where theatre is not usually performed. Finally, through work with a principle called *barter*, in which the perspective is beyond the actual theatrical situation and rather in the social consequence of the meeting of two different cultures.

Odin Teatret has at the present (1991) several productions which underline its plurality. There is *Talabot* (1988–91) based on the biography of a Danish anthropologist, Kirsten Hastrup, on meetings with other cultures and confrontations with history and the figures of the past who become visible to the living.

There is the street performance *Rooms in the Emperor's Palace* with previous Odin figures, like 'the demon', 'Death walking on stilts', 'the dwarf', 'the drummer in white', 'the polar bear', all recurring from earlier street performances, and now constant, classic Odin figures that are being developed over the years.

There are the solo performances *Judith* (Roberta Carreri) about the female figure from the Bible who cuts off the head of Holofernes, and *Traces in the Snow*, an artistic autobiography by Roberta Carreri, where the secrets behind the performance are shown.

Wait for the Dawn (Richard Fowler) is based on *The Stranger*, a novel by Camus; *The Castle of Holstebro* (Julia Varley) is about Death telling stories, a young woman herself confronting this figure, and other figures from previous Odin performances; and *The Echo of Silence* (Julia Varley) is about the actress's voice and the secrets behind the process of creation with text-subtext and score-subscore.

Memoria (Else Marie Laukvik and Frans Winther, a musician) is based on two Jewish stories about people who survived the hell of the concentration camps by virtue of their beliefs and strength of will. But it is also about the pain of having to hold on to the memories of the past as something better than just senseless and incoherent fragments.

Finally, *Itsi-Bitsi* (Iben Nagel Rasmussen, Jan Ferslev and Kai Bredholt), a very personal performance based on Iben Nagel's professional biography as an actress, is related to her meeting with the Danish rock musician Eik Skalø, in the 1960s, about their travels together and their relationship to music and drugs up to his unexplained death in 1969 in India.

All these 'small' performances reflect a trend in Odin Teatret. The material is mainly produced by the actors themselves as a result of training and previous performances. Thus the basis of *Itsi-Bitsi* is Iben Nagel's previous working demonstration to which is added a dramaturgical context. The professional biography in terms of former characters from different performances is revived and begins to speak and act in relation to the story of her life with Eik Skalø. The theatrical characters become a language: words, movements, sounds, gestures, a personal language which permits a dialogue with the past.

The past is dancing. This proves that the theatrical characters have been created from actions which are part of the actors' languages, which are not limited by a certain context and by a certain performance. And this language, which is part of the actor's reality, often acquires a new and unexpected meaning in a new dramaturgical context, and this meaning disconnects it from a biographical origin.

THE ACTOR'S WAY

Odin Teatret is also an educational institution which shares its techniques and experiences. But what can actually be communicated? First of all an attitude to the practice of the actor. What is decisive is not a specific technique which can be learned, but an ability to dilate and shape the actor's presence on stage and the spectators' perception. Odin Teatret has examined the possibilities of developing the principles which help the actor to learn how to learn.

Contrary to many theatre forms, which use as their starting-point the spontaneous behaviour of daily life, Odin Teatret has worked with another body technique or body architecture, by changing the 'natural' tensions and ways of reaction. Often it is simple actions like walking, sitting down, looking, etc., which are being examined in the so-called *training*, when the actors develop, renew and vary their individual energies and their ways of being present physically and mentally, irrespective of the dramatic context, a specific figure or character.

Over the years Odin Teatret's training has been developed. At first the actors all did the same exercises – often, very dynamic, acrobatic exercises, motivated personally by each actor with an inner 'movie'. This created an individual intention, created space and time for each individual.

At a subsequent stage they started to work with properties and instruments like a kind of dance. Training became individualized, based on a variety of very concrete principles and actions: losing one's balance, throwing imaginary objects, using contrasting movements, dividing movements into precise points of start and finish, dividing the movement of the body into segments with one part moving at a time, etc.

At a third stage this 'dance' training was further inspired by the fact that the actors travelled in Asia and there learned various Oriental ways of dancing. They studied the principles on which the Oriental dancers' very traditional and codified behaviour is based, which makes them extremely present.

These were not studies of folklorist dances but experiments with technical principles of behaviour, developed during training. Thus training is not just part of the actor's education, but also a continuous activity helping the actors to find unusual solutions.

New improvisations create new material, or old material is done in different ways, just as a jazz musician creates variations on a specific theme. The result obtains depth and force through this long and patient work, during which the actors' actions are mounted, cut and brought into a rhythmical and dramatic context, which finally leads to a complex staging of the spectator's attention.

THE THEATRE OF MEMORY

As an art form theatre is transient and exists only in the concrete meeting in time and space. The performance can be repeated, but it cannot be reproduced, and it lives on only in the memories of the spectators.

'The past' and 'the dead' are quite central metaphors in the history of Odin Teatret. Death has always, as in *Anabasis*, for instance, been a faithful travelling companion. It is a concrete character in the theatre's gallery of characters, a reminder of the need for immortality – in the theatre as well. The dance with the dead is a way of keeping alive the memories of the past as an important factor in life, biographically as well as professionally.

> There are experiences which cannot be forgotten without losing the thread that leads us back to the child with whom our adventure began. We must not forget that death exists, that you have to account for all your actions in life. If we do not understand that a thread guides us back towards that which is essential in ourselves, then we are living in a present in which we cannot put down roots. It is important to have ancestors, not only biologically, but also professionally.
>
> As a man of the theatre I have a grandfather – Konstantin Stanislavski. He was unique, as an artist and as a human being. Through the changing fortune of his profession and of history, he managed not to lose himself or the ethos, the values which sustain life. Not only artistic, but also social values: how to live with other people and build a community that wants to work together.
>
> To remember means not to lose your dream. Although the flame has gone the ashes remain. We must protect the ashes. That is why it is important to remember that in our youth something existed which was essential for us.
>
> (From an interview with Eugenio Barba,
> *On the Way through Theatre*, video, 1992)

Perhaps it might even be argued that the value of the theatre is that in 'the re-creation of life' it always reminds us of what is perishable, of life's inconsistency, and eventually of death.

Theatre is not a contemporary art form, it does not at all reach the level of the advanced communication channels of modern society permitting information, knowledge and expressions to be communicated in spite of time and space, and to create simultaneity all over the world between receiver and sender. Thus, according to Barba, the theatre as an empty ritual has to find its own meaning and justification. This can be seen through the history of modern theatre, where different political, didactic, therapeutic, or spiritual meanings have been attributed to the theatre in the re-creation of lost rites or social contexts. For Odin Teatret the answer lies in the recognition that the theatre creates a meeting between human beings on a human scale: based on a direct relationship in a room where a limited number of spectators must be able to see, hear and feel – not necessarily the same things, but equally well.

Barba says that the actors and the spectators must be able to talk to 'the part of us which is in exile'. He draws parallels to the previous function of the Church as a place where one could find God, who was actually 'another' part of oneself. It is a mental and emotional space in the borderland between the reality we know and the one we do not know (or which we have forgotten). The performance room does not re-create the picture of reality. On the contrary it is, as in abstract art, a space in which different points of view and ways of thinking are present at one and the same time, becoming concrete and sensory.

THE ANTHROPOLOGICAL JOURNEY

Talabot is a story of what happens when you see what is strange and unreal. Odin Teatret has dealt with people forced into exile for political reasons (in *Brecht's Ashes*) or with people who settle in foreign countries because they want or need to (in *The Million* and *Anabasis*). Odin Teatret's actors are themselves people who have left their own culture because of nonconformity and a feeling of being a stranger. Exile may be a way of assuming this strangeness, of making it visible and legitimate. In *Talabot* we find an anthropologist who studies another culture and in doing so builds a bridge between her native culture and the foreign culture, and we see the double reality and identity which arise when you belong to a specific culture, but find another one and enter its spirit. 'The bridge' is the possibility of returning to your own culture as an 'expert' and a 'communicator' of a foreign culture.

In *Talabot* the Danish professor of anthropology 'Kirsten Hastrup' is a professional spectator of foreign culture as she is confronted with the dead people in Icelandic culture, the hidden people, but also the dead of our era (among others Antonin Artaud and Che Guevara). The anthropologist becomes the point of identification for the spectators and for Odin Teatret on a journey into the past and into the land of the dead. Through her personal biography she represents the necessary and subjective points of view of history, tradition and the inheritance which is passed on.

Talabot was last performed in September 1991 in Holstebro, as a part of *Waterways*, a performance staged over nine days and nights, produced by Odin Teatret in association with Hotel Pro Forma and Akadenwa from Denmark and Teatro Tascabile di Bergamo from Italy. *Waterways* took place all over the town, which became a large stage: in the squares, on the roof-tops, on the church tower, on the river, on the bridges and in the parks. It was dedicated to the 'Columbuses': the explorers who face novel experiences with new impulses, fresh perceptions.

On a large flat roof in the middle of the town a boat was built during the performance, while Odin Teatret among others performed fragments from *Talabot* in new costumes, with new music and text; here called *Klabauterpeople*.

At the end of the week the boat was completed and was then buried in the park with Golem (the man with no soul) by the klabauterpeople and other figures from Odin Teatret: Death on stilts, Mr Peanut, the polar bear, the masked drummer in white, the demon dancing on stilts, Trickster or the Angel, etc. – all those figures that represent the history of Odin Teatret. The park had become a living fairyland. Earth was thrown on the boat by the figures. Finally a tiny boat tied to a white balloon sailed up towards the blue sky.

Erik Exe Christoffersen
Aarhus, January 1992

INTRODUCTION

The first time I saw an Odin Teatret performance was in 1972. It was *My Father's House*, being shown in connection with a seminar on *commedia dell'arte* (the art of the Italian actor, 1600–1700) at Odin Teatret in Holstebro.

It was something of a shock to see *My Father's House*. Its intensity, musicality, atmosphere and tension went beyond what I had thought possible. It was a whole new form of theatre for me. Something I didn't understand very much about. But it had an unbelievable effect on me and that excitement and fascination stay with me still, twenty years later. Not many theatre performances have such a long lifetime in one's memory.

I have since seen most of Odin Teatret's productions and they have given me a series of intense experiences. At the same time, they have shown a continuous development and evolution of craft.

Odin Teatret has pursued a slow and consistent exploration of the theatre medium and the behaviour which characterizes the actor's work on and during the various productions.

In contrast to many other theatre groups of the 1960s and 1970s, which legitimized their activity politically and ideologically in relationship to society's cyclical conflicts and movements, or in relationship to a public, Odin Teatret explores the theatre's own anatomy, its possibilities and limits and its connections to other theatre cultures. It is an exploration of the theatre's ethics.

The history of Odin Teatret becomes *theatre history* because it expresses certain general tendencies in theatre culture. Tendencies which have been present in the history of modern theatre since around 1600, when the first professional actors, in Italy, went out travelling. Odin Teatret's history links the history of European theatre, from the *commedia dell'arte* to Stanislavski and Grotowski, with the traditions of Asian theatre.

I asked some of the actors from Odin Teatret to talk about their work, their craft, their training and technique, and about what motivates their work. And not least about the personal and social meaning of what they

1

do. Is there perhaps something incongruous about letting actors express their opinions about these issues? Actors usually 'talk' by means of their body movements, dance rhythms, tone of voice, and in any case, definitely not by means of the written word, a form of expression in which they are perhaps not skilled and for which they perhaps have neither qualifications nor training.

Traditionally, it is not the Odin Teatret actors themselves who write about their work. This function has been filled first and foremost by Eugenio Barba. The actors must relate in their own language and in particular must relate something they know about, something which is irrevocably linked to a form of expression which cannot be limited to the written word without being reduced, because their form of expression is a part of the immediate moment.

And yet, it is perhaps time to break down certain boundaries in order to attempt to give form to the secrets behind the movements in space: the ability to draw attention, to restore presence, to create life. An ability which is based not only on God-given gifts, on the grace of talent, or on the genius of spontaneous inspiration, but also on self-discipline and the will to repeat something over and over again in training.

The principles which govern presence have become visible at Odin Teatret. Over the years, the training has transformed itself into a culture: a way of thinking, a way of reacting, a way of seeing and perceiving the world, a way of being-in-the-world. And they become a way of telling, which I have attempted to capture in this book. A way which is specific to Odin Teatret.

A ROOTLESS TRAVELLER

The 1960s saw an explosion in the theatre world. Alternative theatres, experimental theatres and street theatres were formed. The groups were varied but had in common their revolt against the traditional, text-dependent, established theatre. Some of the old avant-garde theatre reformers' ideas about the actor in the theatre were kept: reformers like Stanislavski, Artaud, Meyerhold, Brecht, Eisenstein, Piscator. Like them, theatre people in the 1960s looked back to traditions such as the *commedia dell'arte*, Molière, Shakespeare and, not least, to the older Asian theatre traditions, such as Japanese Noh and Kabuki, Indian and Balinese dance, Chinese 'opera'. These Asian theatre forms were thoroughly studied, not only as exotic forms of expression, but also as technique, training and principles for behaviour in performance.

Twenty or thirty years have now gone by and most of these groups have disappeared. New generations of group theatres have appeared and have made their own developments, found their own results, had their own successes and fiascos: positive and negative experiences. There have been movements in various directions, some following new paths, other paths opened up by the 'elders'.

What does this chapter of theatre history tell us? What happened to the people who tried to make theatre the basis of their lives? Was any experience gained which has value beyond its time? Is there a pattern which remains when time has washed away all other traces? Did this period change the theatre and, if so, how?

The point of departure for Western theatre has been, and often still is, the dramatist, the text, or the director's political, ideological, or aesthetic ideas. In a few cases, it is the music or the architecture of the space.

The theatre usually starts with a dramatist's text, in which the actions and the relationships between the characters are already determined, and then a director is engaged to illustrate the text on the basis of a general concept and, finally, actors are engaged to render the text's actions visible.

But there is another possible point of departure: the gathering together of a group of actors and saying, 'Let's see what we can find.' As Eugenio Barba has said, when wondering why the actor in our Western theatre tradition, in contrast to the traditional Asian actor, limits himself or herself to one character in each production: why doesn't the actor research the possibility of creating all the story's connections, with many different characters, with jumps from the general to the specific, from the first to the third person, from the past to the present, from the whole to the part, from person to thing, from role to role? Why is a distinction made between a singer, a dancer and a character actor?

Traditionally, the actor's work is limited to what the spectator sees: performance. This is, however, only the result of the actor's work. The process which leads to this result is equally important. The process is the actor's improvisation work – a lifelong process which is an exploration of personal resources, personal material. It is a journey into the unknown.

The painting *The Wanderer* by Hieronymus Bosch (1450–1516) shows the travelling 'actor'. It is the same figure as that found in various images of the fool on medieval Tarot cards.

The fool is a wanderer, journeying without a geographical home, without roots, always on the way towards something new, always undergoing transformation. His journey is full of dangers. He is walking on the edge of a precipice, at the limit of the permissible, the understandable, the usual. On the edge of society.

The painting is about inspiration, beginning, freedom and choice, but it is also about doubt and ambivalence, expressed in his hesitant attitude. The whole body reflects the paradox of this person. One part of the body is going forward, another is going back. And then he has different shoes on.

Is the actor a rootless traveller, a wanderer on the edge of society?

When, over a period of years, actors work with a body technique which is different from their daily body technique, their behaviour takes on another

Figure 1 Hieronymus Bosch (1450–1516): *The Wanderer*. Museum Boymans-van Beuningen, Rotterdam.

form. It slowly becomes a part of their identity and personality and creates a framework for their existence. From this perspective, from the theatre world, the actors can establish a relationship to the outside world. An actor's identity is a possibility for a particular kind of existence, one which contains a particular and definite kind of life.

But actors can also be 'swallowed up' by their craft, lose their ability to move in and out of a role and that particular form of behaviour which is characteristic of the theatre process. They thereby lose the ability to turn otherness on and off.

How does one move from daily life to theatre life and back again, for years, and still keep these transitions dynamic and hence variable: dramatic?

And what will the actors find in the end? Maybe not what they were looking for. It is like the story about the man searching at night. The act of telling the story makes at the same time, fragment by fragment, a living image. And in the end you have a surprising montage tied to the story.

In a little round house with a round window and a little triangle of garden there lived a man. Not far from the house there was a lake with a lot of fish that the man caught and sold in the town.

One night he woke up and heard a terrible noise. He went out into the darkness to find out what was wrong. He ran to the lake.

Here the storyteller began to draw the man's route, as on a map of an army's movements. He ran southward, he tripped over a stone in the middle of the road, and later on he fell into a ditch, got up again, but fell into another ditch, up again, fell into a third ditch and got up again. He now understood that he was wrong and that the noise did not come from that way, and he ran back northwards. But when he got there he thought he heard the sound from the south, and he ran back, fell over a stone, a little later he fell into a ditch, came up again, fell into another ditch, got up again and fell into a third ditch and got up again. Now he could definitely hear the noise from the end of the lake. He rushed there, and saw a great leakage in the dam through which fish  and water ran out. He started to mend the hole and worked all night and did not return until dawn.

When he woke up the next morning he looked out of his little round window, and what did he see: a stork.

(A retelling of a story from Blixen, 1963: 213)

Life is of course lived forward and proceeds more or less haphazardly, but when later it is looked back upon and interpreted, it is seen to consist of patterns which create meaning out of the randomness of its actions. The man does not look for a stork but carries out his project in a sequential manner and completes his task. It is when he first sees the stork that we understand that the series of seemingly arbitrary occurrences had a purpose. He must have laughed out loud.

Is this an image of the actor's search for theatre?

In the courtyard of the old farm which is now Odin Teatret, there is no stork, but there is a tree. A dead tree without roots, painted white, as in Japanese theatre, but it nevertheless seems to be alive. A tree which has taken on an artificial life with no connection to the earth it is planted in. With a trunk and branches, all of which help to create the tree's pattern, the tree is an image of Odin Teatret's many and varied cultural activities – theatre productions, seminars, and individuals with widespread interests, new buds on the theatre's trunk. One can meet and become acquainted with this pattern or with parts of its branches, one can measure oneself against it, understand or misunderstand it. One can discover one's own identity in the difference between it and oneself.

The pattern as such cannot be assimilated or reproduced but one can learn from the principles which govern the tree's life, principles which are different from those governing the life of a natural tree. Precisely because Odin Teatret has always given importance to not 'only' creating theatre productions but also to exploring the general principles of life, discovered in or through the theatre.

THE HISTORY OF ODIN TEATRET

The history of this theatre could be written in many different ways. One could write about the productions but then the actors' daily lives, training and preparations would not be part of the story. One could concentrate on Barba and his reasons for making theatre. Or one could simply choose to examine the broader lines, the factors which have created the continuity in this group's work: the repetition of central themes in the productions, each of which is performed for many years, the presence of the same three or four people, the fundamental training principles.

But there is also discontinuity: many changes in the company of actors (about thirty-five actors have worked at Odin Teatret over the years), the jump from the first, closed performances for few spectators to the open, street theatre performances, from dramatic theatre to dance performances, from serious theatre to clowning.

How does one describe Odin Teatret in a way that reveals the rhythm which has been typical of its history, the oscillation between apparently incompatible poles, between discipline and freedom, between revolt and submission, between continuity and discontinuity, between the accidental and the necessary?

The history of this theatre group is dynamic, rhythmic, a constant displacement of weight, a constant avoidance of the static and the predictable.

I have chosen to divide this history into four phases, and have structured the book accordingly.

'The study years': the first phase is made up of the period of time which Eugenio Barba spent studying with Grotowski from 1961 to 1964 and of a shorter period he spent at the Kathakali actors' school in southern India in 1963. These studies were his basis and qualifications for the founding of Odin Teatret in Norway in 1964.

'The closed room': the second phase is made up of the establishing years from 1964 to 1974, when Odin Teatret moved to Holstebro and there set up a theatre laboratory devoted to the education of actors, the production

6

of performances and the pedagogical and theoretical presentation of the art of the actor.

This phase is entitled 'The closed room' because during it work was done on developing the actors' possibilities for expression, in protected seclusion and isolation. The productions *Ornitofilene* (1965), *Kaspariana* (1967), *Ferai* (1969) and *My Father's House* (1972) were performed in spaces where the number of spectators was limited to between sixty and eighty.

'The open room': the third phase is the travelling years, 1974–82, and began with Eugenio Barba's return home to southern Italy with Odin Teatret. Here the cultural identity which the group had gradually created became apparent. The group opened up, literally: for the first time ever, the actors trained outdoors. They began to do street theatre and parades and established a closer relationship between training and performance work. They practised barters, an exchange of dance and song between local people and the theatre group. This activity became a central part of Odin Teatret's activity during its travels in the following years.

The group made connections with various other theatre groups which were working with similar principles. This led to the manifesto on the Third Theatre (Barba, 1986a: 193) and, as the result of contact with a number of European and Asian actors, ISTA (the International School of Theatre Anthropology) was founded (1979). The travels were also reflected in the productions made during these years: the meeting between various cultures and the exile existence were central themes in *The Book of Dances* (1974), *Come! And the day will be ours* (1976), *The Million* (1978) and *Brecht's Ashes 2* (1982). This period was as expansive as the army in the street performance *Anabasis* (1979). With Eugenio as commander, the actors wandered the world over.

'The dancing time-space': the fourth phase began with work on *Oxyrhincus Evangeliet* in 1984. From the open room, filled with big movements and powerful energy, the group returned to the almost immobile. Travel in space became travel in time and the landscape of dreams. The actors turned the energy of violent dance into an expansion of the moment: energy in stillness.

The production *Judith* (1987) also contained this interest in the minimal, which became expanded and enlarged like a close-up on film.

POINTS OF VIEW

The central element of this book is the actor's culture, what epitomizes it and how it is transmitted.

One aspect of this culture is the actor's body technique (both a physical and a mental technique), which makes possible the transition from a daily behaviour to a theatrical or scenic behaviour. Daily behaviour is typically economical and efficient. One aims for the straight road and saves as much energy as possible. Theatrical body technique, on the other hand, is characterized by an exaggerated and unnatural body tension, with the result that the actor alone, with his or her presence and dynamics, is able to capture, hold and direct the spectator's attention. One could say that the actor's technique makes energy visible as presence.

A second aspect is the artistic or aesthetic level: the conditions for the dedication to and the execution of the actor's craft, the actor's social position and concrete and symbolic meaning in a particular historical context.

A third aspect is the actor's personal motivating force, his or her talent and reasons for being concerned with the theatre in the first place, the way in which individual resources are administered, developed or blocked, which themes the actor plays out or gives form to through training, improvisation and performance.

The aspect of the actor's culture is a 'living book', 'written' in the actor's own language by means of movements, gesture and sound, and irrespective of the dramatist, the director and the theatre. It disappears with the actor like footsteps in the sand.

A fourth aspect is the scientific level. A series of experiences can be summarized and become abstract knowledge and hence the basis for a dramaturgy which is concerned with the actor's behaviour, with the relationship between actor and spectator, with the relationship between actor and text, with the actor's meaning and function.

How are these experiences described, disseminated and developed further without their connection to the sensory and concrete point of departure being lost?

Odin Teatret's productions are difficult to describe because they are constantly changing. Not only in the way that any theatre performance does so from night to night, but also because the productions are slowly changed over time by both the director and the actors. My descriptions and the actors' explanations can never be identical to the real actions or the performances. Actions and performance must be re-created so that they become images and experiences in the reader's own inner performance space. Many of the questions I put to the actors have not been included in the text; neither does the text follow the chronology of the conversations I had with them.

These actors, who have worked together for so many years, are extreme and radical in their search for the possibilities for the actor's existence. It is precisely for this reason that they might be able to relate something essential about their profession, something which is not only connected to personality but which is also an independent, living language, no matter how different it may appear to be for each actor.

Figure 2 Anabasis, Peru, 1978. On the way. Photo: Tony D'Urso.

1

THE FOURTH FLEW INTO THE FIRE AND BURNT UP

The study years: 1961–4

If we wish to understand the principles which are the basis of Odin Teatret's productions, we must go back to the point of departure and look at the conditions which influenced Eugenio Barba's perception of the theatre.

Barba was born in 1936 in southern Italy. His father, who died in 1948, was a general in Mussolini's army and took part in the field campaign in Ethiopia. At the age of 17, Barba left home, hitchhiking. In 1954 he ended up in Norway. He worked as a plumber and later in the machine room on the freighter *Talabot*, bound for Asia. Back in Oslo in 1957, he began to study at university. At the age of 23 he received a scholarship to study directing at the Warsaw State Theatre School.

In Poland in 1961 Barba saw the work of the 'Theatre of the Thirteen Rows', a small experimental theatre which had been led since 1959 by Jerzy Grotowski (born in 1933), an actor and director from Cracow. As a result of this meeting, he moved to Opole to follow Grotowski's work there until 1964, in which year he was denied re-entry to Poland by the Polish bureaucracy. In 1963, he made a study trip to India to gather material on Kathakali theatre. He stayed in India for six months, part of which time was spent at the Kathakali school in Kalamandalam.

Since it was not possible for him to return to Poland, he went back to Norway and there sought in vain to enter the theatre world. So he gathered together a group of young people who were in one way or another interested in the theatre, several of them having tried unsuccessfully to get into the established theatre schools. A completely fortuitous collection of fourteen young people were present at Odin Teatret's first day of work on 1 October 1964.

INDIA

The time Barba spent in India had a great deal of influence on the way in which Odin Teatret later developed.

Twenty-five years after his stay in India, Barba wrote:

10

The long nights of Kathakali gave me a glimpse of the limits which the actor can reach. But it was the dawn which revealed these actors' secrets to me, at the Kalamandalam school in Cheruthuruty, Kerala. There, young boys, hardly adolescents, monotonously repeating exercises, steps, songs, prayers, and offerings, crystallized their ethos through artistic behaviour and ethical attitude.

(Barba, article, 1988c: 126)

In an article on Kathakali theatre written in 1964 (Barba, article, 1967), he refers to an old Bakt tale about four butterflies who had heard about fire. They went to see what it was like. The first butterfly approached the fire. The second skimmed it with its wing. The third flew over it. The fourth flew into it and burned up. The first three saw the body of the fourth be consumed by the fire, transformed and melted in the flames. But it could no longer share its knowledge.

One cannot penetrate the secrets of the Kathakali actor, much less copy his training or technique, because to be a Kathakali actor is not a choice but a 'calling'.

Training of a religious nature: one becomes a Kathakali actor not by choice but by vocation. The training begins at the formative period of the child's character, at the time when he is the most receptive to the stimuli of his environment. He is taught absolute respect for his guru, who initiates him in a Tao, the secrets of which he is not allowed to reveal. One cannot incarnate a god unless one believes in a god – thus, religious faith is the very basis of this theatre. The child is constantly immersed into the *mysterium tremendum et fascinans* of religion. Acting is not a profession, it is a form of priesthood. The quality of his vocation is tested by eight years of training, harsh almost beyond endurance, which will mark him for the rest of his life and will endow him with a sensitivity different from that of the layman. Moreover, the Kathakali began as a form of yoga and retains some yoga characteristics. The *chela* (novice) is literally 'initiated' by the guru through a long and crucial apprenticeship. He who wants to come near the gods, must move away from what is human; his technique is a means to reach the metaphysical. It is also an offering and a consecration like that of Karma-Yoga. For the Kathakali actor, acting has an intrinsic value and is its own reward. It is a form of prayer and a true method of psychic transmutation.

(Barba, article, 1967: 49)

By means of his craft, the Kathakali actor dedicates himself to an identity and a life-style which go beyond both the performances and the technique:

A Kathakali actor has no fixed salary; he cannot offer his services for money in a theatre – there are no theatres. He plays three or four

11

times a month, and admission is free. He cannot have another job, because he must practise several hours every day. Some actors become gurus, open a school, and take students for a fee. Others earn their pittance by acting as servants in the temples. Most of them are indigents. We may well wonder why they become actors. The answer is that the actor-priest of the Kathakali offers his body to the gods like the Juggler of Notre-Dame in the medieval legend who offered his juggling to the Virgin Mary.

(ibid.: 50)

As a result of his education and his theatre work, the Kathakali actor undergoes a slow transformation. He is set apart from society by his otherness and is initiated and integrated into a new identity-creating world, the theatre's world. Obviously, a Western actor cannot adopt this way of being an actor, but the basic attitude can be formulated as a paradox which has been a guiding principle for Odin Teatret.

How does one become an actor, not out of respect for the public's need, nor in order to be accepted by the public, but in order to satisfy an inner 'calling' and one's own inner need? How does one become an actor without being dependent on 'the theatre'?

Barba's studies of the Kathakali actor's dramaturgy and his description of the Kathakali actor's theatrical language and forms of expression reveal certain limitations in the European way of perceiving the actor's work and dramaturgy.

The Kathakali actor is not like the European actor: he is not limited by the dramatic action, the actions of a role, or by the condition that the actor must represent a daily reality. The Kathakali actor makes use of a hermetic language which re-creates and symbolizes reality with the help of 'secret signs'.

The Kathakali actor is a story-teller who narrates by means of mime, pantomime and dance-like, rhythmic movements and gestures. The hand and finger movements are mostly narrative, while the face expresses the emotional and the dramatic aspects of the story. He can change point of view with respect to what is being told, he can jump in and out of his role with an almost cinematic technique. Eugenio Barba analyses a simple scene as an example:

Let us imagine that the protagonist finds himself near a river. His hands indicate the place with *mudras* [hand gestures] describing the landscape: trees, boats, people. The face, and mainly the eyes, which keep looking at the hands, express the reactions of the character. Suddenly, the hands tell of the appearance of a crocodile. The face immediately expresses the emotions of the character at the sight of the crocodile: surprise, terror, desire to flee. Then the hands tell the end of the story: the crocodile is killed. On the actor's face the audience can read the effort, the disgust, the pride of the victorious hunter.

From this simple example one can imagine what effort of concentration and imagination is required from the actor to compose his acting technique so that the audience will understand him. Moreover, the performance lasts eight or ten hours.

(Barba, article, 1967: 40)

The scene is performed with the body. A fictive landscape is created and analysed at the same time, so that the spectator can both perceive the outer universe and its mechanisms and react to it subjectively. The actor describes a mountain: one can read its height in his eyes at the same time as one sees his body climb it.

The Kathakali actor's language does not describe daily life. His behaviour is rendered extremely theatrical and artificial by means of a deformation of daily behaviour.

The very stylized, symbolic rituals or freely invented suggestive movements are based on the actor's language. The extreme opening of the eyes, often in contrast to acrobatic movements, makes it possible for the actors to be very expressive with the eyes alone. The movements of the hands and fingers, almost like the hand movements of a sign language, become an epic language. There can be different rhythms in different parts of the body: between the legs and the hands, for example. There are sections of pure dance which have nothing to do with the actions of the role. The performance itself can be interrupted: one actor can withdraw and freshen his makeup or change his costume while the other actors continue, and then undergoes a rapid transformation, entering the fictive world once again.

The artificiality, the theatricality and the deformation of daily behaviour create the performance's ritual character and its magical reality. The spectator is pulled out of normal time by means of rhythm, music and the actor's transformation.

The actor's costume is an essential part of this transformation. It is an instrument and a prop for the actor and gives him the opportunity to make the body oversized and to strengthen its expressiveness. The makeup is likewise an element which helps in exaggerating expressivity.

Both the process of making up and the putting on of the costume are part of the preparation for the performance and the actor's slow transformation for the ritual. It is just as much a psychic preparation as an external one, making deep concentration possible.

The Kathakali actor first becomes a master when he is able to give technically complicated actions a touch of immediacy, when he has gained *Manodharma*, performance skill, which makes it possible for him to go

13

beyond the fixed score and cast himself into improvised and spontaneous actions and thereby increase his own contribution to the drama.

POLAND

The second essential part of Eugenio Barba's professional preparation is his stay with Grotowski and the 'Theatre of the Thirteen Rows' (later called the Teaterlaboratorium) in 1961–4.

Barba follows the work at Grotowski's theatre as assistant director on *Acropolis* (1962) and *Dr Faustus* (1963) and works as director on Dante's *Divine Comedy*, which is never finished. He writes a series of articles and *Alla ricerca del teatro perduto* (1965) ['In search of the lost theatre'] about Grotowski's theatre.

Grotowski's work is characterized by the search to find a way back to the theatre's essence, to go behind the literary theatre in order to eliminate those elements which are not necessary for the theatre. The theatre is reduced to the poor theatre, to 'what happens between the spectator and the actor'.

It is an attempt to re-create the theatre as 'ritual', where both the spectator and the actor are participants.

In this 'ritualized' theatre the traditional separation between the stage and the auditorium does not exist. The spectators are observers who are themselves observed. And they are also part of the performance as some kind of witnesses to the actor's actions. Mentally and physically, the spectator is part of the action.

The spectator's destiny is to be an observer, but also something more: to be a witness. A witness does not stick his nose into everything, doesn't try to get closer to or interfere with those who are acting. A witness keeps a certain distance, he does not want to join in. He wants to gather evidence, wants to see everything that's happening from the beginning to the end, preserve it. The image of what he has seen must remain within him. I once saw a documentary film about a monk who set himself on fire in Saigon. A crowd of other monks was present and observed what took place. Some of them helped the one who set himself on fire. They gave him the fuel, prepared everything, but the others stood apart, almost hidden. They stayed immobile while it all happened. You could hear the fire crackle, you could hear the stillness. No one did anything. They really participated. They participated in a ceremony which was also a testimony, a testimony to the most extreme action in the world and in life. And, since the man was a monk, a Buddhist, they also participated in a religious way. But they did not interfere. They kept their distance. The Latin word *respicio*, 'to respect the thing', expresses the function of the true witness. It does not mean to intervene with one's own little role, with one's self-demonstrative 'me, too', but to be a witness, that is, to not forget. One must not forget.

Putting the spectator at a distance means giving him the opportunity to participate, in the same way that the witnesses participated in the action of that monk who set himself on fire in protest.

(Grotowski, 1973: 62)

The spatial relationship between the actors and the spectators is determined by the logic of each particular production. The architecture of each production is therefore different and the placement of the spectators within the space is determined according to their function in the production as a whole.

Barba describes the actor's interpretation more as a process than as an actual role:

For the actor, the interpretation of a role is not the same as identification with the character: he is just as far from 'living in' the role as he is from representing it with '*Verfremdung*'. For the actor, the role is an instrument which he uses to challenge himself, to reach certain hidden sides of his personality, to render his most intimate details visible.

Jerzy Grotowski considers the theatre to be a collective self-penetration. If the theatre is to reawaken and stimulate the spectator's inner life, it must counter all opposition, shake every mental cliché inhibiting access to the subconscious. This theatre can be compared to a veritable anthropological expedition.

(Barba, article, 'Mod et sakralt . . .', 1965b: 3)

The underlying dramaturgical principle is what Barba calls 'scenic polemics'.

This principle is expressed on various levels. One such level is the contrast between the text and the actor's action. An action must not just be repeated or illustrated by the actor. The actor can work in spite of the action or in direct opposition to it. The same applies to the music, which can also be contrasted to the action.

The actor's body can also be made to obey the principle of opposition: it can be divided up and execute different, simultaneous actions which work against each other – the face can express courage, the arms fear and the legs panic. All parts of the actor's body become a part of the role or action:

Every movement, every gesture, the way of walking, all the kinetic possibilities, the corporeal expression, the colour of the voice, its intonation and nuances, all these elements must be part of a composition whose effect is dependent on their physical shock value, which the actor must consciously work into the role's structure. A brief

15

movement is already, in and of itself, a micro-pantomime which informs us about the character, about his intentions and plans. Every single sentence is made into an action by means of the intonation of the voice. Every sentence is seen to contain a whole series of other sentences which are not part of the logic of the spoken words.

The structure of a role is closely linked to the actor himself. His psychosomatic characteristics are a skeleton upon which the entire role is based. This is not to say that the actor must play himself but that he must take his particular attributes into consideration, by polarizing them, for example (an ugly Romeo, perhaps?).

(Barba, article, 1964b: 76)

The actor does not interpret a role but creates an action through a modulation of energy and the innermost and smallest impulses. This creates a state of tension in the spectator and mobilizes the spectator's inner psychic energy, so that he or she becomes part of, is made co-responsible for, the dramatic action.

As in Kathakali theatre, there is no place for passive decorations, props, or costumes. All the physical elements are brought alive as the actor's co-performers, they extend the actor's actions or work against them. The voice has a musical quality or rhythmic value, just as in European opera. The text is not recited in a traditional manner but becomes part of the 'performance text'.

Training is a very central activity in this theatre. As a daily activity independent of performance work, training is something new for the European actor – or is perhaps the resumption of a tradition which has otherwise remained alive only with circus artists, ballet dancers and singers.

Training does not serve the same purpose for an actor as for an 'artiste': it is not the working up of 'numbers' or the learning of particular skills. It can, however, lead to the acquisition of skills or abilities which, when mechanically repeated, can in turn threaten personal energy or motivation. Training must be continuously transformed and individualized in order to present new resistances, in order to create new obstacles for the actor.

Training is therefore an individual process. The basis is ethical: the individual reasons and necessity for how, why and when a particular series of exercises is done. The effect of these exercises is equally individual.

As far as actor training is concerned, Grotowski was influenced as much by Indian as by other forms of classical Asian theatre. But he had known from previous experience that one could not transfer signs and movements from Indian theatre to European theatre as anything other than clichés.

Training, as developed in the Grotowski laboratory, is far removed from traditional apprenticeship or the learning of particular skills. It is actually closer to modern psycho-therapy, as found, for example, in the work done

16

by Wilhelm Reich in the 1930s and developed further by Alexander Lowen in the United States. The essence of this therapy is the unlocking of the muscle armour which blocks the flow of emotions.

Psycho-dynamics is one of the concepts which Odin Teatret later rejects as a useful point of departure for the actor.

The essential aspect of training in Grotowski's theatre is the basic principle of the process: the principle of elimination or *via negativa*. The actor's driving force is not the desire to 'express'; on the contrary, it is that which resists his or her actions. Non-action opens up creativity as a disorientation, an improvised action in the true sense of the word: that is to say, an action which is not prepared, an action which is unpredictable and which brings the actor into contact with his or her unfamiliar psychic landscape.

There is another fundamental principle which is applicable to the actor's creative process. It is found in the contradiction-filled relationship between discipline and spontaneity. The discipline lies in the repetition of an exercise or training beyond the limits of the actor's will or immediate, spontaneous desire so that the training becomes the physical, concrete forming of a structure against which the actor fights and to which he or she establishes an active relationship.

Grotowski reached the limits of theatre with his theatre laboratory. The actors' technique and the precision of the performances created an indissoluble boundary between the actors and the spectators, a boundary which could be breached only beyond the theatre. *Apocalypsis cum figuris* (1968) was the Teaterlaboratorium's last production (performed until 1978).

Grotowski slowly distanced himself from theatre and moved towards what became called post-(para-)theatre, in which the boundary between the actors and the spectators is no longer present. Everyone participated in a meeting, a meeting often stretching over a long period of time, sometimes weeks; a course of events which was not structured with respect to aesthetic principles or fiction. It was a very concrete form of meeting based on a series of specific actions which brought the participants into a non-daily form of fellowship and rhythm. These events often took place in natural surroundings such as woods, fields, or mountains, with many hours of physical activity, running, singing, dancing, chanting, climbing, completely outside normal time rhythms, often with the use of natural elements: fire, earth, water.

This movement out of the theatre – beyond the theatre – corresponds in many ways to similar movements, undertaken by other theatres, away from theatre institutions and their buildings: Odin Teatret, which in the middle of the 1970s moved to southern Italy and to other areas without traditional theatre culture; Peter Brook, who went to Iran on research trips with his actors; Théâtre du Soleil, which went to India and later Japan at the end of the 1970s. In contrast to Grotowski, these groups have since 'turned back' to the theatre. For the moment, we must conclude by saying that the Teaterlaboratorium was closed in 1984 after a slow period of dissolution. Many of its members have died and others are working in various new situations.

One of them, Ryszard Cieslak (a collaborator of Grotowski's since 1961), was at Odin Teatret in connection with various seminars at the end of the 1960s and passed on elements of his training. He reached a point where it was no longer necessary to do theatre:

> Let me use this image, because it has meant a great deal to me: we are running down a road. The road is a metaphor for life. We run because we must run. But at a certain point we can stop to rest. And it is possible to rest all of your life. But if you know that you have to run because you really have to run, then the landscape around you will be transformed.
>
> Sometimes, you'll run the wrong way. So you'll have to turn and start again. Sometimes, you have two roads in front of you, one to the left and one to the right. And you have to choose.
>
> Along such a road, you will fall many times. And so you must be strong in order to get up again.
>
> Sometimes, it is also necessary for you to be hard on yourself. Sometimes, it is necessary for you to relinquish something that is important to you. But you can choose. You can do it, or you can not bother. It depends on what you really want to do.
>
> (Cieslak, 1982: 21)

Ryszard Cieslak, who died in 1990, performed in Peter Brook's *Mahabharata* (1985–8).

2

THE CLOSED ROOM: 1964–74

Ornitofilene, Kaspariana, Ferai and *My Father's House*

Our theatre does not wish just to entertain, nor does it seek to defend a thesis. It seeks merely to ask questions, which each of us must find answers to, because 'engaged art' does not offer the right answers; it just asks the right questions.

(Ornitofilene programme, 1966)

'The Bird Lovers' was the title of the unfinished manuscript which Jens Björneboe made available to the newly formed Odin Teatret in the autumn of 1964. The training and improvisation work were built up around this text, which was much cut and in fact completely changed structurally. Björneboe comments as follows on this amputation or adaptation:

> After Barba's surgery, not even the torso of the play was left. Just the heart and lungs and brain. But the miracle was that it was alive. The dialogue and the connecting plot, exact and developed – completely gone. Just the conflict remained intact – the conflict between humanity and bestiality – between freedom and bondage. This conflict was still there, as a brutal, vulgar and completely convincing reality.
>
> And it was the same play.
>
> It was completely different, yet the same – that is, not any other play in the world. It was completely and utterly 'The Bird Lovers', but simpler and more crudely seen, from another point of view.
>
> For me, the essence was a new insight: that all of our inherited dramaturgy, the theory of the plot, 'the work with the plot', was finally rejected. A drama can live without a plot, it can be nourished by pure conflict, pure war: disjointed and violent.
>
> (Björneboe in Barba, on the productions, 1970: 12)

Ornitofilene was premiered on 1 October 1965, and was performed 51 times in Norway, Denmark, Finland and Sweden.

There are four actors in the production, performing various small roles and the three main roles: the father, who is a bird hunter, the mother and their daughter. The performance takes place in the whole room, which is a

19

kind of meeting-room, court-room or church. The actors and the spectators sit at tables, around which and on which the actors also perform.

The performance begins with the chairman bidding everyone welcome to a discussion meeting: certain foreign bird lovers would like to build a tourist paradise in this little Italian town; this new activity will be of benefit to the local people, new revenue will invigorate the local economy. 'The foreigners' have one condition: the local hunters must stop hunting birds.

Among those present at the meeting are the daughter, mother and father; they protest against the proposal. The father refuses to stop hunting birds. It becomes clear that the 'bird lovers' had previously occupied the town, during the war, and not as tourists, but as soldiers in Nazi uniforms. They had tortured and killed the town's citizens.

The performance jumps back in time to the war, when the father was jailed, tortured and condemned to death. He rises from the dead, a lullaby is sung for the daughter (a death song, which is used again in *Brecht's Ashes* 2). The daughter maintains that she also wants to be a hunter. At the same time, the townspeople recognize that they must forget the past and the father recognizes that times have changed and that the 'bird lovers' had had a difficult job to do during the war. He remembers the persecution of the Jews and one hears a train coming into the station; the four actors rush about the room trying to hide but end up by peacefully resigning themselves to destiny. Hunting is forbidden and the bird lovers are made welcome.

The father tries to hang himself but cannot, and gives up at the last moment. The judge gives him his hand and the tourists give him money.

The daughter embraces the father and spits in his face. She says: 'Fathers who betray their children shall atone for them.' She then hangs herself. The mother sings a psalm and the father laughs at the audience and says, 'Our children!'

A year after the opening of *Ornitofilene*, Odin Teatret was offered premises in Holstebro, Denmark. Else Marie Laukvik and Torgeir Wethal moved there with Eugenio Barba, but with no production, since the other actors had left the group. Work was begun on a new production, with new actors. It was ready in June 1967.

Odin Teatret was now also called 'The Scandinavian Laboratory for the Art of the Actor'.

The laboratory concept is a manifestation of the obvious kinship with Grotowski's theatre. It also emphasizes the scientific and research aspects of the group's attitude towards the theatrical profession.

Concurrent with theatre and performance work, Odin Teatret undertook a series of other activities which became central for the new theatre in Holstebro: the publishing of the magazine *Teatrets Teori og Teknikk* (TTT) ['The Theory and Technique of the Theatre'] which, with twenty-three issues in the period 1965–75 and the publication of five books, dealt with

Figure 3 Rehearsals of *Ornitofilene*, 1965 (Anne Trine Grimnes and Else Marie Laukvik). In the air-raid shelter, winter.

central theoretical theatrical topics from the *commedia dell'arte* to Asian theatre, from Stanislavski, Eisenstein and Meyerhold to Grotowski, Fo and Peter Brook: a series of books and articles which describe and analyse that part of theatre history to which Odin Teatret belongs.

Moreover, a series of seminars was arranged with theatre people from all over the world, such as Barrault, Decroux, Dario Fo and Grotowski, and with Asian actors. Films were made on the actor's technique and about the main productions.

The new production *Kaspariana* was presented 74 times. The group of seven actors was dissolved within a year and only three actors, Else Marie Laukvik, Torgeir Wethal and Iben Nagel Rasmussen, remained.

Kaspariana was based on a scenario by Ole Sarvig, a series of scenes which the actors used as a basis for improvisation and for the creation of a performance text. The performance text was the composite of the actors' movements, dialogue, sounds, songs, scenic elements, costumes and

21

props, and the relationships between the actors and between the actors and the spectators.

The point of departure for the production was the myth of Kaspar Hauser, who appeared in a square in Nuremberg in 1828 and who was mysteriously killed five years later, without his background ever having been discovered. He was 21 years old.

Kaspar turned up in Nuremberg as a stranger with neither language nor 'identity' and the production shows the attempt made to integrate him into society. He is subjected to a social experiment.

During the performance, the room is transformed. Each of the actors has his or her own construction, which is that actor's 'house' and which can be taken apart and put together in various ways, moved around and set on edge. These constructions were also used as musical instruments and props.

The production describes Kaspar's social birth. He is given a name and is told the story of the son who was betrayed by his father. He is taught and is given some of man's knowledge. He must show what he has learnt – but he has forgotten his role. He is prompted and remembers. A party is held to celebrate.

Kaspar is thought to be sick – he is examined: he needs a woman. Kaspar and the chosen woman are brought together – their relationship develops contrary to the others' intentions. Kaspar experiences love, but the others kill the child born of the union and separate the lovers.

Last phase. Kaspar is initiated into the art of war.

The French theatre critic Marc Fumaroli described the production's beginning and end in this way:

Six actors dressed in makeshift costumes enter in a stream of light. Each climbs up on one of the crooked platforms criss-crossed with wooden slats. These platforms are strongly lit from within, giving the impression of a pyre. One involuntarily thinks of Artaud's remark: 'Actors must be like martyrs, burnt alive, signalling to us from their pyre.' Slowly, and with movements which remind one of weightless astronauts, the actors fashion their costumes before our eyes by modelling around their bodies the pieces of rough material which were lying at their feet.

One of them, the leader of the chorus, leaves his 'launching pad' and spreads out into the room like a large, uncertain bird. One by one, the other actors join his flight in larger and larger concentric circles. A concentrated atmosphere of boorishness is created to the sounds of raw and shrill voices, a bird of prey's banquet. Suddenly, and without our knowing why, a revelation becomes visible, a revelation which radiates fragility and innocence: a young man steps

22

forward, dressed in a simple white loin-cloth. *Ecce homo*: Kaspar Hauser (played by Torgeir Wethal). From here and there around the room we hear expressions of astonishment and fear. The young man collapses, unable to withstand the sight of these disturbing vultures who resemble him. They throw themselves upon him, as if he was the dessert in their cannibals' banquet. The transcendental nature of Torgeir Wethal's appearance from the depths of night can only be described by comparing it to northern European Gothic painting or sculpture, to Memling or to Dierick Bouts' *St Sebastian* and especially to Riemenschneider's white stone Adam in the Würzburg Museum.

The end:

The chorus is suddenly still and the warriors stand face to face, with a knife between them. The knife is seen to be more of a sign than an instrument of war. On top of the platforms which they have set up towards the dark sky, the choristers stand like the gods of wind and storm and create with their breathing and humming a winter land-scape full of sinister warnings. Are we perhaps in that valley where Oedipus, on the way to Thebes, met his father and thus his fate? Are we perhaps on that plain where Cain made ready to avenge himself on God by offering Him that blasphemous sacrifice, his brother Abel? The two warriors are now a two-headed monster with the knife-sceptre raised at the ready. The room goes dark. We never find out whether Kaspar chose the fate of Oedipus or Cain or Christ; whether he assumed the role of executioner or sacrifice, sacrificial priest or sacrificial lamb. It is Kaspar's last incarnation: Hamlet, the quintessential modern hero, with his unresolved situation.

(Marc Fumaroli in Barba, on the productions, 1970: 35)

In 1969, Odin Teatret premiered *Ferai*. The production was shown at the Théâtre des Nations theatre festival in Paris and subsequently performed 220 times. The spectators sat across from each other in four slightly curved rows, two rows on each side of the performance area: seen from above, a whale or a boat.

The production is based on a text by Peter Seeberg and is a weaving together of Euripides' play *Alcestis*, about a young princess who sacrifices herself for her husband Admetos because it has been foretold that he must die unless someone else gives up their life for him, and the story of the Danish king Frode Fredegod, as told by Saxo Grammaticus.

In *Ferai*, the legendary Danish king has already died, leaving no heir, and the power of the throne and the hand of the king's daughter Alcestis are to be given to the winner of a contest. Admetos wins the contest and thus also the power in Ferai, and Alcestis. Admetos wants to reform the society and rejects the former king's authoritarian way of ruling and wielding power. Admetos wants the people of Ferai to have their freedom and the chance to live in brotherhood. But the people are afraid of the freedom offered to them by Admetos and they ask for punishment and constraint, as under the former king. Admetos refuses to carry on the old king's traditions, even though Alcestis herself begs him to do so.

The people try to bring the old king back to life again and even though he is dead, they find him more attractive than the new king. They revolt. Alcestis involves herself in the conflict and sacrifices herself by committing suicide.

Alcestis' sacrifice can be seen in the light of Jan Palach's suicide on the streets of Prague, where he set fire to himself to protest the Russian invasion of Czechoslovakia in 1968. At the same time, her action is an image of the 'actor's' sacrifice and transformation.

Peter Seeberg's text was considerably reworked. Text and characters were removed and new scenes were added. The work with the text followed the method which we saw in connection with *Ornitofilene* and to a certain extent with *Kaspariana*. These three productions constituted a first phase in Odin Teatret's dramaturgy, which had to do with 'scenic polemics' or a consciously sought-after confrontation between the text and the production, as a means of bringing the textual space alive, with the spectator as a kind of 'witness'. The action had parallels with other texts and images from the Bible, from the story of Jesus and from the tragedy of Hamlet, and, because of these textual dilations, was ambiguous and very open to interpretation.

The performance took place in a closed room. The spectators and the actors were so 'bound' to each other and the room that, for example, it was not physically possible to leave the room during the performance or to enter it once the performance had begun. In the closed room, communication was central, protected and respected as a kind of unbreakable 'contract'.

Ferai was performed until 1971 and was Odin Teatret's first international success. But the group was dissolved and re-formed: only Iben Nagel Rasmussen, Torgeir Wethal and Else Marie Laukvik remained. New actors joined the group and the work took a new direction, both as far as the training was concerned and with respect to the way in which productions were made.

My Father's House was premiered in 1972 and subsequently performed 322 times. No outside author was used. The production was created exclusively from the actors' improvisations, as a montage without linear action.

In April, 1971, the actors and I agreed that our next production should deal with Fyodor Dostoyevsky's life story. Certain events

24

from his life interested us: his relationship to his father, who was murdered by his own serfs in revenge for his habit of abusing their under-aged daughters; his meeting with the liberal intelligentsia in St Petersburg; Petrasyevsky's literary salon and illegal discussion-Wednesdays; his arrest and staged execution on Semyonovsky Square; his stay in a death-house in Siberia; his passion for gambling; his turbulent love-life.

We soon discovered that the objective, biographical elements were beginning to blend with Dostoyevsky's own vision of his experiences, as he had distilled them in his novels. His epilepsy was seen through Fyrst Mysjkin and Smerdyakov's illness; his conflict with his father was seen through the confessions of the brothers Karamazov; his love-life as a constant choice and suffering: one woman between two men, one man between two women. The biographical details seemed to begin to blend with the universe which Dostoyevsky conjured up in his writings.

In this floating world, the work took a new direction: the historico-literary relationship led us to new associations, sudden changes in thought, personal questions, the discovery of 'Dostoyevsky-ism' in ourselves, a vision of a cosmos-Russia which was also inhabited by Leskoff's, Gogol's and Goncharoff's characters.

The production is the result of the meeting between Dostoyevsky and us. Hints and situations from his life and works can be glimpsed in the production, but everything has been filtered through our own truths, experiences and longings. A wandering of recognition in *My Father's House*.

(Barba, 1986a: 39)

When one reads the spectators' comments in *Breve til Min Fars Hus* ['Letters to My Father's House'] (Barba, on the productions, 1974), it is clear that many spectators could not understand the action of the production, but were nevertheless swept away by an atmosphere, as if by a kind of torrential wave, an unbelievable, almost erotic yet dangerous attraction. As if they were being pulled towards a precipice.

It was as if the ground under one's feet was uncertain and one was in danger of losing one's balance. This sensation is actually very precisely described by a picture drawn by a 7-year-old spectator: the house is teetering on a rocking stone and is threatened because it is out of balance. Beneath it one sees 'the Russian motherland' on which Dostoyevsky fought to gain a firm foothold.

A black cloth obliterating the floor makes it difficult for the actors to keep their balance. The production shifts from light to total darkness broken only by occasional flashes of open flame. At one moment there is peaceful calm and ecstatic happiness; immediately thereafter, stormy

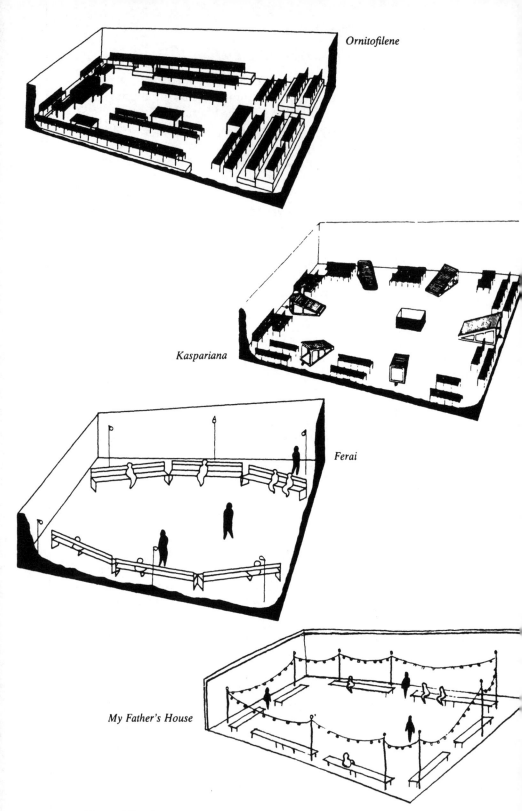

Figure 4 Scenic arrangements for (top) *Ornitofilene*, (middle) *Kaspariana*, (lower left) *Ferai* and (lower right) *My Father's House*.

suffering. There is constant agitation, in keeping with the nature of Dostoyevsky's life.

Something else quite remarkable appears in the spectators' letters. It's as if the performance didn't end. Many people saw it several times and found it difficult to leave the room when it was all over. The production had an almost transforming power so strong that many people remember it years afterwards as a series of glimpses, images, situations, movements, feelings in a dream.

Many spectators felt that they were experiencing a direct creative process:

> What struck me most was the structure in your rectangular room, defined by the benches, that is, by the 'spectators' themselves, an empty room which came alive and stayed alive from the moment the 'actors' arrived, but also because of the 'spectators' ' presence. . . .
> Then this theatre-like room took on a truly 'religious' meaning. Something magical and miraculous came alive. A ritual was consummated, with a maximum degree of participation and fellowship.
>
> (Barba, on the productions, 1974: 40)

With *My Father's House*, Odin Teatret does not attempt to re-create or illustrate a text but independently 'composes' an 'other' reality where the actors are not limited to the psychology of single characters.

This is seen, for example, in the way the two waiter-musicians, one blond and playing the accordion, and the other dark and playing the flute, use their instruments as parts of their 'characters', parts of their physiognomies. The flute is a growth on the actor's face, like a beak or trunk, and the accordion is a defence, something to hide behind, something to spy from. But also an extra stomach.

At the same time, the 'sounds' and the 'voices' from the instruments are not limited to these characters. They can comment on the drama, make ironical statements about the 'rich'; the music can become a dialogue between the two of them and between them and their master, whose actions are observed. But as waiters and musicians, it is also their duty to create environments for their master: the winds on the Siberian tundra, the hooves of galloping horses, the fire's flames.

3

JOINING ODIN TEATRET

ELSE MARIE LAUKVIK

You were 21 years old when you took part in the founding of Odin Teatret in Oslo, 1964. How did it happen?

In August of 1964, I tried for the second time, and still without success, to be accepted by the theatre school in Oslo. I was sure that I had talent, so my picture of the world fell apart. But there was nothing to be done. So I thought, 'You'd better try something else.'

One evening at the dinner table, I told my family that I had decided to go to business school. At the very moment I said this, one of my girlfriends telephoned and said, 'You're going to do theatre.' 'What?' I said. 'Yes, there's this man, his name is Eugenio Barba, he's been in India and Poland, and he's going to do a Jens Björneboe play, and it's going to be really hard, it's very Oriental. I'll call back as soon as I find out more.' I was completely surprised, speechless. It was almost like a sign. I don't actually believe in fate. But that moment was a kind of fate for me, because I had just decided to do something completely different.

After a few days, my girlfriend called back and said, 'We have to talk with a contact person at the university.' So we did. On the way out, a dark-skinned man got into the lift. He was dressed in a dark blue velvet jacket and rust-brown tie. I myself was wearing a rust-brown skirt and dark blue velvet jacket and I thought, 'We must have the same taste. We're almost related.' He stood there and talked to another man about Indian Sanskrit. I stared at him in fascination, thirteen floors down in the lift. And then he disappeared into the crowd.

A week later, my girlfriend called again and said that I had to come to a meeting at Halling School at 6.00 in the evening. On 1 October.

Like a frightened rat, I looked carefully around the classroom filled with people in black tights. But then I caught sight of the man from the lift and suddenly felt completely at home. I went up to him, smiling, and said, 'Hi! I'm Else Marie.' He didn't answer, looked at me in a serious way, and nodded briefly. I understood that now it was going to get serious. I began

Figure 5 Training at Odin Teatret, 1965 (Torgeir Wethal, Else Marie Laukvik,
Anne Trine Grimnes and Tor Sannum). Photo: Odin Teatret.

to do the same exercises as the people in tights. In the following months, I
never asked myself whether this was better or worse than theatre school,
whether it was good or bad. There were eleven of us when we first started,
but after five or six days, there were only six of us left, and after four
weeks, we were but five. As the romantic and superstitious person I was, I
felt that destiny had shown the way.

The first exercises we did were purely physical. I remember that we had
to crouch down and roll our shoulders at the same time. But it was
impossible for me to roll my shoulders as much as a millimetre, in spite of
the fact that Eugenio sat there on a stool like a pillar of salt and repeated
over and over again, 'Up with the shoulders.' 'There certainly are a lot of
strange things one has to go through to become an actor,' I thought. And
my wonder at the profession and the people and situations in it is certainly
one of the things that has stayed with me most over the years. But the first

training was very difficult. It was pure endurance training. And I wasn't accustomed to doing gymnastics and physical exercises. I thought, 'You'll never manage this.' I was so stiff and sore, I could hardly go up and down stairs.

There were various kinds of exercises in those first months. There were Kathakali exercises, eye and hand exercises, there were some yoga exercises from Grotowski's training, there were mime exercises, ballet training.

A few days after we had begun, we were told that we were to prepare, at home, an improvisation for the following day. I asked another girl in the group what improvisation was. She answered that it was to pretend that one was doing an action with something or other that wasn't there. 'Ah!' I thought, 'I'll have to find some household task that's easy to do.' And so my first improvisation was baking a cake in the kitchen, since that was something I was quite good at. It was unprepared, because I couldn't bring myself to flail with my hands in the air at home in the kitchen. It was the first and probably the funniest improvisation in my life. All the others laughed when I, with great appetite, ended the improvisation by tasting the dough with my index finger. The following years were to show me that there was more to life than baking cakes. My biggest obstacles have been tiredness and my back. Sometimes I win, and sometimes I lose. I've many times fought my way through and then asked myself why life can't be a little more comfortable.

The performances

At first, we worked for three hours every evening. After Christmas, we started work on Jens Björneboe's script and worked every day from 9.00 in the morning until 4.00 or 5.00 in the afternoon. We prepared the first sketch of the production and showed it in May of 1965. We were three women and two men. But one of the women left and so there were four of us. And it was we four who developed the actual production, *Ornitofilene*.

We worked first in a classroom at Halling School. After Christmas, we had a room in the Architects' Centre in Oslo. It was a good room, and there we made the first version of *Ornitofilene*. But unfortunately, we couldn't use it any longer and so moved to an air-raid shelter. In this room, with its dripping walls, the production was finished. The temperature inside was 13°. But it was a fantastic place in which to work with the voice. We often stood 20 m apart from each other, early in the morning, when we started with voice training. It was here that I felt that my voice really opened and once in a while took on a power beyond myself. My voice bounced back to me from the space and I was completely astonished.

It was difficult for us to understand exactly what it was that Eugenio actually wanted. Group theatre and alternative theatre didn't exist at that time, or, at least, I didn't know anything about them. It was hard to understand what he meant when he talked about Grotowski and his ideas.

We improvised both alone and together. And many things were also done purely technically. In the first version of *Ornitofilene*, I was the daughter in the family. It was a very little role. I was somewhat disappointed, since I had typed the script on the typewriter, pounded it out with leaden shoulders and cramps in my neck. It was stencilled and given out to the four other actors. I didn't get even one speech and was completely ignored, without any explanation whatsoever. It was difficult not to let my disappointment show.

But the other girl left, quit and went into traditional theatre, and I had to take over her part. So I ended up with a double role.

Many of the things we did we were told to do by the director. It was very specific: 'Do this' or 'Do that'. Or things happened in the training or during improvisations which were then woven into the action.

When I began at Odin Teatret, I was tremendously shy and felt insignificant. Eugenio asked me to sing and I simply refused.

But the air-raid shelter had its own life, and something happened there that could never have happened in the same way anywhere else. There's a scene which I remember very strongly. It's the 'burial scene', and there I sang for the first time. A very 'hot' scene, very violent. The father is condemned to death. The mother and the daughter, mad with despair, loosen their hair and, crying, sing 'Yonder in Gethsemane . . .', while he is being executed. Then they approach the body and wash and care for it. The daughter washes his feet with her hair, just as Mary washed Jesus' feet. She is crying and the crying turns into crazed laughter. I discovered that when an emotional state is taken to its extreme consequence, it can turn into its opposite. She screams, '*Ecce homo*': 'Behold the son of man'. She puts the corpse on her back as if it were a cross and carries it around the room, laughing crazily. The mother walks in front of her and sings a burial song.

But the father is not dead after all and the women, joyful because of his resurrection, sing hallelujah.

Ornitofilene was performed in a very changing and dynamic style. A great deal of text and song, very rich in imagery. The theme had to do with double standard morality.

Many of the scenes were ambiguous, such as the scene we called the 'rose monologue'. One of the actors made a slight change of costume and became a German general while he talked about roses and about what a shame it was to dig them up.

The same applied to another scene, the 'pogrom', where the actors crawled up to the windows, hid under the tables and chairs and ran around the room in confusion. They pounded on the doors and walls, trying to get away from the massacre which awaited them. Panic became resignation

Figure 6 Ornitofilene, 1965 (Else Marie Laukvik). Photo: Odin Teatret.

and, bleating like lambs, they went into the 'gas chambers'. We made a tableau on the table in the middle of the room, with arms and legs sticking out in all directions: a stiff, mute cry.

During the rehearsals we did an improvisation in connection with this scene. Eugenio played a record of music and songs that we were to react to.

Without ever having heard the song before, I found myself driven to the walls. I stood for a long time with my face to the wall and then felt my way along it, like Rachel crying at the wall in Rama over the loss of her children.

I had experienced a pain that was very old, about the tragedy of the Jews (the cry in Rama). I expressed that pain in the only way I could. Eugenio explained that the song was a very old synagogue song which the Jews sang on the way into the gas chambers.

The song had struck an inner chord which first came to full theatrical expression and life twenty years later in my work with the Jewish tailor Zusha Mal'ak in *Oxyrhincus Evangeliet*.

I didn't have any particular relationship to Judaism but that song happened to call up certain images, images which as a child I had seen in the Bible: 'the crying wall at Rama'.

One evening I spoke with a woman who had just seen the performance. She had experienced the ghetto scene as a sexual orgy. It was a shock for me to discover how differently a scene or a performance can be perceived.

After Ornitofilene *the group changed the nature of the training and the 'style' of the performance work. Why?*

After each production, it is important to return to zero. We cleanse ourselves: clean up, tidy up, create light and clarity. We create a new working situation by making new rules, we change the dressing-rooms. We have to leave the old production behind, we have to tear the 'old' to pieces.

In contrast to *Ornitofilene*, which was very dynamic, rich in imagery and full of light, *Kaspariana* was dark and slow, like slow motion. It began in the dark and ended in the dark. And the actors had a completely different way of moving.

We made a conscious choice to work with slow-motion training. We also had an inner motivation while we worked, an inner motor, which coloured our actions. *Ornitofilene* was composed of more coolly planned action patterns interspersed with some 'hot' scenes, that is, scenes which were emotionally stronger for the actors. *Kaspariana* was a completely 'hot' production. In our terminology, we differentiate between 'hot' scenes, in which the actions are influenced by an inner narrative, a stream of images, like a movie, and 'cold' scenes, which are purely technical movement forms without personal motivation.

We began to work on the various characters who met Kaspar Hauser in the square in Nuremberg. We were not defined as personalities; our actions were determined by the situation. At one moment, I was the goddess of learning who raped Kaspar with a Bible. The next moment, I was the bird-mother who had to teach her child to walk. The mother who said farewell to her son as he left to go to war. The mother who sang the song of lament during one of the scenes where Kaspar was suffering. I taught him to walk, I taught him to tell stories. He was born out of a carpet and I sang lullabies, I was the mother he never had. I was the mother figure throughout the performance, but when Kaspar was to be married, my role was more that of a giggling wedding guest. So we changed characters. There were no definite, clearly defined roles.

The actor builds up an inner score and then has to learn to change motivation with lightning speed. That's where the secret lies. Learning to change motivation quickly. Sometimes, one has to change motivation in the course of seconds.

While *Kaspariana* was dark, slow and sonorous, *Ferai* was more dynamic, lighter, with a lot of text and a clear sequence of actions. Before *Ferai*, we again changed the kind of training we did.

Just before *Ferai*, we had been doing stamina training, training that went on for many hours. We also did a lot of composition training, training with acrobatics, mime, slow-motion movements, and we all took part in the same exercises, although we also trained individually, each of the actors on their own.

In Ferai, Alcestis is a closed character, dressed in a dark cape which hides all of her body. She has a cloth tied around her head so that her hair is hidden. There is something shut and aloof about her. Something nun-like. Something pent-up. She is both innocent and nearly diabolic.

Alcestis sacrifices herself. She impales herself on a knife. The knife is also a whip, the same whip she flayed the 'people' with at the beginning of the performance as her father's last 'gift'. The whip represents her father. She submits to her father's power and enjoys the subjugation – which is also a liberation.

After the death of her father, she takes 'him' off. She removes her costume and out of the empty mantle which falls to the floor, a new being is born, the 'bride', with long, loose, blonde hair. The 'shadow', the 'inner angel', is liberated, something 'pure and celestial' floats away.

Her action of sacrifice has created another reality. Admetos begins to play the flute (the knife and the whip are transformed) and shows that the prop contains a third possibility. A poetic possibility? He exits, playing the flute. The people follow him.

What is your perception of the ending in Ferai?

It was a very long scene, one of the longest scenes I have ever performed. It was based on an improvisation, most of the elements of which were used. I played Alcestis, and our theme was suicide. My motivation in the production was very closely tied to this first improvisation. You have to be faithful to your motivation, which contains various inner pictures and action impulses, forming a pattern. For me, these images were very clear. The scene was set and then could not be changed. My inner images remained very much the same from performance to performance.

Are they personal images which then become the 'character's' images?

Yes and no. I created the character and it is certainly not a traditional one. If I was to play Hedda Gabler, for example, I would analyse the part and try to bring out the images found inside her. But here the sequences were created by me, their life comes from my imagination and it unfolds

Figure 7 Ferai, 1969 (Torgeir Wethal and Else Marie Laukvik). Photo: Odin Teatret.

completely independently of the director and the author of the script. But the images don't have to be personal, if by personal one means coming from one's own life. What goes on in the actor's head is a private domain, something we very seldom talk about.

Nearly everything I did was completely imaginary, material from my subconscious. On the other hand, I am probably more of a Stanislavski-type actor than the other actors at Odin Teatret. The images which come up are very detailed. They enrich me. I think that if you only use motivations from your own personal experience, then your possibilities for expression become limited.

Ferai was constructed on the basis of the work of the individual actors and on a number of recognizable main roles. At that time, Torgeir [Wethal], Iben [Nagel] and I had worked together for a whole year, so we had the most experience. The new actors didn't have the same range but they did perhaps have the same intensity.

My Father's House was more collective. All the roles were equally large. The training was much shorter, more intense and freer. It was no longer skill training but impulse training, which is a warm and expressive training, a wave flowing through the body, causing the body to act without stopping, fluently, but yet with variations. One doesn't stop and differentiate the elements. It's just like in music. If one trains a movement in a particular way, it is technical skill training. But with impulse training, one combines the elements in a rhythmic sequence. The important thing is the driving force which directs the actor's body, the wave which moves the body.

Neither Torgeir nor I trained very much during that period. We were tired after all the perfection training. But Iben continued to work and found new possibilities.

My Father's House was a very lively yet softer production. It unfolded in a more flowering way, whereas *Ferai* was more strict and rigid. Perhaps in reaction to five years of discipline training: a kind of liberation. We learned that language was not so important and invented our own 'language'.

In many of the places we performed, people could understand *Ferai*, even if they didn't necessarily understand the language we were speaking, because we also used a body language in addition to the language of the text. But in those countries where people could understand the spoken language, they often had difficulty following the performance. Movements are stronger than sound and the spoken word. If one makes a movement at the same time as one speaks, the words are not heard. In *Ferai* we had worked a great deal with intonation, with changes in voice and tone, often in opposition to the meanings of the words, and this created difficulties for those spectators who could understand the text. We solved this problem in *My Father's House* by working with the text in a different way.

My Father's House was based on the actors' improvisations and not on a script. We had a theme, on the basis of which we made choices, but it was the actors' bodies, their movements in the room, which formed the production. At the beginning, my 'score' was divided up into a series of different roles but gradually, as we performed, this changed.

At the beginning, I felt very distant from *My Father's House* and was unsympathetic towards it. I didn't want to do it, didn't want to accept it. But then I was drawn into it and was taken over by it.

In the first production I saw, you had long hair. But later your hair was cut very short, which completely changed your appearance. What did this mean for you?

After I cut my hair, it was as if I had given in. It was a kind of penalty. I had a guilty conscience and had to punish myself. Maybe it was in order to return to zero. My hair was as short as a prisoner's, but in a way I felt I had freed myself by cutting the 'old' off.

I was in conflict because I didn't want to be at Odin Teatret at that particular time.

Before we started work on *My Father's House*, I felt like performing something funny. I said to Eugenio, 'I want to play a clown.' 'I'm not interested in clown productions,' he answered. I went and took a clown course with Jacques Lecoq in Paris and when I came home, we were supposed to begin work on *My Father's House*, so I didn't get the chance to play a clown. But I managed to sneak some half-grotesque things into the production. A hint of something humorous which satisfied me.

Can you reconstruct the sequence of events in My Father's House?

I don't think that one could make an actual reconstruction of the action. It would vary so much from actor to actor, since we each have our own understanding of our actions and our characters. The director has perhaps a completely different justification for our presence.

The framework of the production is the 'thousands of strange things' which a condemned person experiences on the way to the scaffold. This actually happened to Dostoyevsky and is something he probably never got to the bottom of. One finds traces of it throughout his writing. It was a kind of psychic torture which he and several of his friends were put through because they had become involved in politics. They were pardoned at the last minute.

Confrontation with death is an important part of the production and is connected to yet another theme: the absence of God and the Father. This is something which Dostoyevsky deals with in both *Crime and Punishment* and *The Brothers Karamazov*. If God is dead, everything is permitted, there is total freedom. This is a reference to Dostoyevsky's own father who was a tyrant and a drunkard and who raped the women on the estate. He

Figure 8 My Father's House, 1972 (Else Marie Laukvik and Ulrik Skeel). The beginning of the performance. Photo: Tony D'Urso.

was murdered by the peasants. The absent father figure lies like a shadow over the production.

How did the performance begin for you?

The spectators come in and sit on the benches, which are lit with bare light bulbs. I enter with two musicians, toss a flower on to the floor and whisper, 'To you, Fyodor Dostoyevsky.'

I toss the flower in Dostoyevsky's honour in the same way that I imagine a Buddhist would lay a flower at Buddha's feet. I give myself to the performance. I do the action in a way that is a complete opening. Not pleasure, not happiness, not fear, but humility. I am humble *vis-à-vis* Dostoyevsky and his fate. A pure action, because one who offers a flower to a god must be motivated by pure thought.

It's the same kind of feeling I have when I enter an empty work room. I have a reverence for the empty theatre room, for the empty space, for the latent possibilities.

Someone whistles, the other actors enter. The musicians play a Russian melody. I dance with one of them.

The condemned man is led to the scaffold. A black blindfold is put over his eyes. I kiss him.

A black cloth is spread out over the floor. The lights go out. Accordion music in the dark. Suddenly, matches are struck in the dark behind the spectators. Faces are briefly lit. I go over to the condemned man, who has fallen on the floor. I lead him over to a white sheet. In my hand I hold a little light, which flickers like the spark of life which is about to leave him. I move the light over his face and mine so that it almost burns us. A woman sings in a high, falsetto-like voice, 'Fyodor Dostoyevsky . . .' I blow the light out and the room goes completely dark. We are moving over into a new dimension. Perhaps it is the moment just before death, when one's life passes in front of one's eyes. Or is it perhaps like having an epileptic seizure?

Light. The white sheet is now covered with earth, or ashes, or maybe it's blood. It is the night of the wake. I sing a lament over the body of the dead man. He is now also the Father who has committed rape. I pull the white sheet up to my neck so that the earth collects in a pile in my lap. I feel like 'Mother Russia', I stand up and scatter the 'Russian earth' out over the black cloth. A path is made which is then peopled with the various characters. They dance and sing.

I feel that the 'Russian people's soul' is very present. A Russian wildness.

The condemned man is no longer blindfolded. I lie down beside him and sing as I caress his body with my hair.

In what now happens, he is almost a spectator of the events that take place all around him.

There is a scene between a woman and two men, a very poetic and beautiful scene. They run as if over a grassy meadow.

Then comes a very violent and dynamic scene, like a troika gallop, a four-in-hand is rushing at great speed, like in *The Brothers Karamazov*, when the brothers drink vodka and dance with Grushenka.

The black cloth is now pulled to one side.

I am now a poor peasant, barefoot and wearing a brown leather skirt, like Sonya, the prostitute in *Crime and Punishment*. She who opens 'the way' for Raskolnikov, so that he assumes suffering and guilt and is 'resurrected' or 'reborn'.

The other characters have collapsed after this orgy, after the intoxication of wildness. Then the peasants come forward, with an even greater wildness. It is the peasants' feast. I pull the master's boots off, throw them up in the air, howl and shout with joy. I put the boots on and walk in triumph around the room. The musician plays the accordion and he drinks a whole bottle of beer. I dance in ecstasy until I collapse on the floor.

The room has become a battlefield; I look with fear out over a strange landscape. It reminds me of the scorched earth policy (when the earth is burned to hinder an enemy's forward march). I feel burnt out myself, like Joan of Arc. I have taken the boots off and hold them up in the air, towards the sky, I am a witness and my action is an accusation. I slowly lower my arms, still holding the boots, and embrace my body, as if I were embracing my lover on his way to Siberia. And then I go round the room whistling with a beer bottle, like a happy child. I taste the beer and gulp it down.

I throw the boots and the beer bottle into a canvas sack. The musicians have spread out the black cloth again. I stand in the canvas sack and stamp my feet.

The condemned man asks (in a language which the spectators can understand): 'What is a great idea?'

I answer: 'To change stone to bread is a great idea.'

'Is it the greatest?'

'It's a great idea, but not the greatest. When a man is no longer hungry, he asks, "What shall I do now?" '

The two musicians are standing behind the spectators, in the dark. They extend two long poles with flickering lights on the ends into the performing area. The lights flutter like birds and briefly illuminate the two men, who confront each other. One of them offers a crucifix, the other answers with a switchblade and with it kills the woman he is obsessed by.

I come in with an oil lamp and the light plays over the dead woman. At the beginning of the performance, I threw down a flower in Dostoyevsky's honour. I now have a second flower between my toes, and am holding a third flower in my hand. I make it fly like a butterfly and then tear it to pieces. Its petals fall over the dead woman, who has been draped over the man's knee. It is as if I am tearing her to pieces, as if she were a delicate flower or a butterfly, sacrificed to a destructive power.

When the lights come up, the condemned man is once again blindfolded. Another character has put on the condemned man's jacket and is almost hiding behind it. He stands alone in the middle of the room. All the other characters stand behind the spectators and throw money at him. He is stoned with the coins, like a Judas. He falls, gets up, tries not to succumb, falls again and stretches his hands out towards the condemned man, who helps him up while still throwing coins at him. The condemned man takes off his blindfold. The two men embrace, become brothers, are united. Perhaps the condemned man assumes his destiny of suffering, as Raskolnikov did. Perhaps he has found himself. Perhaps it is a rebirth, after the final torture. The jacket protects the two of them. They exit. We dance and sing and follow them.

TORGEIR WETHAL

What happened the first time you met Eugenio Barba in Oslo, 1964?

'My God,' my mother said, 'he's a foreigner, Italian or something. Now you be careful.'

Ever since I was 9 years old, I had been running back and forth between the theatre in Oslo, where I had played small juvenile roles, amateur theatres, where I performed and directed, and the old film studio outside town, where I had also worked. And somewhere in the middle of all that I also tried to go to school. My parents gave up their opposition to my interest in the theatre by the time I was 11 or 12, and they tacitly supported me.

But now my mother was really nervous. 'Foreigner, Italian or something.'

And a foreigner he undoubtedly was, the broken Norwegian on the telephone left no doubt about that: 'Hello, my name is Barba. We need to meet.'

'Oh? What about?'

'Theatre, of course.'

'OK. Where shall we meet? Where can I find you?'

A restaurant we both knew. 'I'm dark-skinned and will be reading *Dagbladet.*'

Foreigner, dark. My mother wasn't happy at all. But . . . the dark little man with the blue jacket and the correct tie had set the *Dagbladet* to one side and spread the strangest pictures out over the table-top.

He smoked roll-your-owns, that didn't seem so foreign – almost Norwegian. The pictures, on the other hand, were foreign.

Close-up shots of two men using their fingers to spread their eyes wide open. A woman, making the most frightful grimaces. A man in white robes, standing on one leg on a table. A man lying on the floor with his legs spread in the air, while another man flew between them. Two men, hitting each other with sticks.

'These are the actors in Grotowski's Teaterlaboratorium, where I have been studying for the last few years. Look! Faust is standing on one leg, way out of balance, while he recites a long monologue. The spectators are sitting around a table, which is the performing area. The actors undergo preparation through long training. The facial exercises which you call grimaces have been taken from Indian dancers – Kathakali. They practise bio-mechanics, which is a kind of acrobatics. The actor must be able to fly. They work with physical training, plastic training, voice training – but when they begin work on a production, the psycho-technique is the most important.'

Madness – pure and simple madness, but exciting – and above all, excitingly told. A table as a performing area! Neither I nor anyone I knew had ever seen a theatre without a stage. And flying actors! And psycho-technique!?

He wanted to gather some people together and start a theatre group which would work with the same principles. Did I want to join for a trial period and see what it was all about?

I can't imagine that I had understood anything. Anything other than that it had something to do with the theatre. And that I wanted to do theatre was one of the things that I was very sure about.

It might have been his eagerness – his nervousness – his definiteness – which enticed, charmed and beguiled me.

'I want to have a meeting with those who are interested. Are you coming?'

I was 17 years old. Still plenty of time to try a lot of things. 'Yes.'

My mother's anxiety was justified.

I had never imagined that I would do anything other than theatre. I had been bitten by the traditional theatre and had made a definite decision to enter it. I had been to an audition at the theatre school when I was 17 but had not been accepted. They thought I should wait a year. When they asked me, 'What will you do if you don't get in?', I replied, 'I'll come to the auditions next year.' So if Eugenio hadn't turned up, I would certainly by now have had my thirtieth anniversary in one theatre or another in Norway. I would certainly have been completely satisfied.

The profession

For me, Odin Teatret has always been a specific point of reference from which to relate to the outside world – and this point of reference has at the same time always been variable. Within this point of reference – these

42

Figure 9 Training at Odin Teatret, 1968 (Lars Goran Kjeldsted, Eugenio Barba at the table, Torgeir Wethal, Dan Nielsen, Stanley Rosenberg). Photo: Roald Pay.

changeable frameworks, in Odin Teatret – I have experienced situations and periods of time which have contained the greatest possible concentration of life – situations in which I have, within a very short time, experienced and learned more about myself and my surroundings than I would have outside Odin Teatret. This has sometimes happened, for example, as a result of my confrontation with a difficult work task, but what I am most of all referring to now is what we call improvisation and 'the creative work'. The experience gained through the concrete and specific search for the basis and form of expression for a production influences and infects one's 'private self', as does all experience.

Yet I have never gone into these situations in order to have a private experience – it always had something to do with my work.

We use specific work techniques. The verb 'to improvise' – to do the unforeseen – has led to an endless number of forms of praxis and interpretation. I believe that within Odin Teatret there are just as many different ways of approaching an improvisation as there are actors in the group. How large a part of the work process improvisation is also varies and some of the actors have made many more and deeper experiences in this area than others.

I myself no longer use this 'technique' so often, but it is nevertheless my basis and an important professional experience.

My own improvisation story began in the attic of Halling School – Odin Teatret's first room.

We began with work on studies. This was a kind of illustration – an improvisation: you walk through a wood – push the branches to one side, one of them hits you in the face – you come to a creek – hop from stone to stone – halfway across you almost fall into the water – you reach land on the other side and step on swampy ground – etc. A sequence is fixed, and the work contains a specific inner visualization. Nature and all the details of the experience were to be seen with the inner eye. In my first work journal, from the fall of 1964, I find written:

Concerning Studies: Feel, before you express something. Consider and see something specific before describing what you have seen. Hear before you answer. Sight – hearing – smell – taste – recognition (feeling) must always be taken into consideration.

The verb 'to feel' is later taken out of my work terminology. Feeling is the result of a meeting between yourself and your surroundings. If you begin by feeling something, then all you can reach afterwards is a tense, stressed expression. A feeling cannot be forced out – it is the result of many factors. But apart from this aspect, these words from 1964 still have value. They have been fundamental to my way of doing improvisations through the years, but as time has gone by, I have taken the contents of these improvisations from worlds which are bigger and more complicated than when I first began. My wandering in these 'scenes' has often brought me to the unknown – the unconscious. My reaction to these meetings has often followed a pattern which earlier I had not recognized as my own.

I remember my first improvisation alone with Eugenio. It was after the ordinary work of the day was over. Eugenio tried to explain to me what I should do:

'There are certain people who are more important to you than others; there are situations you have lived through, desired, or dreamed about that are more important to you than others; there are places, seen or unseen, which are more important to you than others. Begin from a situation which is a combination of a known face and a definite action in a definite place. Let this world come alive, follow it, live in it. There are no rules. Everything can change along the way. Maybe it's like a day-dream, or a dream. Maybe it's something you remember. Take your time. Begin from the position which is most comfortable for you.'

Perhaps Eugenio's explanation wasn't exactly like this. It has probably been concentrated by my memory over the years. But I remember the situation very clearly:

I lay down on the floor and closed my eyes. It was quiet. I was 17 and

rather inexperienced in many aspects of life. But nevertheless – or therefore – I had a strong imaginative and dream power. I often had very strong
experiences without doing anything at all.

First I met the heavy and comfortable darkness. Then slowly I let spaces,
people and actions appear. Friends, parents, girlfriends . . . faces passed
by, stayed with me. I finished some old, interrupted experiences from the
past. Formerly withheld reactions were expressed. It was sometimes
chaotic. It flickered with various faces and actions, all mixed up together.
This occurred most when the thought that something had better happen
pretty soon – surely I wasn't meant to just lie there on the floor with closed
eyes – worked its way into my other consciousness. I don't know how long
it lasted. My perception of time disappeared, it still does during improvisations. Finally I opened my eyes and got up from the floor, where I had lain
motionless the whole time.

When I think back on all this today, it can seem absurd. Most directors
or teachers would have interrupted the actor after a short time to say that
they obviously hadn't explained the task very well. In the course of the
hour or hour and a half that I suppose the improvisations lasted, Eugenio
sat still and watched, he didn't interrupt me, and neither did he criticize me
afterwards. The hour without physical actions contained an intensity which
it took years for me to bring alive in the theatre space.

My first improvisation was like a film shown by a projector with no bulb.
All the images were there and passed in front of my objective eye, but the
room was dark. For some actors, the improvisation must be projected in
space and the body must be its three-dimensional screen. For other actors,
at another level, it's simpler: the body lives and carries out its part of what
is happening. But whichever way the actor works, everything and everyone
'around' him that he does something with, that do something with him, are
invisible to the spectator. The improvisation must not illustrate this world.
The actor must simply react completely, both physically and emotionally,
with respect to what is happening, to what he is doing. His improvisation
takes place in space. The actor who uses the 'screen' will usually first see
his images and then show them in space.

Eugenio then said:

'Each improvisation is the other's speech, and he doesn't behave as we
do. In daily life, we behave according to a certain pattern – the other does
not use this pattern. He uses another language and it is this other language
which we must find our way down to. Ninety per cent of every improvisation must be the other's speech. And the other 10 per cent is the introduction. This has nothing to do with originality. It has been said that the actor
who plays himself is empty after two productions and has nothing new to
say. That's not the way it is. You excavate. Like an archaeologist on a dig,
you always find new layers underneath the layer you have already un-
covered. I believe that the people who are meaningful to us, who are

45

important to us, are actually monomaniacs. They're always confronting the same problem – they dig deeper and deeper into it.'

There is nothing to prevent an action in an improvisation from being transferred to and expressed with another part of the body than what may be realistic, or the direction of an action may be changed. 'To put your hand on a man's shoulder' can perhaps become an action where the outer action is determined beforehand, yet done at the same time as you go down on your knees. But all the dynamics, the qualities and the intentions must be kept, the idea is not enough: I use the knee instead of the hand, I use the floor instead of the shoulder.

The actor often prefers not to show certain parts of his imagination directly. In such a situation, he can use the 'transfer principle': letting other parts of the body execute the action. He's hiding, in a way, but at the same time he can, when he has become accustomed to doing so, fully live the inner life without being disturbed by 'censor thoughts'. And outwardly, he hides the fact that he isn't hiding.

Let us suppose that we have to do a love scene. Many actors will make use of a part of their memories which is completely parallel with the contents of the scene. The literal action corresponds to an equally literal content. The action is an illustration based on memory. There are other actors who use a part of their memories which does not correspond to the scene's outer action. Perhaps, while the love scene is being played, they relive one of the most beautiful fishing trips they've ever been on, or something else which has nothing at all to do with the action. They do this in order to give a completely different, more exciting 'colour' to the act of love. Perhaps they will bring the spectator further. The action pattern must start from one's own memory warehouse, one's own need to express, and then perhaps be used in a completely different context.

For the actor, the simplest and most ordinary phenomena are often the most important. The person you have been happiest with, or a person who has died, or something you once did. The problem is to transform this into something literal, to make what is the most important for you, in you, into an action and to show it.

During one period, I made use of improvisations where I wandered in the deepest, darkest tunnels, like going down a throat, like skiing down grooves that were really wrinkles, like being blown over by a storm from the nose. These experiences became concrete actions that I could remember and re-create. A kind of slalom movement with specific swings from side to side could emerge from and respond to the caressing of a wavy wrinkle on a forehead.

If you are searching for something other than a directly epic, outer illustration – which doesn't contain secrets – then you have to find a way to create and combine multiplicity, you have to work with several things at a time, or translate what is happening into another language, into something corresponding, whose quality nevertheless derives from the literal part of your imagination.

Everyone can improvise and all improvisations can, in one way or another, be memorized and used as a fixed, repeatable action pattern. This is a kind of material which the actor and director share and can form further and adapt to the needs of the production. The inventive director, or the director who knows what he wants to do with his work, can get something fruitful out of most improvisations, but it is a mistake to neglect to respect – or to avoid respecting – the fact that the 'depth' of the actor's material is important. The actor who acts with his outer self can be an important teller of the director's story but he will never be the one who makes that story greater.

I don't care where the actor gets his power from – where his depth lies – as long as he finds the way out of his shell. Improvisation can be a means for the actor to learn to know and to accept many of his own powers, both the light and the dark. In any case, the point of departure for such work can never be therapy. The goal is theatre work: the production.

> The wind is strong. I lean against it. I spread my arms. I see the valley far below. I stand on the edge of the cliff. The wind holds me up. I rest against the wind. A gust hits me in the stomach, catches me and throws me backwards – up. I lie down and fly with the wind. It whistles and lifts me up. I whistle back. It gradually changes direction and spins me around. I land on my feet, on the cloud's soft carpet. Quilt – sprung mattress. I walk over the fantastic fields. My feet sink deep and are pushed, sucking, up again. I walk towards bright colours, towards strong light. I run with slow seaman's strides towards the sun. I approach the sun, feel its warmth, run into it, burn up. Am not. Am. The dust of my ashes floats slowly down, down over Studenterlunden. Down over the town's main square. I see the teeming life from the air. I land softly, among the hurried and noisy crowds.

This was the way that Kaspar Hauser's awakening ended on the square in Nuremberg. For me. In me. This scene in *Kaspariana* was assembled from fragments of several improvisations. When I now read my work notes from that time in 1966, I can see that every time Eugenio asked me to make a change in the outer action – changes I wrote down – I immediately changed my inner sequence of actions and wrote down the new montage. And it was this new montage that I concentrated on remembering.

In the actor's inner world, anything can happen. He doesn't need to defend or explain its logic. But the director both can and must work on what the actor lets out, on how he manifests his inner world. At the beginning, the director must also help the actor find the areas in himself which have power, not only within him, for himself, but also outwardly, as form and life in space. This he must do without speaking 'personally'. The security shared by the director and the actor is protected by the fact that they always talk about the task at hand and the visible result. No matter what the actor translates the director's words into, no matter what parallels he finds within himself and works from, they must speak together on the basis of the world of the theme or about the work's general problems.

What form has your training taken and what has it meant to you?

Since Odin Teatret began, a great deal of our work has had to do with the actor's training. For the most part, the purpose of the training has not been the acquisition of skills for later use in performance. The purpose of the training has been to help the actor to break down his conditioned reflexes, to help him to work on his own daily movement patterns and to overcome his learned fatigue limits. Our training was also intended to lead the actor to an understanding of the elemental rules of physical expression.

For a long time, the training was technical: a study of the relationship between various muscle tensions, a search for the laws which govern corporeal expression and the relationship between the body and space.

Just as a good mechanic is familiar with the relationship between the different parts of a motor, we have knowledge of the ways in which movements can be technically combined and of the ways in which movements influence each other. Some mechanics will also search for technical improvements, get ideas from other mechanics, try new combinations. But to teach mechanics to avoid the mechanical can also be difficult.

The first year's training was made up of fixed elements, of exercises we had learned, many of them from the physical and plastic training which Grotowski and his actors had developed. We always did these exercises with a motivation, a personal justification. You saw images and furnished the room with them, they were a part of stories which you lived.

With time, this work began to limit us in a negative way. Most of us slowly became caught up in 'psychic clichés', expressions of 'feelings' which stuck to us when we worked on a production. A kind of inner banality settled in, it was as though our imaginations and emotions began to wear out.

When we became aware of this, we chose to go the opposite way. Training became hard and physical, like athletic training: a physical obstacle to be overcome, a result to be made better, improved. It was hard. I don't believe it taught us anything as actors (but it was undoubtedly one of the reasons for the aggressiveness and inner competition which characterized the *Ferai* company). And yet some of us developed a psychic conditioning. If you could manage to survive that period, you could survive anything.

Since then the training has had many different points of departure and has taken many different forms, but its essence has always been technical. We have used our training to search for forms of expression, not content.

The biggest surprises which have occurred in the development of our training have come about because of the actors who, in spite of what Eugenio and the other actors thought, insisted on developing new work because of their own needs. Working against the group and for themselves, they brought us all further.

At ISTA [the International School of Theatre Anthropology] in Holstebro in September 1986, you demonstrated a training sequence. Can you describe it?

It was a strange experience, doing that demonstration. The training sequence I showed was from 1966–7. At that time, our training, as I have mentioned before, was done using personal motivations. Irrespective of what we did, tiger jumps, leaps and falls, whatever, we did it with a definite motivation and with specific details. You knew, for example, where you did it, whether on grass or on small stones, etc. We built up an inner universe which permeated the fixed patterns of the physical exercises. And the part of this training which for me was closest to performance work was the 'cat chain'.

During the preparations for a production, it often happens that many actions are constructed because they are required by the story. We call these actions 'technical passages'. In such a situation, the actor has the shell of an action which must be filled out, must be given a motivation. The pattern and the main action are set but there can of course be changes in tempo, rhythm and nature. This was also the case with the 'cat chain', based on five or six set physical exercises, more or less difficult to execute – going into a bridge, arm bends towards the floor, shooting the spine upwards, standing on one's head. You allowed an inner action sequence to live within these exercises. You were in a completely personal situation in a particular place at the same time as you were doing the exercise, precisely and concretely. Your inner movie has a great influence on the details of an exercise, the rhythm, the tempo. The exercises become something you do in relationship to someone or something, or they are done against you, or with you.

During ISTA, Eugenio asked me if I could do the 'cat chain'. I remembered the inner movie perfectly well, even though I hadn't 'seen' it in twenty years, but I had trouble remembering the order of the exercises. I trained for several days, trying to do the exercises. It became clear that it wasn't going to work. Then I discovered that the work journals I was using to refind the sequence of the exercises were from an even earlier period. I had later changed the order.

I showed the sequence to the other actors in the group who knew it from

Figure 10 The cat chain, 1987 (Torgeir Wethal). Photo: Torben Huss.

the past, and they perceived that it was as it had been. But I kept wondering about one thing: was I showing the same exercises, or was I showing myself as I was when I did the exercises back in the 1960s, as 'Torgeir, who did the "cat chain" twenty years ago'? Was it an old image I performed or re-created? The answer to this question was not clear, but the sensation I had was that 'now Torgeir was moving his fingers, the way he moved them back then and for the same reasons'. Naturally, it gets all mixed up, because memory and experience work their way into it. Naturally, a technique becomes a form of experience one carries with one. It becomes a kind of language in the body. One makes use of various things at the same time. Today, the training is based on an almost cold, technical analysis. Eugenio will never interfere in the actor's 'why', he is only interested in the set action patterns and in the usable energy which they contain. It is left completely up to the actor himself to fill out and motivate his action, or not.

For me, the specific motivation, the inner movie, that was built into the exercises was so specific a driving force that twenty years later it re-created the same physical effect because it was not a representation of something that had happened – it was alive in the present.

I did it in the same way as a performance, where the order of the movements is also set and becomes physical memory.

Seen from the outside, the 'cat chain' contains a very powerful build-up of energy. One can see how the energy slowly moves up through the whole body until it finally explodes. Can you describe what you experience?

Yes, if we only talk about the end of the exercise, then, yes, I can. This is because I decided a long time ago to keep the whole story to myself. It all takes place near a particular river, a place where I have often been and felt safe and at home, a place I still long for, a place which belongs to my childhood and youth, a place I shall not see again. During the improvisation, I experience being in love, love itself, eroticism, ecstasy, separation and loneliness. What happens at the end of the exercise is that someone leaves me, and the river, and goes over the nearby hills and slowly disappears down into a soft valley; it's not actually very dramatic. I catch sight of her again, high up on the hill-tops. And, in fact, what then happens is simply that I shout to her, shout across the fields. A great shout to that person, a physical shout that begins under my feet and moves up through my whole body. The quality of the shout, its motivation, its basis, is of course dependent on what happened earlier.

I did the 'cat chain' alone, without having to take a production's dramaturgy into consideration. And I did it with closed eyes. Whenever I had to do it again, it only worked if I closed my eyes.

When you do an action for the first time in an improvisation, when you have time and space at your disposal, you can live it completely. When it then needs to be set, you first repeat it relatively technically. And yet, when you are in a production and are working with other actors and have to react precisely to them and have to execute an action, or a part of an action, taken from an improvisation, the memory of the original reason why you did that action will continue to colour the action, give it the same tone.

IBEN NAGEL RASMUSSEN

Why did you join Odin Teatret?

Something very crucial happened to me when I saw Odin Teatret for the first time. Until then, I had only experienced theatre as something deadly boring. There wasn't really anything in it that held or interested me. But when I saw Odin Teatret perform *Ornitofilene*, I immediately realized that this was something I would like to do. This was something I felt I could invest myself in. I was invited to come to the theatre for a trial period. When I arrived in Holstebro in 1966, what I found was a farm which was to be turned into a theatre – but it wasn't finished yet. The cows had just been taken out of the stalls that were to be our training-room and the pigs were still grunting in the part of the building that was to become dressing-rooms and a 'library'. We worked in a nearby school from 7.00 a.m. to 12 noon and from 5.00 p.m. to 8.00 p.m. in the evening. The first part of the day was devoted exclusively to various kinds of training while the evening hours were used for improvisation and performance work. From the very beginning, we knew that we were on the way to a production, that this was our goal.

The day began with acrobatics and martial exercises. My first surprise was that we began with the physical work right away. I had expected that we would begin with a meeting and that things would be explained. But no – for the first time since I was 6 years old and started school, which above all consisted of reducing my life to words, I had to learn to do something with all of myself. After a few hours' work with acrobatics and martial exercises, we moved on to work with the 'cat chain'.

It was Torgeir who first showed us the chain. I remember that afterwards Eugenio said: 'So, now it's your turn to do the same.' I gaped and couldn't understand what was happening when the others in the room began to stand on their heads or tried to make a bridge. Because what I had seen was not an exercise. It was Torgeir's 'world', something fine and light that shone through his body and the ten exercises. What impressed me was not that he went into a bridge or stood on his head, but the amazingly astral way (so it seemed to me) in which he did it. I didn't see an ordinary body but a kind of spiritual, shining body.

We learned the exercises and put them together. The chain was to be motivated with a personal story, personal images. We showed the work one at a time. This moment was extremely important for us because it contained a little moment of performance. We saw how each person's chain was different from that of the others, even though the exercises were exactly the same, and how the whole sequence became a kind of training poem, where rhythm and energy were modulated following dramatic principles.

At the beginning, the physical challenge to reach the limits of one's ability was unbelievably important. For the first time in my adult life, I was obliged to mobilize all of my will: to use maximum power to get the body to fly and maximum awareness so as not to hurt myself. At first, my 'power and awareness' was heavy and a little chaotic, like someone who is made to fight for the first time with a sword that is all too heavy. Today all my power and awareness can be contained in a very still scene or a nearly immobile fragment from training. The extreme effort at the beginning was a necessary step: it helped me find a vital centre in myself.

What was your first improvisation like?

All four students were given the same theme for an improvisation: we were to walk through a wood, preferably with an imaginary partner. It was made clear that this partner must not be mimed. For example, you were not supposed to mime that you were walking with a dog on a lead. We were to arrive at a house or a castle. There was a door we could open. And, as far as I can remember, here we were to meet our prince or princess.

So we were to improvise one at a time with an imaginary partner. I chose one of my friends. I realized right away that the notion of this person being with me might hinder me so my first action, which I myself felt to be rather clumsy (perhaps because it was an outward, descriptive gesture), was to wave goodbye – and off I went, alone, into the wood.

A strong wind blew against me. The ground was muddy and slippery and there were many obstacles, branches blocked my way. I crawled upwards, I fell, I yelled out loud. Helplessness – desperation – perhaps defiance. I came to the inhabited 'castle'. I knocked on the door (the actual door of the room). No one answered. I knocked again, and perhaps a third time. Still no answer. Then I did something which has made me uncomfortable every time I have since thought about it: I curled up in a ball in front of the door and fell asleep, waiting.

I remember no other details from that first improvisation. My own reaction to and criticism of my work was that I didn't use the space adequately, although we hadn't been specifically told to use the space.

Eugenio's criticism was that I had screamed in a wild and inarticulate way.

The two actions in the middle of the improvisation, the fall and the scream, later became two of the most important elements in my work. Just as it is said that gypsies can cry in any language, through their songs, I learned to articulate my scream, so that it could be heard and perhaps understood in many different places. The fall has been central for the development of my personal training and it has been one of the elements that I have repeated in new forms in various productions.

The improvisation work began quickly and was aimed at the coming production: the story of Kaspar Hauser and of the world which Eugenio conjured up for us with his words.

He told us about Kaspar and about the production we were about to build together. He told us about the ideas he already had. Concerning Kaspar's social birth, Eugenio said, 'We will portray the rich society that meets him. We can illustrate it through our costumes. They are going to be sumptuous. You will put these costumes on in full view of the spectators.'

We worked with the costumes for several days. We used rectangular pieces of cloth – nothing was sewn – and fashioned the various costumes out of them. If we tied, wrapped, or folded them in one particular way, they became 'everyday clothes'; arranged another way, they became 'party clothes'; another quick change and you had made a carnival costume, another change and we were soldiers.

Not even the shoes were sewn – they were pieces of hide held together with leather laces. Here again, the same: each of us improvised with his or her pieces of hide and found at least three or four different kinds of footwear.

Eugenio had had the idea that each actor would have a 'home' which consisted of a little platform. Each actor made a design for this 'home': one was an oval, one a rectangle, one a hexagon.

The way the chairs should be set up was also proposed by each actor. It was decided that they should be arranged in little groups around each platform and should be set facing the actors as much as possible, not directed towards the middle of the room. This solution turned out to be one of those good but impractical ideas one sometimes gets, because there were places in the room where, to put it mildly, it was hard to see (this arrangement of the chairs was later changed).

The roof of each platform was made of slats of wood. A light was placed on each platform and shone up through the roof. Our pieces of cloth were laid over these slats and used to make human-like figures on the tops of the platforms.

The performance began like this: the spectators come into the room; we are outside the room, on the other side of the door; the lights go out, the door opens and we come in, one by one, slowly. We are wearing leotards but have bare legs. The men are wearing shorts or swimming trunks. The lights under the platforms are turned on. One after another, the 'houses' are lit from within. We get dressed in front of the spectators while we sing and laugh. Each actor has her own speech, her own melody, which builds in volume.

Even the way of coming in and getting dressed was of course set by means of individual improvisations.

The most important thing for me as a new student during these long rehearsals was Eugenio's concentration and seriousness, whether it had to do with the placement of the chairs or the working out of a costume. All the small details. How the party shoes were tied, what kind of a figure to make on top of each platform. Everything, *everything*, EVERYTHING was important. No chatter, no superficial talk. We rehearsed in order to find specific solutions, not just in order to rehearse. If somebody came with an idea, it was tried right away. If it worked, it was immediately set. There was an atmosphere of excitement, a feeling of being on the way to something. We were attentive to the unexpected, the possible. We had a direction, a trail to follow, but we had to discover everything.

The improvisations were meaningful, surrounded by respect, silence, concentration. The improvisation work was always done in connection with the building-up of a production. Some improvisations were used almost in their entirety. I personally did few improvisations in those first years and I always felt that there was something incomplete when a montage was made of the improvisations. I believed that the improvisations should be left as they were, a result in themselves. Later I learned to consider them as a sketch which must be worked on by the director and which found its true life later. Sometimes only after the director had completed the production.

The montage in *Kaspariana* and *Ferai* was much simpler than in the successive productions. The scene in *Ferai* where the people cry over King Frode's body was built from individual improvisations which had a common theme: trees in anguish. I think this was the first time Eugenio used a more complicated montage technique, but the order of nearly all the actors' actions was kept as it had been in their improvisations. I thought it was exciting to work out that scene because it contained an interplay of impulse and rhythm with which I associated strongly.

All in all, I didn't do more than three or four improvisations for each of the first two productions. The rest was composition (by composition I mean, for example, to walk in a certain way, to move like a bird, to use one's costume to deform the body).

When we started work on *Ferai*, I tried to make my improvisations as short and as specific as possible. I wanted to be sure to be able to remember everything. I played a peasant in *Ferai*, and this production has always represented the earth for me: brown colours; weight; steady, solid, sure steps; singing which never moved out of the chest resonator. The only time this did happen it was choked off by another peasant. But no matter how 'specific' I tried to be with my logic, no matter how much I struggled to visualize my inner world, it never became a connected sequence of actions. It was more like a montage of images, a selection of details. At this stage of my development, however, this was not an incorrect way to proceed. I kept to the over-specific, I cut off, denied, anything that was deeper than I could immediately understand.

With *My Father's House*, I began to fly like the figures in Chagall's paintings. I no longer held on in a cramped way to what was logical but let myself be carried, permeated, as if by an inner vein of warmth, light and softness. I let go of the daily logic I had sought for in vain and found a dramatic logic that was alive. Actions are, they do not pretend to be. But the accent in the inner, personal themes also changed; I no longer tried to describe the 'dark' – suffering – or, better put, it was as if the 'dark' was finally permeated by a power that could no longer be dominated. In *My Father's House*, this power was love in the form of erotic power.

When Odin Teatret first made a dance performance, in Carpignano in southern Italy in 1974, none of us knew that it was to be the beginning of a whole new era. But the beginning of a new language could be glimpsed. A new form of danced drama which was not controlled by aesthetic principles alone, based on a language which was neither psychologically preoccupied or politically simplistic. A language with which the actors could not declaim or bore their spectators. A completely simple physical power and presence were necessary if one was to take up the fight outdoors where there were crying children, barking dogs and a public which in many cases had not sought out the theatre but quite the reverse.

The dance performances have a development possibility and a future. In Odin Teatret's 'traditional' productions, there are sequences which are very close to dance. There is a connection between what we call physical actions and dance.

In Asian theatre, every performance contains sequences of pure dance, moments which usually indicate a climax, an emotional outburst. It can be difficult for Westerners to accept the transition from meaningful actions to dance, where steps and movements do not have specific meanings.

The dance performances exploded our training. But it is important to remember that there was a long period of previous work which prepared us for this explosion.

ROBERTA CARRERI

You were 21 years old when you first met Odin Teatret in Bergamo, 1973. What was this meeting like?

It wasn't actually an accidental meeting. When I was going to high school, I had a very special teacher. He meant a great deal to me; he was my 'master'. He was very interested in the theatre and was the director of a theatre in Bergamo.

In 1973, I was studying art criticism at university and this former teacher of mine came and found me one day. He told me that he had invited Odin Teatret to come and perform in his theatre. 'You mustn't miss the chance to see them,' he said. Certainly not! At that very time, I was studying Artaud, Grotowski and Barba and was about to take an exam in theatre history.

It was 31 May. Odin Teatret was performing *My Father's House*. We drove to Bergamo and I remember that I was expecting to see a really good performance.

We park in front of the theatre, in the town's lovely medieval square. The air is warm and soft. The theatre's little foyer is crammed with people. The lights in the ceiling make the colours in the spring dresses shine brightly. I am one of the first spectators to enter the theatre room, the floor of which has been covered with planks, giving the air an unusual smell. Wooden benches form a square around the room, a metre from the walls. Over the benches hang bare light bulbs. It's cooler in here than outside and you can feel the cool air on your skin.

All the spectators are now in and are sitting on the benches. The actors enter. A daisy held in someone's toes, a voice, a name, 'Fyodor Dostoyevsky'. Accordion music, dancing, beer which runs down a neck and is sucked up by the wooden planks. Smells, darkness, silence. A little

56

Figure 11 The Book of Dances, 1974 (Roberta Carreri). Photo: Tony D'Urso.

flame which casts light on a flower in a glass of water. The glimpse of a young woman's face as she is lifted off the floor by one of her colleagues.

Music again, light. Endless dancing. Meeting, collision, embraces, darkness. Small flames in the darkness, casting light on long hair, hair glued by sweat to burning faces.

It's become tremendously hot in the room, I've lost all sense of feeling in my body. All I can feel is the heat on my face, which is burning. A large black cloth is lifted into the air and floats down to the floor.

A man wearing a white shirt and a blindfold smiles hysterically while another young man with long blond hair and a jacket over his shoulders falls in a cross-fire of coins thrown by the other actors. The blindfold is pulled off. Glances meet and melt in a moment of wounding beauty. An embrace. The jacket covers the shoulders of both men.

My eyes fill with tears.

The musicians lead the actors out of the room and leave us breathing air heavy with burned-out passions. We leave.

Between the theatre room itself and the actors' dressing-rooms there was a narrow passageway which had been blocked off because of the performance. I knew about this passage because I had often been in this theatre. I rushed into the passage like a hunted animal and hid in the dark and cried so hard that I shook.

I first began to understand why four years later. During most of my childhood, both of my parents were working, so I spent half the day in school and half the day on the streets. I could have gone to stay with my aunt, who lived nearby, but in fact I spent all my free time playing on the streets. I was the only girl in the group I hung out with. I had very short hair and you couldn't really tell that I was a girl. It was pretty rough. We fought with stones and with blow-pipes loaded with pins. You had to be sure to hit your target and then run. I ran very fast. There was an incredible solidarity, but not many words. You were what you did, not what you said you were. You couldn't lie. You were your actions.

That's how I lived until I was 11, until my father realized that it wasn't suitable for a girl to live on the streets, where I peed against a wall, standing up, just like a boy.

It was very hard to have to say goodbye to all my street friends. As an only child, I was lonesome. I began to draw. I got good at it. It was my escape. But it was as if a part of me was paralysed. A wild animal moves in a different way in nature than in a cage. That's how it was for me. My behaviour changed. It was like I was carrying a huge boulder on my back.

What happened nine years later when I saw *My Father's House* was that my body recognized in the actors' behaviour that form of presence which I had had with my friends on the street. That form of harmony in extremity, a way of giving everything, of being what you do and not what you say.

I was tired of role-playing. I was one person with my parents, another with my boyfriend, another at the university or in the left-orientated grass-roots movement, 'Avanguardia Operaia'. I was a whole series of different people formed by my surroundings.

From the time I had left the streets, everything had become a world of words, and the words were different in different situations. I discovered that you can't trust words. They become round and can mean many things. People can always misunderstand each other and hide behind words.

I also experienced this contradiction between words and action in the grass-roots milieu. It was the 'Year of the Bullets' in Milan and the time when terrorism was springing up all over Italy. If I hadn't ended up at Odin Teatret, I probably would have become a terrorist or a drug addict. My anger and sense of powerlessness were very strong.

In December of 1973, Odin Teatret came to Milan and gave a workshop at the university. I sneaked into this workshop. I was extremely nervous because I didn't have anything whatsoever to do with the theatre. But at that time, Odin Teatret was very interested in dance, so we danced to rock music five hours a day for seven days. And dancing was one of the few things I could do.

Four months later, I met Odin Teatret again. In Pontedera. Torgeir and Eugenio were on their way to southern Italy to find a place to work from May to September of 1974. A kind of theatre meeting was taking place and I spoke with Eugenio and asked him if I could come to Denmark and watch them work. He said I could. And so I came to Holstebro on 25 April 1974.

I arrived late at night and Iben and Torgeir met me at the station and took me to a hotel.

At 6.00 a.m. the next morning they drove me to the theatre. I changed clothes and was led into the white work room.

Eugenio told us to improvise, one at a time. My turn came. I had never improvised before. Eugenio whispered a theme in my ear. 'You are afraid, but someone takes your hand and . . .' I remember that I closed my eyes, moved a little bit, and sat down on the floor. I didn't know what I had done.

It was all a misunderstanding. I had come to spend a week and see how Odin Teatret worked. But Eugenio thought that I had come to stay. I found out that it was the new production we were working on and that if I didn't want to be part of it then I couldn't stay and watch the work in the room.

A few days later, I knocked on Eugenio's door and told him that I had to go back to Italy to organize various things, but that I wanted to join them in southern Italy. He answered cryptically, 'If it's God's will, we'll meet again.'

On 19 May, I went to Carpignano. And there began the destruction and rebuilding of myself. We were in Italy but it was just as far back to Milan as from Milan to Holstebro. In some ways the culture that we met there was just as strange to me as it was to the others. Neither did I understand the actors' language. I felt as if I belonged neither to one culture nor to the other.

I had to begin to move again. It was hard. We got up and started work at 5.00 a.m. every day. I was physically and psychically a wreck but kept going. I was split in two. One part of me wanted to escape, but still I got up every morning and kept on working.

We were working on *The Book of Dances*, which was based on the training, in order to be able to show the local people something, to show that we were actors, to keep our identity. So that they could consider us in terms of our work and not as tourists. But I didn't have any training to offer. So in fact my dance in the production was imposed on me. Eugenio worked with me for several hours every afternoon. It was exhausting. I had two small 'torches', sticks with strips of cloth on them, that I was supposed to dance with. I felt like a fish wearing boots. What for the others was an organic process that had grown out of several years of work was for me nothing but choreography that I had to learn to fill with a form of presence that I first had to find. The production was premiered two months after I came to Odin Teatret.

For the first twelve years of the group's work, Eugenio was in the room every morning when the actors trained.

I came in the tenth year. This means that after the first two years of my apprenticeship, during which time Eugenio followed my work very closely, I was left to myself in the training. I learned very quickly to train alone. Eugenio watched my training every once in a while and gave me certain key words with which to work further.

I was the last actor to be trained by Eugenio himself, from zero. Other actors came after me but then it was some of the older colleagues who took on the responsibility for teaching them. Iben [Nagel] and Tage [Larsen] started what became called adoption.

The theatre was formed during those first ten years, both through the professional fight to create its own culture and through the political fight to establish itself and become recognized.

Eugenio and the older actors created Odin Teatret, and I miss that experience. I miss not having lived through those mistakes and struggles with them.

4

THE OPEN ROOM: 1974–82

The Book of Dances, Anabasis, Come! And the day will be ours, The Million and Brecht's Ashes

In January 1974, Odin Teatret went to Sardinia with *My Father's House*. There the production was presented in completely unusual places, in situations with neither a social nor a cultural tradition of theatre.

The production worked in those situations as well. And for the first time, the closed room was opened up. The production was done in public squares, with the spectators standing around the playing area.

Later, in May 1974, Odin Teatret returned to Carpignano in southern Italy at the request of the Italian Research Council, to begin a project investigating the role of a theatre group in an economically under-developed area. This led to *The Book of Dances*, a series of dramatic dances directly derived from the training. This was a new phase in Odin Teatret's development: with several new members, the group began to work in the 'open room'.

The four earlier productions were made over a period of ten years and were presented to a limited audience of between sixty and seventy spectators. In contrast to this first phase, five to six new productions were made from 1974 to 1978: all were kept in the repertoire and were presented to much larger audiences.

At first glance, one could consider this development to be a rupture with the earlier, closed period, but it can also be seen as a consequence of that period.

> Our daily work, our training, which we believed concerned only the individual actors in the group, turned into something else as soon as we opened it up to the outside. . . . The 'secrecy' which we had sought only in order to guarantee ourselves the best possible conditions for our professional development had produced an unexpected result: the crystallization of a 'group culture'.
>
> (Barba, 1986a: 193)

In addition to training and performance work, the group worked with 'barters'. Odin Teatret has since participated in barters over most of the world, in big cities like New York and Tokyo as well as in the most remote areas, such as with the Yanomami Indians in Amazonas, Venezuela.

The idea behind the barters is not to find a 'new theatre language' or a new form of aesthetic expression. Rather, the barter is an attempt to use theatre in another way, in an organizing or political way: to create a situation which allows for contact between actors and spectators in spite of their differences and respective individuality and precisely because of the fascination engendered by difference. The barter is an exchange between different cultures in the form of dance, music, song and ritual, training and performances.

THE FLOATING ISLANDS

As a result of Odin Teatret's travels, barters and meetings with various theatre people from various cultures, there arose the need to characterize and define something which was found to be common for many theatre groups.

In September 1976, an international workshop was held in Belgrade, as part of the Theatre of Nations, under the auspices of the United Nations Educational, Scientific and Cultural Organization (UNESCO). It was the first meeting of the Third Theatre and was led by Eugenio Barba.

On the basis of this meeting, Barba drew up the 'Manifesto on the Third Theatre' (1986a: 193). Six similar meetings were later held, with participants who felt connected to the Third Theatre concept, in Italy (1977), Peru (1978), Spain (1979), Mexico (1981), Argentina (1987) and Peru again (1988).

The Third Theatre is differentiated from both classical and traditional theatre (the First Theatre) and avant-garde theatre (the Second Theatre) in that it takes the actor's culture as its point of departure. Daily work with theatre motivated by personal and aesthetic need.

Barba calls these theatre groups 'floating islands' because they belong to a theatre culture found in niches and reservations outside the dominant and established centres of culture and are without political or economic anchorage. As floating islands, they nevertheless establish among them a network of common endeavours, the goal of which is not to create a common aesthetic or theatre style, but, by means of comparison of their professional activities, to extract and share common knowledge of the actor's work and the conditions for the actor's presence. What they have in common is not a specific method but an attitude: that the theatre is not limited to institutional frameworks and that diving into the universe of fiction is not a simulation but an existence.

Figure 12 Come! And the day will be ours, 1976 (Tage Larsen). Barter with the Yanomami Indians in Venezuela. Photo: Tony D'Urso.

THE PRODUCTIONS (1974–82)

The Book of Dances (1974–80) was a production, performed 350 times, in which a montage was made of particular movement patterns, rhythms and energies in the form of dance.

Dance – as found in popular or folk cultures – is not connected to the written word or to an action *per se* but simply to the dancer's physical presence.

A society is partly characterized by the way its members dance. A society's norms and history can be read in a living book, in the body's way of being alive. Hence the title, *The Book of Dances*. In this production, the dances were woven together with the history of the 'group', its hopes, the personal dreams and associations of its members, and with the danger and the constant risk that threaten to destroy such a world.

Johann Sebastian Bach (1974–9, in three versions) was a comical street performance combining circus clowning and *commedia dell'arte*, often combined with parades done on streets and squares, where the principle of the dramaturgical exploitation of space took a new direction.

The early Odin Teatret productions were characterized by the fact that each production created its own space and its own continuously changing architecture. The actors tried to transform urban space in a similar way. They used their parades to create new experiences meetings, by creating dramatic tensions between 'high' and 'low', as in the relationship between the stilt figures and the dwarf, by exploiting levels, towers and statues, by discovering new rhythms and new points of view for the spectators.

In 1977, the parades were put together into the street performance *Anabasis*, ['Ascent to the Sea'] (performed 180 times 1977–84, in four versions). The production was based on Xenophon's *Anabasis*, an account of the march or wandering of ten thousand Greek mercenaries as they headed home from the war in Persia in 401–400 BC. During this march they suffered many defeats and lost their commander, the rebel Cyrus. Over plains and mountains, across rivers and marshes, with the enemy and death at their heels, they eventually reached the sea. Odin Teatret's *Anabasis* was the story of 'immigrants', of an army of actors armed with flags, drums, masks and trumpets, advancing through the unknown, occupying the town, the towers, the buildings, the squares, followed by the two tall stilt figures: two figures of Death.

The journey ended in a black cloth by the sea. The actors were wrapped in the cloth and smothered. Their voices and sounds fell silent. As an image of homecoming?

Come! And the day will be ours was performed 180 times, from 1976 to 1980. The performance space was a combination of Buffalo Bill's Wild West Show, where the Indian chief Sitting Bull performed until he was shot in 1890, and a native sun-dance circle with a pole in the middle. The theme of the production was hinted at by the room's architecture: cultural destruction which has already become a form of entertainment.

The title of the production is a quote from a letter written by General G. A. Custer just before he was wiped out at Little Big Horn in 1876 by an army of diverse Indian tribes led by Crazy Horse.

As in *My Father's House*, the actors did not represent actual or identifiable characters. In the programme, they are described by their association with a thing or an instrument: the man with the book, the man with the violin, the man with the guitar, the woman in white, the woman with the drum, or the woman with the banjo. The actors are the 'Indians' and the 'pioneers' who meet, conflict, mix. It is a meeting between the civilized and the uncivilized. The production deals with the destruction of culture, the elimination of the different in the name of progress and civilization. A destruction in the name of unity, universal truth and justice where the 'different' finally becomes integrated and exploited: culture as folklore.

But it is not a moral story of the 'bad whites' against the 'poor redskins'. It is a more general story, with texts taken from Shakespeare's *Romeo and Juliet*, for example. It deals with Odin Teatret as a group, with the group's experiences on its journeys and with living as 'others', living in a reservation.

The Million – First Journey was premiered in April 1978 and was performed in four versions until 1984. In all, 223 times. *The Million* is in the same vein as the other dance and street productions. Characters such as the tall demon figure from *Anabasis* are used again. It is also thematically related to earlier productions, since its theme is the journey. At the same time, it contains dances and dance culture from all over the world. So the production ties together some of the important aspects of Odin Teatret's history in the period, during which the group worked with barters, of which *The Million* was also a part.

The Million was a collection of experiences from journeys to South America, Asia, Bali, Norway and other places. And these experiences were shown as dances and as scenes with song and music. There was no actual plot in this cabaret- and musical-like show. But the individual scenes were woven together by a representative of the Western world: the missionary-anthropologist.

The cultures shown are never authentic, they are already processed, extracted from their original contexts, their content altered. Hence the various dances are often parodies of themselves.

While the theme of *Anabasis* was the journey homewards towards the sea and death, *The Million* once again is based on internationalism and journeying as a way of life. The production is dedicated to and named after Marco Polo (1254–1324), who was the first European to explore the Far East. After an absence of twenty-five years, Marco Polo travelled back to his home city, Venice, which he had left when he was 17 years old. He described all the many strange things he had seen and experienced, but his fellow Venetians laughed at him and nicknamed him 'The Million' because they thought he exaggerated and magnified everything.

Thematically, the production is a parallel to *Invisible Cities*, by Italian author Italo Calvino, about the journeys of Marco Polo: movements in space and time. A journey is never an even movement forward. A journey's theme is both the past, one's homeland, and the future. A journey is not merely a geographical displacement. It can also be an existential movement, occurring in one's imagination: an inner journey with no physical change.

The Million's journey is disconnected in space and time and hence the production's structure is neither linear nor continuous but jumps from place to place, juxtaposes the most diverse cultures, mixes together fragments from various cultures.

While the spectators are being seated by some of the actors, other actors are getting ready, putting on makeup, putting on their costumes, or tuning their instruments. We see their 'transformation' into the Asian characters taking place as a number on its own.

The Missionary or Priest enters wearing a backpack, glasses and a black hat. He is also wearing a black cassock with a purple waistband. All the other actors have gathered together as an orchestra on a podium at one end of the room. The Priest suddenly realizes that they are there and greets them. He turns around and goes to the other end of the room, where there is a throne-like chair draped in gold fabric. Beside the chair is a large Balinese parasol and a trunk filled with barter goods, fabrics, jewellery. He sits in the throne-chair like an Emperor or a Chancellor and is entertained by the various exotic dance rituals and sketches which are then presented to him as a 'show'. The Priest is thus the spectator's representative and reference point in the round trip which follows. He signals to the orchestra, which begins to play. The stage is draped with exotic fabrics, forming a background for the colourful musicians who are playing various Asian and Western instruments. The musicians come down from the stage and perform on the floor in front of it. The orchestra is an obvious mixture of styles: an Indian Kathakali dancer plays an electric bass, a 'Balinese' dancer plays an accordion. The orchestra creates a sonorous backdrop of melodies, often isolated as a series of clichés. The Asian culture has absorbed various elements from Western culture, just as much as the opposite has taken place.

The orchestra plays a kind of circus music to which the three 'Balinese' dance. The Priest stands and announces to the spectators: 'Here begins the Million's first journey.'

Next, a Japanese 'Kabuki lion' and a fantasy animal dance together. The dance becomes a kind of fight; the animal's head is hacked off with a machete and offered to the Priest. The rest of the animal runs out on its own. The Priest puffs on a fat cigar, much as Brecht was fond of doing. He once suggested that cigar-smoking ought always to be part of the theatre.

The sound of a ship's bell is heard. A couple dance intensely and acrobatically to 'I Left My Heart in San Francisco'. The man takes off his hat and his pants and continues to dance, in gold shorts. The woman is holding a white flower in her mouth. She gives it to her partner.

Two other actors are watching this 'romantic happiness'; the woman asks, 'Do you remember when the wind was made of green and purple whistles?' The man answers, confused, 'No, I don't remember that, it must have been another.'

A Balinese dancer wearing a monkey mask approaches the Priest, who tries to escape. The monkey-man jumps up on the Priest's back and forces him back to the throne.

Two more Balinese dancers, playing accordion and castanets, dance with the monkey-man, who plays the saxophone. The Priest suddenly tosses fire-crackers into their midst. The fire-crackers explode and the three dancers flee.

The orchestra plays a samba. A character on stilts, wearing a white mask, dances carefully, followed by a smaller figure, also on stilts, and wearing the same costume (mother–daughter). Both figures have at one and the same time very human traits and are very moving and yet have something supernatural about them, something mystical and magical, something reminiscent of South American carnival and witch culture from Bali or Tahiti.

A provocative woman in a purple wig, black silk stockings, a mini-skirt and high-heeled shoes dances with a man (played by a woman) dressed in a black jacket and soft hat. He pursues the seductive woman but she evades him. Suddenly they change roles: the woman chases the man. This reversal happens several times. Finally the woman catches the man and kisses him until he faints. The woman dances on, without the wig and shoes. She dances with a fur-covered animal, a kind of bear, and finally jumps up on its back.

'Death', wearing a Balinese mask and wielding a large scythe, moves threateningly towards the spectators and the Priest. He places the scythe around the Priest's neck and pulls him out on to the floor.

The mini-skirted woman induces the Priest to dance with her. At the end of the dance he collapses, exhausted. She carries him back to the throne, sits on his lap and they begin to flirt. She puts on his hat, they share a glass of wine and together they watch the next scene, a kind of 'show dance'. A man and a woman dance the tango. The dance becomes increasingly acrobatic and brutal. The man swings the woman over his shoulders, between his legs, he spins her around, she finally gives up and is carried away. The man spits on his palms, polishes his shoes. He smears his hair down with his spit and combs his hair with a 'switch-comb' as he lurches back to the orchestra.

The Priest's woman is now sitting on a piece of fabric on the floor. She rinses a glass in a bowl of water. The squeaky sound is amplified by a microphone hidden in a bouquet of flowers. Meanwhile, another couple is dancing a love dance.

The Priest starts a metronome – its rhythm is very slow. It sounds like a clock running too slowly. The orchestra plays a slow version of 'Mack the Knife' and the two stilt figures come out on to the floor. The taller of the two is carrying a staff to which is affixed a head with a bandit-like mask, a moustache and a black hat. The stilt figure rides the staff as if it was a horse and then uses the head to strike a blow towards its own face, its heart, its groin. Meanwhile, the shorter stilt figure 'gives birth' to a little puppet, a miniature version of itself, and dances around the room with it. The tall figure covers its puppet with a white cloth and strangles it. The music suddenly stops and only the metronome is heard, a kind of rhythmic expression of time passing. The organic process is interrupted.

The Priest places the skeleton of a child in the woman's hands: the issue of their meeting. She sings a lullaby to the child and walks around the room, followed by the other actors, as if in a funeral procession. They suddenly burst into cheerful song and dance as if at a funeral carnival. All disappear, except for the Priest, who shuffles around the room like a train, with a whistle in his mouth, while the orchestra plays 'Oh, Susannah'. He suddenly interrupts his nearly ecstatic fever and announces, 'And here ends The Million's first and last journey.'

But the performance is not over. The stilt figures come out once again. The Priest is frightened, is chased by the tall stilt figure, who takes hold of the Priest's purple waistband and unwinds it. The stilt figure pulls off the Priest's backpack and cassock. The Priest hides between the stilt figure's legs, under its skirts. He reappears wearing a top hat and evening coat. He dances wildly and ecstatically, like a new man. The tall stilt figure begins to sway and falls into the Priest's arms. The Priest lays the dying figure on the floor and says, 'We survive everything.' The 'newborn Priest' is now presented with a machete on a pillow. The remaining stilt figure, shaking with fear, tries to escape. It is still carrying its puppet. But the Priest is merciless and fells the stilt figure with a blow to its 'legs'.

He sets the machete back on the pillow which is then proffered to the spectators. The performance is over.

Brecht's Ashes (1980) and *Brecht's Ashes 2* (a second version premiered in 1982) were performed until 1984, 166 times. The production was dedicated to Jens Björneboe. Just as *My Father's House* was a meeting with Dostoyevsky, *Brecht's Ashes* is a dialogue with Brecht, his life and works. The essential part of this confrontation with Brecht is not a political or an aesthetic attitude but an examination of Brecht's situation as an exile, as an immigrant. The production focuses on Brecht's exile period, from 1933, when he flees Germany, until he returns to East Berlin after the war.

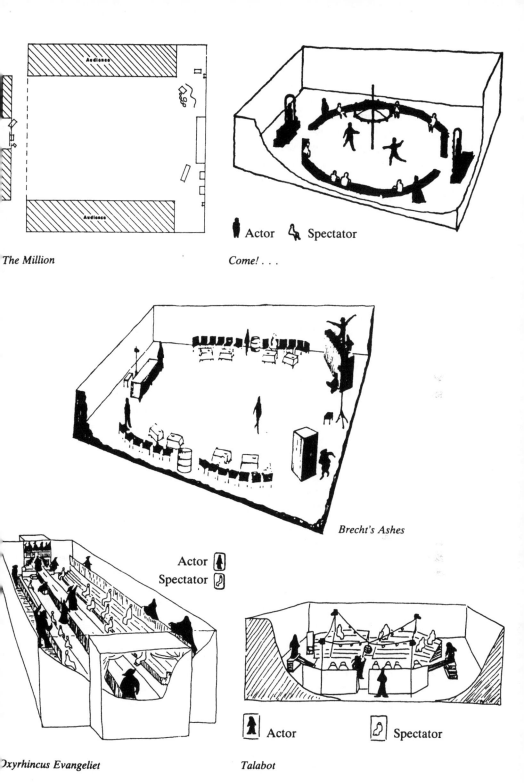

The Million

Come! . . .

Actor   Spectator

Brecht's Ashes

Actor

Spectator

Oxyrhincus Evangeliet

Talabot

Actor   Spectator

Figure 13 Scenic arrangements for *The Million, Come! . . ., Brecht's Ashes, Oxyrhincus Evangeliet* and *Talabot*.

Sixteen years as an expatriate. A situation very reminiscent of Odin Teatret's own immigration.

The production examines both the German author's forced exile and his use of the intellectual's weapon, an ability to distance oneself from social life. Brecht kept himself out of the 'fight' in order to be able to reflect on it, examine it and write about it. The Brechtian '*Verfremdung* concept' was not merely an aesthetic technique, a theatrical technique, but a social necessity connected to the desire to defend the right to what in many situations can resemble an escape or an excuse for not involving oneself. Brecht distanced himself from the centre of events in order to be able then to dissect and examine the dynamics of history with much greater energy.

The balance between what is emotionally lived and vital, and cold, analytical distance is expressed in the relationship between Kattrin, the mute daughter of Mother Courage, and the cool, distant Brecht.

Torgeir Wethal, who plays Brecht, embodies Brecht's withheld energy. Dressed in normal, everyday clothing, he 'walks' around the playing area and connects the various situations by creating a network of tensions between them. Only in certain specific instances does this withheld action become an explosive discharge of energy, at which time it is a rupture which demonstrates that this withholding demands optimal control.

Brecht's Ashes takes place in a square space, with the spectators on two sides, some seated at small tables draped with white table-cloths, as if in Brecht's culinary theatre. The spectators must keep an analytical overview: they can smoke cigarettes or drink beers during the performance, and yet can also be directly provoked, such as when, for example, Arturo Ui suddenly kicks one of the small tables.

The production's montage shows Brecht's long journeys through Denmark, Sweden and Finland to the USA and finally his homecoming to East Berlin. At the same time, situations, characters and actions from his works are woven into the action as a form of reflection in relationship to the biographical sequences. Walter Benjamin's suicide at the Spanish border in 1940 is contrasted to Galileo Galilei's scientific examination of 'oppression'. Brecht's denial of having been a member of the Communist Party is juxtaposed with Galileo's abjuration of his knowledge of the earth's journey around the sun.

The production is bilingual and Brecht, who speaks German, is translated by Mackie Messer into the language of the country where the production is taking place. Both are observers of 'history' but whereas Brecht is portrayed as the passionate scientist, Mackie Messer is the pragmatist, without feeling and devoid of hope. In the scene where Kattrin is raped and condemned to death, the Brecht character shows an emotional engagement as well as a necessary and painful distance, while Mackie Messer curiously follows the action in order to 'measure', coldly and clinically, the degree of suffering.

Similarly, in the scene where Margarete Steffin dies, Brecht reacts in an emotionally explosive way, while Mackie Messer excuses Brecht's outburst, which he says is not sympathy but the fear of being left alone. The opposition between the two characters becomes a double portrait of Brecht: the author's two sides, different, but nevertheless a unity. As Ruth Berlau, another of Brecht's faithful consorts, once wondered: 'How could this socialist and idealist be as shameless and remorseless as the archcriminal Mackie Messer?'

Figure 14 Brecht's Ashes, 1982. Galileo Galilei (Brecht) dissects the fish while he drinks a glass of red wine and Andreas Sarti watches with fascination. The scientific examination takes place while the field cook burns Brecht's books in a frying pan. The context is an image of the ultimate objectivity, the ultimate conformism: the Nazi gas chambers. The uncompromising search for knowledge can, after the dissection of the atom, no longer avoid the subjective need for enjoyment.

The 'fish' reappears in *Oxyrhincus Evangeliet* ('Oxyrhincus' is the name of a holy fish which the Egyptians were forbidden either to eat or kill) and also in *Talabot*, torn apart and battered, literally 'cleaned'; finally in *Waterways* (1991), a tiny boat tied to a white balloon is resurrected and sails towards the blue sky.

Photo montage: Jan Rüsz and Catherine Poher.

5

TRAINING, TECHNIQUE AND THEORY

THE ACTOR'S SELF-DISCIPLINE

As mentioned earlier, the very fact that training becomes an independent part of the actor's work is something new with respect to traditional theatre. In traditional theatre, training is often a part of the preparation for a particular production and a specific role.

At Odin Teatret, training as a necessary process is inspired by Grotowski's actor training, elements from Asian theatre and, in particular, by the development of the ideas of Stanislavski and Meyerhold. Barba himself refers to Stanislavski as the 'primal father of modern Western theatre', first and foremost because Stanislavski's vision of theatre is based on the actors' truth in their presence on stage more than on their being there for the spectator, and on their daily practical training. Rather paradoxically, Stanislavski considered the theatre to be 'the actor's worst enemy', referring to the desire to 'show oneself', to create illusion, to entertain. According to Stanislavski, the actor must 'do' and not show.

In Odin Teatret, training works on this 'doing' by virtue of the actor's work with himself or herself, with the self-discipline which creates presence and with the ability to establish certain rules, which are then broken.

Training does not teach how to act, how to be clever, does not prepare one for creation. Training is a process of self-definition, a process of self-discipline which manifests itself indissolubly through physical reactions. It is not the exercise in itself that counts – for example, bending or somersaults – but the individual's justification for his own work, a justification which although perhaps banal or difficult to explain through words, is physiologically perceptible, evident to the observer. This approach, this personal justification decides the meaning of the training, the surpassing of the particular exercises which, in reality, are stereotyped gymnastic movements.

This inner necessity determines the quality of the energy which allows work without a pause, without noticing tiredness, continuing

72

even when exhausted and at that very moment going forward without surrendering. This is the self-discipline of which I spoke.

Let us understand each other, however: it is not by killing oneself with exhaustion that one becomes creative. It is not on command, by forcing, that one opens oneself to others. Training is not a form of personal asceticism, a malevolent harshness against oneself, a persecution of the body. Training puts one's own intentions to the test, how far one is prepared to pay with one's own person for all that one believes and declares. It is the possibility of bridging the gap between intention and realization. This daily task, obstinate, patient, often in darkness, sometimes even searching for a meaning, is a concrete factor in the transformation of the actor as a man and as a member of the group.

(Barba, 1986a: 56)

In Odin Teatret's first phase, all the actors learned the same exercises, most of which were acrobatic in nature, even though the individual motivations behind the exercises were different. Later, in the 1970s, the training became more orientated towards individual rhythm and pulse. The actors began to construct their own exercises and to organize an individual training with individual goals. With the introduction of props to the training (staffs, flags, stilts, costumes, instruments), this difference became even more accentuated. Seen from the outside, the training began to approach improvisation and performance work. And, in fact, elements from the training were transferred directly to the productions.

The training became a way of composing various tensions in the body, ways of moving in space and ways of working with and giving life to various props; it developed into variations of rhythmical movements in space which were then set and repeated. By the end of the 1970s some of the actors were training with Asian theatre forms, such as Balinese dance, Indian Kathakali, or Japanese Noh dance, in order to learn not the outer characteristics or aesthetics of these dances but the hidden principles which help Asian actors transform daily behaviour. Such a trait could be perceived as 'style' but it is also a technique which forces the dancer to create a new kind of tension in the whole body. The comparison and exchange of analogous principles have placed Odin Teatret somewhere between Western and Asian theatre traditions.

The work of more than twenty years with Odin Teatret has led me to a series of practical solutions: not to take the differences between what is called 'dance' and what is called 'theatre' too much into consideration; not to accept the character as a unit of measure of the performance; not to make the sex of the actor coincide automatically with the sex of the character: to exploit the sonorous richness of languages, which have an emotive force capable of transmitting

Figure 15 A decided body. A dynamic immobility is sustained by many opposing forces, as if the body were the centre of a network of tensions. Training at Odin Teatret, 1983 (Silvia Ricciardelli, Roberta Carreri, Julia Varley and Francis Pardeilhan). Photo: Christoph Falke.

information above and beyond the semantic. These characteristics of Odin Teatret's dramaturgy and of its actors are equivalent to some of the characteristics of Oriental theatres, but Odin's were born of an autodidactic training, of our situation as foreigners, and of our limitations. And this impossibility of being like other theatre people has gradually rendered us loyal to our diversity.

For all these reasons I recognize myself in the culture of a Eurasian theatre today. That is, I belong to the small and recent tradition of group theatres which have autodidactic origins but grow in a professional 'village' where Kabuki actors are not regarded as being more remote than Shakespearean texts, nor the living presence of an Indian dancer-actress less contemporary than the American avant-garde.

(Barba, article, 1988c: 128)

Odin Teatret differs from the dominant Western theatre tradition based on text and the psychology and actions of characters. The point of departure for an actor in the Odin Teatret tradition is not a fictive character but a fictive body. The network of physical energies imagined by the actor pushes, pulls and touches the body, makes it lighter or heavier. These mental 'descriptions' create another physiology but not necessarily another psychology. The fictive body is above all a body with another life or energy: a body-in-life.

STANISLAVSKI

In order to understand Odin Teatret's position between Western and Asian theatre, it is useful to examine the basis of Stanislavski's actor training, which became the foundation for the education of Western actors.

In 1898, the Moscow Art Theatre was founded, led by Konstantin Stanislavski. The Art Theatre met with great success, partly because of its productions of Chekhov's dramas. There was talk of the introduction of realism to the stage. Over the years, Stanislavski developed his method, which was then taken in new directions by his students (Meyerhold, M. Chekhov, Tairov and Vakhtangov). In the 1930s, this method was transferred to the United States by the Group Theater (Harold Clurman, J. H. Lawson, Clifford Odets, Elia Kazan). In 1947, the Actor's Studio was founded, led by Lee Strasberg, and trained such actors as Marlon Brando, Rod Steiger, James Dean and Jane Fonda. This work was based on a method of physical actions and personal expressivity and was called the Stanislavski system.

The Stanislavski performing style is connected to 'realism' and 'realistic' drama (such as that written by Ibsen), where the dramatic action is an interplay between the text and the subtext, between the physical actions and the inner objective. Ibsen's technique is based on a concept of 'action' and when Stanislavski staged Ibsen's dramas, he found that he was obliged to work with 'objectives' and 'given circumstances'.

This tradition, created by Stanislavski for the 'actor's work on himself', was based on the actor's psychic resources and expressivity. The point of departure was a psychological perception of the nature of the role, to which the actor was to give an original and personal life. Imitation and copying were taboo.

It was crucial for Stanislavski to find a technique which the actors could use to transfer to the role their own 'honest' feelings and experiences, their unconscious and unconscious analogies with the role, as visible, physical actions.

It is a dialectic identification process: to find oneself in the role and to find the role in oneself.

The problem for Stanislavski was that feelings are not immediately accessible to the will. One cannot become crazy, be happy, or fall in love on command. One can pretend to do so and one can show certain approved clichés for these feelings. But Stanislavski was not satisfied with imitation.

He wanted the actor really to feel 'truly, reliably and consistently' on the stage.

Stanislavski tried to create a technique which would make it possible for the actor to be consciously intuitive, that is, to repeat a role as if it were real life, without the use of mechanical tricks, night after night. This technique was later called the 'method of physical action'.

The identification process has both an outer and an inner aspect. The actors must first of all activate their own creative subconscious, their imagination and emotions, in order then to be able to do the same for the role. They must begin with the 'magic if'. The actor does not describe the emotional life of 'someone else'. Using the 'magic if', the actor asks: 'What would I do if I wanted to get . . . to change . . .' And a series of specific inner images is thereby brought out of the actor ('I want to do such and such, walk over there, sit down . . .') which activates an interaction between physical actions and inner intentions (subtext) and creates a dramatic, emotional development.

Stanislavski talks of the transition from the 'human body life' to the 'human spiritual life' as a link in the transition from physical action to subconscious emotion. The physical actions are the impulse to an activation of one's 'soul conflicts'. The actor must answer the 'magic if' personally.

The objectives of the role, the 'given circumstances', mean that 'I concentrate myself on the execution of these tasks as if they were my own'. This psycho-technique can be extremely effective but always runs into one problem: what happens to the actor as a private person in this process where more or less hidden emotional structures are laid open – night after night? The actor runs the risk of being locked into specific forms of reaction, specific forms of expression, which are part of the actor's personal psychic potential. The role and the actor slide together and the various roles become identical. Expression becomes reduced to specific, personal clichés. The actor limits energy to a particular pattern. The result is an exploitation of the actor's psychic resources, of the ability to switch from daily behaviour to theatrical behaviour and to move in and out of various fictions.

The problems manifest in psychologically orientated actor technique are the basis of the research conducted by the International School of Theatre Anthropology (ISTA) into the art of the actor from a physiological point of view.

ISTA departs from the Western theatrical tradition. Not because it turns towards the Oriental tradition, but because it turns away from that which has been the subject of every reflection, every 'scientific' research concerning the actor for almost two centuries: psychology. To base the actor's work on a psycho-technique means to direct him

76

towards the 'wish to express' and therefore to avoid the fundamental problem: the pre-expressive bases of the actor's art.

The actor's expressivity derives – almost *in spite of himself* – from his actions, from the use of his physical presence. The principles guiding him in these actions make up the pre-expressive bases of expressivity.

It is our actions which, *in spite of us*, make us expressive. It is not the *wish to express* which determines one's actions; the wish to express does not decide what is to be done. It is the *wish to do* which decides what one expresses.

(Barba, 1986a: 134)

THEATRE ANTHROPOLOGY

ISTA was founded in 1979, as part of Nordisk Teaterlaboratorium, with Barba as its leader, and based in Holstebro. Its aim is to arrange open seminars and congresses on the work of the actor. ISTA has established collaboration with a number of researchers working in various scientific disciplines and with actors from both the East and the West. The essence of this research is the actor's behaviour in the theatre situation.

Different theatre forms and traditions have different aesthetic forms of expression, different body techniques, different ways of using costumes, props, etc. But behind these various techniques is found a common level: the way the actor forms energy and presence, the way the actor becomes 'living' and attracts the spectator's attention. This is called the actor's pre-expressive level where nothing is expressed. In the performance the spectator cannot separate this level from the expressive level. It is an analytical level belonging to the technical process of the actor's work.

Traditional ballet, mime, other Western dance-forms and Asian theatre contain a codified formation of these principles, making exact repetition possible, something which is difficult for many Western actors because the technique is based on psychological empathy.

Most theatre education in Japan, India, China and Bali is traditionally based on study with a master. The acting tradition is passed on from master to student by means of the imitation of movement forms which are to a large extent codified by rules and laws, in an often closed system. There is a disciplined, external apprenticeship which begins at a very early age, as in Western ballet. These movements are worked on long before work with 'expression' and 'role' becomes important.

The actor who is trained in codified movement forms is able to modulate, manipulate, mount and, not least, jump between, various qualities of energy, at the same time as energy intensity and concentration are maintained. A powerful movement (extreme, hard, direction-determined energy in space) can change into a very soft and round movement. The movements can be used as sequences of non-natural behaviour, re-created behaviour, which can be made smaller, made larger, edited. There can be jumps in sequence, repetitions and framing of the movements.

The Asian actor works with specific ways of deforming the body, of binding the body: Chinese dancers who tie their feet in high-soled shoes or the Japanese dancer who has a belt tied around the waist to hold it immobile. The Western actor, on the other hand, is more spontaneous and has freer body movement. There are no definite rules he or she must follow. Precisely because emphasis is placed on original expressivity, the Western actor must often look for 'binding' in his or her personal work.

Asian theatre cannot be reproduced or assumed as an accessible result. It is part of a completely 'other' cultural, ideological and religious context, but it can awaken awareness and be a challenge to the rediscovery and development of similar processes in the Western actor's body. It is not a question of preferring one form of tradition to another but rather of finding a balance between individual need and creative resources and principles which one can discover in spite of differences in tradition, varying aesthetic forms of expression and different actors.

DAILY BEHAVIOUR AND SCENIC BEHAVIOUR

In daily life, energy flows through the human organism in a specific way, a way which is determined by our daily behaviour, by the way we are present and living, visible and attracting attention, or the opposite.

Energy moves as a current which is broken or blocked in various ways, resulting in tension fields. This blocking can be muscular or emotional. Energy impulses such as anger or happiness or sexual excitement can be impeded or blocked: the stomach muscles are tensed, the throat constricts, the mouth and teeth are pressed together, the eyes blink.

A person's character is a psycho-physical structure, a basic attitude with which the individual meets the surrounding world. It can be observed by others even though one may be unconscious of it oneself.

Character generates a typical or habitual behaviour pattern which can be experienced as spontaneous movement but which is in fact a structuring of behaviour norms. The individual person identifies to a greater or lesser degree with a character and does not question it as long as it makes it possible to function.

Character is present and reflected in the muscular system and maintains a balance and logic between inner impulse and expression, between the need to be seen and the anxiety which accompanies this need. Character as such is a compromise between the individual's possibilities and hopes. Character is a testament to a person's living history, to how experience in the past has determined behaviour in the present.

The muscular system is formed during life's stages of development, particularly during the first years, on the basis of a series of essential physical themes: to grab, to let go, to raise one's back, to look out, to sit up, to stand up, to walk. These actions all depend on certain muscle tensions and also contain psychic themes: the expansion of personal space, mobility, independence, etc. The muscular system gives the individual certain movement possibilities but it also contains the possibility of interrupting and withholding the body's energy and such emotional expressions as pain, vulnerability and excitement. In this way, the individual can function purposefully within a given context: an efficient balance between oneself and one's surroundings is assured.

The actor must undo this inculcated behaviour pattern and 'the natural connections' between impulse and expression. To a certain degree, this is a question of a deformation and denial of the actor's way of being and character, followed by a reconstruction of behaviour forms in a new way.

As a general rule, the flow of energy occurs unconsciously, but it can be made conscious. The flow of energy can be blocked, physically impeded and constricted so that the current flows through other channels. Impulse is given a new direction and followed and enlarged.

In Western thought, there is a fundamental differentiation between being (the flow of energy) and the mental consideration of the same (consciousness). Existence is a flow of energy which can take form as an intense feeling; when this feeling is present, one is unable to think. It is not possible both to be angry and to think about one's anger at the same time. One cannot be deeply moved and think about it at the same time.

Training is the process of creating a bridge between energy and consciousness, between states of intensity and states of conscious clarity, a rhythmic oscillation between existence and thought.

Work with technique is a question of creating a non-daily body and physical and mental technique, a 'dilated' body, a reformation of the body's life power: energy, aimed at creating maximum presence.

The transition to the artistic or fictive body takes place by means of specific mental and physical processes. By means of 'magic ifs', the body acts in relationship to the fictive space and to fictive physical laws, as if the body were the mid-point in a network of opposition-filled tensions, as if the body were moving in relationship to a physical resistance of a particular quality (water, sand, glue . . .). As if one's weight became lesser or greater, as if one were made of a different material (a tree swinging in the wind, a little stone rolling down to the water's edge). Or as if one had certain very particular subtexts (hidden intentions) within every movement and action.

The concentration required to execute an action in a particular material, in a particular space, with a particular intention, gives the actor's body a particular quality. It is not the illustrative nature of the action, not whether it resembles something specific, but the work itself as the result of the ability to imagine, which creates the quality of the energy of presence.

Training leads to a new form of behaviour and a new way of being present. The way of being in space, of standing, walking, seeing, sitting and jumping, is re-created in a new way.

Actions are tension-filled, even immobility is dynamic and not static because it is maintained by forces established in opposing directions, which means that dramatic potential is present.

REFUSAL OF CULTURE

In the transition from one form of behaviour to another, there occurs a breakdown of character structure. There is also a refusal of the culture which has created the original structure. The individual sets himself or herself outside that culture.

The refusal of dailiness – the decision to-not-belong-to-it – implies the continual discovery of the transition between the two cultures by means of a training or technique which is not specialized but which is open to the use of various energy forms and resources, a technique which makes possible a modulation of energy without becoming fixed in that modulation. It is important to search for one's own resources, individual goals and personal motivation. Training consists of a self-discipline in relationship to a certain number of exercises which are continuously worked on and repeated. But it is the individual's personal 'temperature' which determines whether or not this training becomes nothing more than mechanical gymnastics and a new form of automatism. It is the personal motor, the individual actor's inner necessity, which determines whether or not the technique is surpassed.

The personal necessity is the meaning which the actor imparts to the work and the profession, to the profession's social and individual significance. The question is whether or not it is possible to avoid being as tied to the profession as one perhaps previously was to the 'character'.

The actor's dilemma is both to lack technique and to be limited by it. To develop a technique that merely makes movements automatic in a different way is to be once again limited by the technique.

The actor is protected by the mask and hides behind it but must still always be present. It is the actor's personal vulnerability that brings the mask alive, but the actor must be stronger than the mask and be able to break it open.

'RULES' FOR ENERGY IN SCENIC BEHAVIOUR

ISTA has so far focused on three energy principles. The first principle is that of the distortion of balance, which is a very common characteristic.

This distortion forces the actor to find a counter-impulse (simply in order not to fall).

Displacement of the centre of weight makes one's balance uncertain with the result that it is necessary to use a great deal of energy to keep one's position. The tensions in the body, necessary in order to keep balance, increase energy and the actor's radiation. The distortion of balance is not only a stylistic or expressive form, but a conscious and controlled way of creating life.

The second rule is the principle of opposition. Energy is always the result of forces being aimed in opposite directions. A movement in one particular direction begins in the opposite direction.

This movement pattern responds to elementary, physical, daily experience: if one wishes to throw a ball, one pulls one's arm back to accumulate energy before the arm is extended forward. The same applies if one is about to jump: one first bends the knees slightly, as if about to run. Energy is accumulated in this movement in the opposite direction and is then released in the desired direction. At Odin Teatret, this is called the 'sats' or action impulse.

Energy moves rhythmically in the form of waves. The dance of opposition is a swinging between the top and bottom of the wave. Energy is accumulated, built up and released in an action. The end of this action is the beginning of a new action. A general trait of Noh theatre is that energy is withheld and accumulated. This means that one does not execute an action 100 per cent in space but works with opposition, withholding part of the action in the body as energy in time. The result could be called an action delayed in time.

There is a concept in Japanese theatre called *jo-ha-kyu*. A movement begins slowly to increase but is held back by a counter-impulse (*jo*: to withhold). The movement is freed from resistance (*ha*: to break) and reaches a culmination or climax (*kyu*: speed), at which point it suddenly stops for a moment. The action is contained just before the explosion occurs. The climax of the action is almost a kind of fast-freezing of speed. The direction of the action is then changed and transferred to a new movement which begins slowly, is built up and, in spite of resistance, is released and reaches a new climax, where it is again contained and turned in a new direction . . . (cf. Barba, 1986a: 150).

This is the play of oppositions. The actor's movement forward is held back as if her hips were being held, forcing her to bend her knees and to press her feet towards the floor in order to advance forward. The hips are suddenly freed and for a moment the action goes quickly forward, almost as if the actor became released from the floor as the knees stretch. The movement reaches a limit which contains a counter-impulse, as if the actor were standing at the edge of a chasm and once again had to use all her strength to hold herself back.

81

Seen from the outside, even the moment in which the opposition is released is extremely effective. It is as though the rule of withholding energy is broken and the energy escapes. It looks as if the actor suddenly develops an impressive strength. This is naturally due to the fact that the knees are being extended. One could say that this breaking of a rule is a fundamental aspect of the dance of opposition and corresponds to the discontinuous and rhythmic movement of energy. An accumulation of energy reaches a high-point where it becomes possible to transform the energy and turn it in a new direction in order to move against the force of inertia. This is also in agreement with a basic principle of dramaturgy and dramatic tension.

Dramatic moments are already occurring in the actor's training as part of the struggle against the predictable, against tiredness, monotony and inertia. This takes place both in the actor and in the room. It is both a physical and a mental phenomenon.

The dance of oppositions takes place in the actor's body as physical and mental energy processes but it also takes place between the actors, between the actors and the props, costumes, lights and sound, and between the actors and the spectators.

In Japanese theatre, we find the tradition of the actor who represents his own non-presence, the *kokken*: the black-costumed helper in Noh and Kabuki who assists the main actor on the stage and who must perform absence. His presence, which neither represents nor expresses anything, is created by means of an extra-daily technique which makes use of a maximum amount of energy and a minimum amount of activity.

This brings us to a third 'rule', concerning the use of discontinuous continuities. It is seen in the omission of an action in a sequence, in the use of withheld or indirect actions (in the same way that the use of subtext is a means to create energy in dramatic language), or in the editing of an action

Figure 16 As in a Western film the performers are prepared: not to shoot or to fight, but to re-present. They are in extra-daily, dynamic balance: the centre of balance has been displaced. The movement begins in the opposite direction: to go forward, one begins moving the arms backward.

It is the position of 'sats', to be prepared or to be decided. Oppositions in the body create a dynamic immobility where the whole body 'sees'.

The learning of movements and rhythms takes place on a pre-expressive level, as a form of dance training without individual expression. Only much later are the learned movements combined with personal motivation, which then leads to individual expression. Actors who work on this pre-expressive level can improvise together even if they do not know each other's language, tradition, or style. They understand and react to each other's body-language, the body-architecture. The dialogue between the actors takes place as a flow of energy, as a physical and mental dance of energy.

ISTA, 1987 (Roberta Carreri of Odin Teatret, I Made Bandem and Ni Nyoman Chandri of Bali). Photo: Tony D'Urso.

by means of displacement actions. The result is an unnatural body which represents neither reality nor daily behaviour. By means of the fragmentation and remounting of the body's behaviour, an artificial body is created. Natural connections are destroyed by discontinuous continuities, resulting in a new body composition. This removal from a daily context makes it possible for the actor to decide.

The essential thing is not the desire to express but to have a decided body.

To be decided is a passive-active form. Etymologically, it means 'to cut away', that is to say, to eliminate or negate.

In Shakespeare's *Hamlet*, Hamlet is decided. He is in dynamic immobility, he can withhold energy. He is only apparently passive or capricious, but he must take a side-route to action. He must negate the social context, which is based on deceit and role-playing. No one is what he or she appears to be and values are dissolving. Hamlet must therefore remove himself and pretend to be foolish and mad, but he is also foolish and mad because he is outside. He no longer belongs to society. He risks his sense of orientation in time and place and he risks his individuality in a conscious separation between thinking (imagining) and being.

As Hamlet says at the beginning of act V, when he is about to duel with Laertes, and when it is obvious to everyone that the King is a murderer and that the duel has been arranged in order to have Hamlet killed: no matter how much one might wish to do so, one can neither anticipate nor procrastinate action. One must only be ready and decided. Hamlet no longer seeks power. He has, in a radical way, negated power. This negation of daily behaviour could be perceived as a dance, a dynamic immobility which manifests the relationship between being and non-being, between absence and presence.

The actor can make a montage of discontinuous continuities in many different ways, but the result is always a tension in the body between complementary poles. The lower part of the body can move with hard, warrior-like movements, while the upper part of the body has round and soft movements.

The actor's impulse is to hit. The action is refused and transformed to its opposite: it becomes a caress. Or there can be a complementarity between the literal meaning and the tonal image of the words the actor speaks.

The work with these complementary principles goes hand in hand with the complementarity of energy itself, with which we are also familiar from daily life. One can speak of the complementary relationship between sorrow and happiness, between love and hate, of the complementarity between powerful and soft energy (animus and anima): focused and extroverted energy aimed in one direction and released at one moment versus circular, introverted, accumulative (non-releasing) energy.

This dynamic polarity between various forms of energy is sometimes the point of departure for those theatre traditions where men play female roles and vice versa. Removing the daily, sex-determined mask makes it possible for the complementary energy, which is absent in daily, convention-determined behaviour, to emerge. The new presence is thus not an expression of a determined sex-identity or behaviour but rather a negation of it, in which case the tension between the daily and the extra-daily becomes particularly noticeable.

6

BUILDING THE THEATRICAL CHARACTERS

The Butterfly's Dream. Chuang-Chou once dreamt that he was a butterfly. A fluttering and happy butterfly which was totally ignorant of Chuang-Chou's existence. Chuang-Chou suddenly awoke and was again completely and utterly Chuang. Now I don't know whether it was Chuang-Chou who dreamed that he was a butterfly or whether the butterfly is dreaming that he is Chuang, although it is certain that there is a difference between the two. So it is with things and their transformation.

ELSE MARIE LAUKVIK

After *My Father's House*, I took a year off to experience something new. After nine years' work, the need for theatre was not so strong and other needs were demanding to be satisfied.

At that time, Odin Teatret also needed to find new ways. What would happen if we performed for spectators who were not accustomed to seeing us? We felt our way forwards to new challenges, new situations, such as training outdoors.

When I came back after a year's leave, the other actors had been doing clown work, and outdoor work and parades had been started which had broken our habitual laws about the use of the theatre space. This was liberating for me.

How did the stilt character in The Book of Dances, The Million *and* Anabasis *develop over the next ten years? This character has become almost a symbol of Odin Teatret and has been performed by many of the actors.*

I began work on that character when I came back from my leave. I worked with a prop, a fringed flag on a staff: a butterfly. When I held it up in front of my face, there was a person in the butterfly.

The character went up on stilts shortly after it got a white dress, which later had a black border added to the bottom of it.

Figure 17 The Book of Dances, 1975 (Else Marie Laukvik). Photo: Tony D'Urso.

Then I made a wig of long, black silk fringe and attached it to my forehead with a red headband. Even the butterfly had had a headband. Later I saw some mummies in Peru. They were a couple of thousand years old and had the same red headband, a symbol of magical power. The red headband I worked with was an expression of something magical and witch-like.

Early one morning in Sardinia, I tried the character out before we were to do a parade. I had worked all night to finish the wig and the parade was set for 10.00 a.m. So I got up at 6.30 a.m. and went out into the streets, to get a feeling for how the character worked. There was nobody around. But then I suddenly saw a woman dressed in black come around a corner. She saw me and was scared to death. She thought I was a vision. Here came a tall white figure with long black hair, walking alone down the street at 7.00 in the morning. She jumped back and ran away. Unfortunately, I couldn't tell her that I was a flesh and blood person, that I was an actor. Maybe she still believes today that she saw a vision, a message of death. Something historical came out of the character. It reminded me of the plague, the Black Death. Not from the 1300s, but from the 1600s. I don't know if this is historically accurate, if there really was an outbreak of the plague in the 1600s. It was a kind of introverted rest. A kind of resignation. Something that crippled a whole town, but also an acceptance of the suffering that people had been afflicted with. The same happened again in a later version of the character, where she's wearing a hat and Death is close by. Here she sees a menacing danger which she can't ward off. She absorbs it. The two characters go together, they are part of the same thing. One is extroverted, the other is introverted.

During a parade, many different relationships come into play. We use a town as a scenic space and 'perform' with the elements we meet. We use streets, windows, walls and openings. We use these relationships in a dramatic way, creating tensions with movements, sounds, costumes and props. The daily rhythm of the street is transformed. Harmony, or the opposite of harmony, is created.

Even though both characters have red headbands, the one in the white dress is different from the tall stilt character in *The Million*, which I would call a Western witch. This character is more innocent. She has something beautiful and holy about her, something clean and life-confirming. Perhaps also something nun-like, an acceptance of cruelty. She sees and suffers and yet is happy.

I'd put on a hat for variety, as part of a parade. It was a South American hat. The trousers were inspired by Rangda, the Balinese witch. She is no longer a nun, but both male and female. The character has a South American soul. Still with the staff and with death in the background in the form of a skeleton. Later on, I felt the need to create an *alter ego*, a shadow of myself. So I made a mask of my face; I added a hat and a wig. I put the mask on to the staff. This was reminiscent of the Indian custom of putting skulls on staffs. It was my own head and so something completely new came into the character. She took on a cruel, frightening quality, but was nevertheless beautiful.

Later, when we began to work on *The Million*, I developed this work further. I had made a tall stilt character, with a black dress and black silk hair. And a white face with the red headband. But with the new prop – my *alter ego* – it didn't work. I had come closer and closer to death, but needed to go deeper, further. So I made a very expressive mask.

The tall black stilt character had the wrong proportions. It was too 'black' and the face was too small. I had to extend the face with a white piece of cloth, just to get it to work visually. To make death more 'alive', I made a mask with a movable red mouth, the red headband and red around the eyes. And then she got an enormous wig of black ostrich

Figure 18 Parade, 1975 (Else Marie Laukvik). Photo: Tony D'Urso.

feathers. I sewed a red dress with black stripes and a black cape with red stripes. She had cotton trousers with white stripes, like Rangda, the witch in Balinese dance, but the character was transferred to a Western context, so I put white lace on the legs. Rangda moved West. And the fingernails were also inspired by Balinese and Indian temple dance. I had long, shiny, curved fingernails made of copper.

The roses at the end of the fingers came later – they're from Thailand. The umbrella is English. The hair was inspired by Japanese Noh or Kabuki. The face, which I made, reminded me of Karen Blixen, almost completely skull-like.

This character was a kind of symbiosis between the original stilt character, the clean, slightly innocent one, and the tall parade character, which had become darker and darker and which, with the little *alter ego*, is a death figure.

The new character didn't need an *alter ego*. It was so visually dominating that it didn't need a shadow but rather an assistant. The assistant became the little *Dyak* (headhunters in Borneo), as we called it. It was a mask Eugenio had given me. I made it into a little child, with a black hat that was too big for it. And the little mask was given wisps of black silk hair, like the earlier character had had, and a white dress.

The mother, the tall stilt character, represented something Asian filtered through the history of the West, an Asian soul with a Western expression.

The colours were red, black and white. Red and black because they are the colours which stand for anarchy, revolt, revolution. They are colours with extreme power, found in many different movements: on the Sandinista flag, in Nazi Germany . . .

The little *Dyak* expresses something I can see but which is hard to put into words, because it is many different things for me. I have, moreover, never heard anyone else try to interpret or explain the figure. For me, it is a kind of symbol of the non-existent Indian, the one who was completely wiped out by the Europeans who infiltrated the West. It has no life of its own, it is an assistant, born in *The Million*.

When I had made the tall stilt character and the puppet, I invited Eugenio into the room to see them. We often collaborate in this way. I show him something, he responds, I work on it some more. Maybe it turns into something completely different, a development suddenly takes a whole new direction.

What possibilities did that puppet have? It had to come into the world, it had to be born, and then it could die. Those are the consequences of the possibilities that a prop has.

In *The Million*, I come in as a pregnant demon on stilts. I give birth to the puppet. I ride around the room on it, with the staff between my legs, as if it were a horse. Then I see that it's an abortion and I smother it by pulling the white dress over it. I take it back to where it came from. It doesn't belong to this world.

The Million was made after all the actors had gone out travelling and had learned various new things. We showed each other the different numbers we had learned. Then we made use of the principle of unconnected connections. We played pieces of music that had nothing at all to do with the numbers they were accompanying. 'Mack the Knife' was played to my dance and it was then that I felt how frightening the character was. Nazism combined with Asian magic, Western colonialism with temple culture.

Later in the performance, she also dances the samba, so an element of Brazilian mafia comes into the picture. This blending of elements was a kind of cultural gene-splicing. For me it is an expression of the danger inherent in transforming culture to such an extent that it becomes something completely different. This character had an evil nature. It represented death culture.

I created the character's 'daughter' two years later, when I returned to the theatre after a year's leave. Ulrik Skeel had taken over the first stilt character in the meantime. The daughter was smaller and much more passive. There was something innocent about her. She was shy and withdrawn. At the end of *The Million* she was hacked down by the Priest; she fell with a cry. She became a kind of sacrifice. The daughter also carries a puppet. While the tall stilt character is negative, the little daughter is positive. She represents the positive qualities of nature people, good magic.

The stilt character was made just as such figures were made in magical prehistory times: a fingernail, a bit of hair. When the various elements were assembled, they created a new reality, another reality. It's not something I play at, but a weaving-together, a montage, which creates a new being. A theatrical gene-splicing. One can't think one's way to the right proportions or to the visual unity.

For me, the creative process comes about through an empty space, a kind of presence, a state in which I am and am not. I open a sluice, I let the subconscious come into its own; and yet the conscious is also always present and can choose from the material which emerges from the creative process. These poles are necessary. I can't force the material out. The empty space is a necessary condition. It helps the door to open. I find a kind of a receptivity towards other characters and let them emerge. They are an expression of another reality. This has nothing to do with my own personal conflicts or feelings. I am open to the accidental possibilities which present themselves. My task is to choose and combine these possibilities. In the same way that Picasso puts various, accidentally found figures and colours together.

I take a piece of fabric and look at it, add a colour, add another element, a headband . . . I develop it step by step. I have no predetermined ideas about the character.

Figure 19 Anabasis, 1978 (Else Marie Laukvik). Photo: Peter Bysted.

When the costume is ready, I put it on and look at myself in the mirror. This is the moment when I first see who I have become. With respect to this way of working, I am probably somewhat different from the other actors at Odin Teatret. It is only when the character has been constructed that I begin to work on the basis of its logic. Much as Chaplin did. He had no a priori ideas about his tramp. It was coincidence that created the character and he responded to coincidence. I have done the same thing with many of the characters I have made.

It is of course essential that one is able to see and recognize a character within these accidentally assembled costumes.

It's as though I put myself to the side. It's like being taken over by music and becoming one with the note. It's another level of consciousness, another wavelength, where space and time are experienced in a different way. It can often be an extremely pleasant experience which you sometimes have almost to force yourself out of.

It's a kind of ritual, with a meaning different from that in religious ritual, where there is a union with God. Here you are united with a note or a movement. It's like flying and becoming weightless. When I create a character, it's not a part of myself I'm trying to show, and yet, of course, it is also a part of myself. The composition is made and it becomes a character. And I can sometimes be surprised by people who expect to find the same character in private life as they see in the theatre. People couldn't understand that Chaplin was not the same person as his tramp, and that as a private person he even began to get involved in politics.

I demand the right to go in every possible direction, in possible and impossible directions. I am a point that can be everywhere: a fly on a stick. I accept a large world-view and I accept differences in people. I pull out different parts of myself to respond to these differences.

What was the training called the Fisherwoman?

This was a kind of training during which we tried out a whole range of different possibilities: working with staffs, hats, roller-skates, cabaret costumes. . . . We showed all these strange fish to each other and to people who came to visit us. We worked with all kinds of different props and out of this work arose various characters. I made a little old lady who was hunched over and walked with tiny steps, kind of Chaplin-like. I made a female clown with a straw hat, red trousers, black skirt and mittens with cut-off fingers. We worked with this character for Mother Courage in *Brecht's Ashes*, work I never finished because I left the production. I worked with cabaret dance and with a Japanese Kabuki-inspired character, with long fingernails, big pieces of jewellery, a big black hat and the mask from the tall stilt character. Not being on stilts gave me more movement possibilities.

We often did individual improvisations that had no relationship to the characters. It was training with props and costumes, staffs and chairs and characters, training in being able to shift quickly between various movement principles. During the same period, we worked a lot with music and played music for the improvisations. So it was a training system that was based on individual improvisation. It was a choice. At other times, we've gone about it in different ways. It also had something to do with Eugenio's way of making a montage, where it is often an advantage to have individual improvisations. Group improvisations can be technically difficult to edit. Body expression often becomes limited, filled with cliché and insufficiently visual. The task must therefore be very specific so that there are no hesitations or pauses when the actor stops to think. The actor mustn't think during improvisation, she must act and let herself be carried by the actions.

Eugenio works on improving the actor's expression, which then later can be woven together with or put in relationship to other actions, according to the principle of opposition.

It has been difficult for me to do only pure training with energy exercises, with energy and impulses. I get bored doing the same exercises over and over again. Once I have mastered a movement and have to keep on repeating it, I feel imprisoned. It's only when music is used as part of this kind of training that it feels natural for me to limit myself to physical expression. For many years, I have been tempted to use the training to enter a kind of 'borderland' where improvisation and imagination have free rein.

I don't believe that there is one single way to train. An actor can't follow a recipe, each person is unique and has particular creative possibilities. For me, training is often a question of being in the best possible physical shape, so that the work I then do is not sabotaged by tiredness or stiffness and lack of flexibility. I need endurance but I must also protect my body, flatter it and not threaten it.

I have to be in such good physical shape that I can let myself be swept away, as if by a wave or a wind. I might want to fly through the space, freed from the floor, but not for very long at any one time. I look for a kind of training which doesn't drain my energy but gives me energy instead, just as performing does. My physical weak points are my arms and my wrists. I've had back pain ever since 1975, when I started on the stilts. Maybe my leg muscles aren't strong enough and I lift the stilts with my back instead of my legs. Acrobatics are impossible for me because of my bad wrists. On the other hand, I work a lot with hand exercises, opening and closing the hands in all possible ways. I also work with exercises that strengthen the back rather than those that wear it down. You can't trifle with your body. You can easily cause damage that lasts for years.

IBEN NAGEL RASMUSSEN

Vestita di Bianco ['Dressed in White'] *(a film by Torgeir Wethal, 1974) is a film about the one who doesn't belong, the outsider and an actor's social loneliness. She is dressed in white, and has a mask on her face. From the world of nature she is coming to a little town. She beats on a drum, as if to awaken something or to announce a message. She is rather child-like, naive, perhaps a town fool. Her best contact is made with children, who imitate her or sit down beside her and watch her eat. Adults reject her – one closes a window, another goes inside his house.*

She is shy. Maybe she cannot talk. There is something animal-like about her, something strange about her movements. She is occasionally happy and jumps up and down like a child. But one has the impression that her message is primarily one of unhappiness, emphasized by the tears on her white mask.

She seems to be homeless. In the cemetery, she perhaps finds a certain degree of peace. She plays her flute and communes with the dead. As she is leaving, she meets a man on a horse-drawn wagon. He offers her a ride. She shyly demurs.

A cortège of cars passes her on the way to a wedding party. She comes to the town square and finds the bride's veil caught in a car door. She puts it on and goes into the party, where she dances for everyone wearing the veil. She suddenly runs away, like an animal that has discovered it is being watched, towards the sea, tosses the drum away, loses the veil and finally makes it down to the water, where a man sits and weaves baskets. She goes out into the water, sings to the water. She throws her mask and flute on to the beach. It's as if she's been blinded, and she protects her face with her arms and crawls into a little fishing boat and poles out into the water.

Without her mask, she is completely vulnerable. She hides her face and goes out to sea. The man on the beach watches her and carries on with his work.

How did you create this character?

The white character with the mask and drum appeared before we went to southern Italy in 1974. I imagined that we would arrive in some town and that I would yell to the people in the houses. The character was a kind of announcer from the very beginning, but I didn't have a clear idea of what it would be used for. Eugenio was a bit against the character: 'The drum is fine', he said, 'but . . .' He had told me about Kattrin, in Brecht's *Mother Courage*, and about the scene with the drum, where she warns the towns-people about the soldiers. It sounded exciting. I bought a drum and then forgot all about Kattrin (when I did perform Kattrin, much later, she didn't use a drum).

The character has been with me ever since. The mask has been changed a bit. I've often thought about making another character for our parades, but then the white character would be missing.

95

I don't know what gave birth to this 'town crier' or why it's so strong for me. I had no model for it. Yet it does have something powerful and poetic about it.

The character has changed along the way. When I see *Dressed in White*, I'm amazed at the rather loose, dance-like way I walk. When I used the character later, in big cities, it was more aggressive and warrior-like. My way of using the character was later influenced by Balinese dance, although not directly so (there are no actual movements from Balinese dance). But the way the character in *Anabasis* walks, jumps forward, reacts sharply, changes direction or is pushed back, reminds me of the way the warrior fights with Rangda (the witch).

So the character is very connected to training and to the way my training has developed.

In contrast to my characters in earlier productions, which were based on very set patterns of movement and action, this character is often improvised in public. The way of coming into contact with the spectators is completely different. Every little detail is important and meaningful – the way the spectators answer, what they tell or show me.

The character has a tremendous security. I am the character from the moment I put on the mask and start out – sometimes alone. The character has a kind of openness. I can do anything – things I would never dream of doing without the mask. Dance in a courtyard for a couple of women, eat spaghetti off a child's plate.

With time, the character seemed to grow technically and gave me more possibilities. I wear the same costume in *The Book of Dances*, but the character is different. I used many of the same numbers in Farfa's street productions [Farfa is a group founded by Iben Nagel in 1982]. The character is something that reaches deep into me and I'm not finished with it yet.

The fact that the character is not dependent on a production is very important. The other characters I have made have all been tied to particular productions and have died with them. The character has given me a great deal of independence as an actor.

I don't actually like being directed, don't like having someone tell me what I have to do. I need to make my own material and develop my own language. This means that I prefer to consider the work with the director as a 'meeting'. There is a part of *Marriage with God* that is taken from another production, a production we made with Farfa. So a piece of actor's material can be used in two different productions. This was an important thing for me to learn, that I could create fragments that could be used in various contexts.

During the first years, Eugenio watched everything. He observed all the training and all of our improvisations. The actors wrote down the various improvisations and Eugenio took part in their reconstruction. Later, when we began to use video to reconstruct the improvisations, particularly

Figure 20 The dancing stranger (Iben Nagel Rasmussen). Photo: Tony D'Urso.

during the work on *Come!* . . ., we were often alone. It was the first step. Eugenio began to withdraw from the actors' preparatory work and training.

In *Brecht's Ashes* and *The Million*, a lot of material was prepared beforehand and I then 'met' Eugenio, who took my material and the other actors' material and made a montage.

It became very important for me to be able to prepare as much material as possible beforehand. This went hand in hand with Eugenio's development and his growing experience with refined montage technique. It became important not to let yourself be swallowed up by his story, but to protect your own search, continuity and 'life' in the material. I think we get on to the wrong track if improvisation, as the term was understood in our early years, loses the meaning and the 'holy' respect it was given when Odin Teatret first started. If one only works with or considers the signs which the improvisation casts off, like flower petals or leaves which can be arranged in a vase according to one's taste, isn't there a danger that the actor's work ends up being sterile?

Training and performance

The relationship between training and performance has become closer over the years. There is a continual exchange of impulses between the two. The ideas about a coming new production take my training in new directions; a discovery made in training can inspire a scene in a new production.

My training is often now divided into two parts: the second part is a kind of improvisation with known elements (the elements I have worked with and developed in the first part). Improvisation in this kind of training consists mostly of the variation of rhythm and context but it is also possible to break through the technique to such a degree that moments from the second part of the training can be used directly in performance.

My character in *Come!* . . ., the shaman, is very active, with a lot of jumps and falls, and if I hadn't developed exactly that kind of physical work in my training, then the character would never have become what it did, would never have had its particular power.

But none of the elements in *Come!* . . . is taken directly from the training. What I found in the training was a particular kind of strength. There were in fact no visual descriptions in the improvisations. Rhythm, speed and composition were the fundamental aspects. During the work, I always had the feeling that I was casting myself into a maelstrom which could sweep me away. And yet at the same time, I believed that I could signal something, with understandable signs, something that I myself perhaps didn't understand at that moment – or to put it in a better way, something that I didn't understand in a rational way.

In *Come!* . . ., I was present with a dramatic nerve that I had strengthened during training. Later, during the development of the improvisation material, I gave the positions and movements I had discovered during the improvisations a more specific meaning, a kind of civilizing process took place that I am not sure was necessary. In any case, the essential thing was the raw material, the signal from the maelstrom.

The dance in *Marriage with God* was based on a training principle which had to do with displacing my balance. I worked with high-heeled boots, which helped me lose my balance in various ways.

I found the various positions in the dance, which are connected with the swaying way I had of losing balance, by imagining religious pictures and actions, such as the Virgin Mary at the cross.

'January 16, 1636. The Kaiser's troops threaten the Lutheran city of Halle. The stone begins to speak. Mother Courage loses her daughter and moves on alone. The war is still far from over.' (Brecht: Mother Courage and her Children*)*

In Brecht's Ashes, *the scene can be described in this way: Brecht places a small game-board on the floor. Kattrin sets some small animals on the board, which is the town of Halle. The other actors are nearby, lounging on the floor, each one with a tin soldier in front of him.*

Kattrin, mute, tries to warn them. She crawls up on a large box and begins to bang two scissor blades together, so that they sound like a bell ringing. This very emotion-laden scene is interrupted by Brecht, who has been sitting and reading.

'Kattrin, don't bare your teeth if you can't bite!'

Kattrin continues and the other actors laugh at her. Finally, she crawls down from the black box. Arturo Ui gathers up her toys and lays her carefully on the floor. He slowly and carefully stuffs her scarf into her mouth. She lies quietly on the floor. Arturo Ui places a large transparent bowl filled with water between her legs. He takes off her hat and lays it carefully on the floor beside her. Suddenly, he immerses his head in the bowl of water. Kattrin reacts as though she were being raped. She tries to defend herself with her hands, but in vain.

Mackie Messer is stretched out on the floor above Kattrin's head and watches with interest. A long time goes by before Arturo Ui lurches up, gasping for air. It sounds like a combination of orgasm and suffocation. He is shaken but gradually regains control of himself. He dries his face, grins brazenly, fixes his hair and carefully puts on his hat.

Yvette Poitier, the whore, comes over to Kattrin and kneels beside her to help her. Mackie Messer gives Yvette Poitier a push with his cane, knocking off her wig. She gets up and kicks Kattrin, turns towards Arturo Ui, goes over to him and kisses him passionately.

Kattrin is judged because of her goodness. Arturo Ui takes her jacket off, so that she is standing with a naked torso and uplifted arms. She is still

Figure 21 Brecht's Ashes, 1982 (Francis Pardeilhan, Iben Nagel Rasmussen, Tage Larsen). Kattrin is raped by Arturo Ui while Mackie Messer watches with interest. Photo: Tony D'Urso.

wearing her red gloves and is still trying to use her hands to warn of the coming danger.

The executioner (the Jew from the concentration camp) drags himself forward, singing, and wielding a kitchen knife which he has taken from the cook. He moves slowly up behind Kattrin and with a rapid movement indicates that her head has been cut off.

A plate crashes to the floor and the field cook shouts, 'Wow, that scene is enough to make you cry.'

Kattrin collapses. Brecht lays a red flag over her. Her hands are still trembling and Brecht shows that his heart is beating in time with her hands.

The character of Kattrin is found in a dramatic text and has its own life there. Is your use of the character connected to the text and its actions? And how did you build the language of this character?

The world that Kattrin moves in is Brecht's world and the world of the war. This is her background, her roots. Kattrin was the first character I ever worked on during training and it was during training that she broke loose from the literary text. She became an independent character which later became a part of the general story about Brecht (it wasn't, after all, *Mother Courage* that we were going to work on, but a production about Brecht's life). The only scene that was kept from Brecht's play is the scene where Kattrin warns the people of Halle that the soldiers are coming to set fire to their houses. But we didn't use Brecht's text, only the actions, which end in her death. One could say that during the training, I worked with the character on the pre-expressive level. The character was ready before we began the montage work. All her ways of walking, sitting, using her arms, using sound, were very precise physical actions without specific meanings and thus they could be used in various contexts.

If the form has a specific meaning, then it is difficult for the director to use it in a montage because he sees something different from what you yourself are doing.

If I do a scene with Kattrin which has a very specific meaning for me, then difficulties can arise if this action is placed in a context where it means something completely different.

If, on the other hand, you work on the pre-expressive level, then both you and the director have a greater freedom.

So my work has gradually become more technically orientated. Kattrin was not created on the basis of improvisation. She was composed as an action pattern which only later was given meaning in relationship to the contexts in which she was used in the production. Even the scene where she bangs the scissor blades together to warn the townspeople has a technical basis in the sign language I worked with, combined with the sound of the scissor blades striking against each other. It was very difficult to make that scene, because of the combination of these various elements. The idea for the montage was Eugenio's, a typical example of how I myself would have stopped much too early and where the director insisted until the scene worked.

What is essential about this way of working is that the actor has something to say above and beyond the technical. For me personally, the essence is the shout, the yell which was already part of my very first improvisation. The first time I developed it was in *My Father's House* where I yelled 'Fyodor Dostoyevsky' very loudly, at the beginning of the performance. When I did the improvisation, I was terrified at the thought that I would have to repeat it, the note was much too high for my voice.

Later, this yell was used in many ways, calling, lamenting, demanding, but with the same extremity for all the characters. The 'white character', the shaman, Kattrin.

Something that helped me a great deal when we did *My Father's House* was the work we did with gibberish, something I also used in *Dressed in White*. I always found Danish very difficult to use in performance.

It was important to discover that Kattrin, although mute, was not deaf.

She was not isolated but was always in contact with what was happening around her. She kept the child within her, her way of being near others, the way she was touching and silly. She saw and experienced a world not yet manipulated by words. In fact, she also 'talked', with her hands, with the sound of her wooden shoes, with her little jumps.

I myself often feel more mute than Kattrin. When I try to talk I know that the words are like the tiny tops of icebergs whose bases remain out of sight. If I try to remember what I used to be like, I remember many different Ibens, and they are all mute. It's a big mistake to believe that a mute is also necessarily deaf to what is happening around her, passive or instinctive like a wild animal.

I am very taken with one particular image of shining people dancing on a beach. If I had told Eugenio about this, he would certainly have shook his head and said, 'That's nonsense, it doesn't interest me. I want to portray things with a historical perspective – the destruction of the Indians, the Greeks' ascent to the sea, and Brecht, the intellectual, and the situation under Nazism.' But I always held on to my meanings – my image – and followed Eugenio through his historical journey. I rolled out my beach in every single production. He has always accepted the strange, dancing way I move. With every character, from the shaman, Bach the clown, to the 'white character' to Kattrin.

In what ways have you been influenced by Asian theatre?

I have been stimulated most by seeing and experiencing the actors, their performances and training.

On the practical level, I have worked very little with Asian actor technique. I cannot emphasize enough how important it has been that I have had a base which was my own personal training. It was this basic training of my own that I wanted to develop. And this training had absolutely nothing to do with Asian theatre forms. It was based on falls, jumps and ways of sitting down. It consisted of a vital use of space typical of Western dance and my main source of inspiration was Isadora Duncan. For my meeting with Asian performers to be fruitful, it was essential that I at no time have wanted to be or dreamed of being like them. I wanted to grow as an actor at Odin Teatret. I was a European, with my confused background; Asian performers were Asians, representing a form of dance and drama that was inseparably connected to its cultural and religious background.

When I came to Odin Teatret, Eugenio's model for our education was that of the Asian actor. He used expressions like 'the Chinese principle' to indicate that a movement or an action should always begin in the opposite direction: if I want to go to the right, I begin with a step to the left. There were exercises for the face which had clearly been influenced by Kathakali. There was stick-fighting, which had a Japanese name. Eugenio explained

Figure 22 Brecht's Ashes, 1982 (Iben Nagel Rasmussen). Montage: the actor is placed in a new context; here not in the performance, but in front of the 'Wall'. It is a kind of dramatic quantum leap from the text to Berlin at the time before the Wall was broken down.

Kattrin speaks with her hands:

When you make me happy, I often think: Now I could die. So I have been happy right to the end. When you are old and think of me, I will look as I do today, and you will have a lover who is always young.

Photo montage: Jan Rüsz and Catherine Poher.

how he had been fascinated by Kathakali when he was in India, and not only by the suggestive night-time performances, but particularly by the Kathakali actors' attitude towards their work. How the aspiring actor got up at 5.00 a.m. to train the voice before breakfast, how the training went on throughout the whole day, interrupted only by short breaks to eat or to do practical work, how they worked and lived together. As our work developed over the years, it was clearly not bringing us any closer to the East; on the contrary, the results were typically the fruit of our own time and situation. When I look back at one of the strongest, most beautiful and most important fruits which our work has produced, it strikes me that I recognize in it many of the elements that had fascinated Eugenio twenty years before, but it has gone through such a transformation that no one, certainly not Eugenio himself, has noticed it.

I'm thinking about our stay in southern Italy, where we made *The Book of Dances* and *Johann Sebastian Bach*. There, under the Italian sun, and with all the daily problems, I think that the last thing on our minds was Asia and Asian actors. We wanted to be ourselves, fully and completely, and yet it was as if Eugenio's old dream melded both with our daily life, and also with the dream that certain young Scandinavians had of being able to live and work in a way that was different from the usual.

Vocal training began at 5.00 a.m., outside town or by the sea. After breakfast, we continued training. After training came performance work. In the evenings we did barters in the surrounding towns. These barters could sometimes, in one single evening, bring an otherwise divided and disparate town back together. We lived together and the practical work in the house was part of the daily programme.

In the technical preparation of our productions, those principles with the exotic names are still to be found, but not as foreign elements. They are the joints and nerves of Odin Teatret's body.

Do you differentiate between different forms of energy?

Yes, at a certain point I realized that all exercises are not equally good. Earlier, we had done many different kinds of exercises, the only condition being that we should do them in a personal way. Later, when I began to teach, I found that different training exercises result in different forms of energy. Some exercises block energy, others give energy back to you.

If you have a training in which you throw imaginary objects out into the space, a form of energy is built up which almost lifts you from the floor.

If you are using Japanese martial technique, which we call samurai training and which is more connected to the earth because one's centre of gravity is carried low, then it gives another kind of energy. You can work in a conscious way with the various forms of energy. You can make a conscious choice to cultivate individual forms of energy.

Energy can flow like a wave. The first time I understood this was when I saw Japanese actors. I understood purely intuitively that they modulate energy as a continuous wave.

I had earlier had a natural resistance to training because it was so tiring. Later I developed a form of training which had a continuity, based on my own elements: various ways of sitting, of losing balance, of falling on the floor, of jumping and turning in the room, establishing oppositions in the body and various directions in space by means of a concentration of energy in a direction opposite to that of the action's final goal. Like when you reach back with the arm before throwing something (the sats).

I discovered that training has 'shadows'. I work with the exercises but they also work with me. A clear example of this is the exercises based on falling. If they are done correctly, there is a little moment of lack of control where the body is off balance. At this moment, it is easy to see if the actor is cheating, if she is attempting to control the whole process herself. This moment of lack of control has nothing to do with uncontrolled training.

During the first years, I worked with real falls, where the body meets the floor and then, by means of turning or rolling, comes up on its feet again and ends the exercise in a standing position. Later, in order to avoid damaging my knees, I developed the exercises so that the body no longer touched the floor. Just before the fall occurs, I take the control back again by moving one foot forward and blocking the energy in a very precise stop, loaded with energy. Further work in this direction consists of learning to use the energy – to send it in another direction, to keep it from dying. When I do these exercises, I change tempo and rhythm.

When I am training I am in a state which is a kind of meditation, even though I may be working very quickly and reacting. I have a kind of inner stillness but I am nevertheless thinking and on the lookout for new physical possibilities. This is a very wakeful form of meditation – you are mentally and physically active and give yourself to the body's rhythms and waves of energy. It is a kind of meditation in energy. Perhaps meditation is the wrong word to use here. Perhaps one should say that training is a kind of improvisation structured according to certain selected principles. You are in a state in which you can observe the development of your work at the same time as you are led by it.

Rhythm must be varied (not staccato) with precise stops at the beginning and end of every exercise. When I teach, I work on continuity from the very beginning. Even if the student is able to do only three or four exercises, these exercises are put together and the student must improvise with the sequence, varying the rhythm and intensity. It is essential not to interrupt this phase with comments, but to give short precise directions or corrections while the work is going on. On the other hand, it is important not to limit oneself to these three or four exercises and repeat only them, but to develop new elements day after day. At this stage, musical accompaniment can only confuse and destroy one's chances of reaching what I call a personal rhythm. It is important to learn to listen to that 'something' within us which I simply call energy, to discover that we can lead it, that it can surprise us, to experience that it is possible to become one with it.

When I say 'dance', I don't necessarily mean an extreme release of energy in space. The Noh style of acting is also dance: the energy which the Noh actor radiates is enormous but it does not explode in space. This energy-laden state is much more difficult to control.

In my work as a teacher I have been astonished by how many resources still remain when, after the ordinary training (where everyone feels they are ready to drop with exhaustion), we move on to dance with music as a partner. It almost never happens (in contrast to training without music) that someone stops in the middle of the process and thereby destroys it. The elements that appear are less thought-out, the very tempo makes thinking impossible. Because of the rhythm of the music, the body is given a push, it leads the work. It becomes obvious that the body is much more intelligent, much richer in proposals, than one would think.

Then comes a very difficult but necessary process: the setting of the various elements, the choosing and mounting of the elements into a kind of choreography. If you don't set and fix the elements, you fall into a false spontaneity, a false freedom. The elements will crumble, will be forgotten. I never use recorded music when I teach. I emphasize that the music we use must come from the body. Recorded music can be a trap, because you can be tempted to believe that you yourself are creating the enormous space that the music opens up.

The rhythm changes again when we begin to work with props. Different props will naturally give different rhythms. A fan will have a different effect on the body from that of a large flag. If the music carries the dancer, then a prop is an even more specific partner. It helps you avoid being self-centred, it helps you direct yourself out into the space in a precise way, to follow, to answer, to work continuously, without playing at acting, but acting.

The work with props gives the actor the chance to 'write' and create dramatic sequences. I am not interested in being set in a specific role. I think that it is important that the director gives you tasks that lead you in a new direction, or in a direction different from the one you thought you would go in.

I need a director to put a spoke in the wheel of what has become all too natural. The older one gets, the more difficult it becomes to renew oneself. The better you know yourself and your possibilities, the harder it becomes to find new challenges. The training therefore also becomes an important means of getting away from your old forms of expression. Or you can work with new ways of using your old material and transform it. We are getting older, and on the technical level this is very exciting. What is going to happen to those of us at Odin Teatret when we no longer have the same physical strength? Ballet dancers, for example, stop dancing quite early. Is the same going to be true for us? Or can we do something exciting, something which is not just an unsuccessful repetition of the efforts of our youth? This is something I was very much interested in during the work on *Marriage with God*.

In Asian theatre, the masters are often 50 or 60 years old or older. If you are trained into top form when you are young, then it is possible to keep the energy in your actions when you are older. The release of energy in space can be diminished without the same thing happening to the intensity.

In *Marriage with God*, my point of departure was the ballet dancer Nijinsky and his wife, Romola de Pulszky, during the period of their lives when Nijinsky was mad. We found a picture of the two of them, when he had just been released from hospital and was healthy again. She is standing in a ballet position and he, a little old balding man, is turning her around. We began to collect pictures of old people and studied their faces, their body language and the experience in their eyes. In the production, the physical score was slower and less powerful, but with the same intensity and energy as earlier.

I have always worked in a fast and vital way, so it was exciting to work with this new form of energy, or with the translation of energy from fast, powerful dance to a slower tempo where the energy is withheld so that it doesn't explode in the room. It is relatively easy to take an action which has occupied a lot of space and diminish it, but the opposite doesn't apply.

This is not because I feel that I am in bad physical shape today. But I have become better at economizing my strength. I don't waste my strength, even though I use optimum energy.

TORGEIR WETHAL

What do you think about training now?

One of the risks we run is that we often begin to think mechanically. And I think that, in certain periods, our training work is often conservative rather than developmental. You know how to prepare the mechanics, or you think that the motor is good enough, and you keep it in shape. This doesn't necessarily lead to a negative development. Awareness of the problem can force us to find new points of departure.

For a long time, I didn't take part in the training. I stopped several years ago, for certain very specific reasons. I wasn't getting any further with it, it had become barren ground for me. It wasn't something which held me. It had slowly become more difficult to materialize ideas and needs as 'sprouts' in the training situation.

Then, when we began to work on *Oxyrhincus Evangeliet*, and were rehearsing and were on tour at the same time, I began to get out of shape. I had kept in good shape earlier, because of having to do the performances: both *The Million* and *The Book of Dances* were active enough to keep me in shape. But *Oxyrhincus Evangeliet* is physically very static for me. So at the moment I am trying to go back to a combination of good old acrobatics and basic physical training. And of course, I would still like to be able to do what I was previously capable of physically.

But at the same time, it's also very exciting right now to find out what possibilities I have to fill a space with presence by using very limited physical actions, with less activity than before. This is a point one should first permit oneself to be fascinated by after having gone through the opposite. Purely technically, it is the same as it is with any form of training or expression. It has to do with certain tensions, certain directions in space and, most of all, with a combination of various directions at the same time. An action which is unequivocal and which follows only its own speed and direction will never be as fascinating as the action which contains built-in oppositions.

With respect to these minimal physical actions, I am currently training with a why for every single movement. I extend my hand and turn my wrist because I am touching or want to touch something specific, rather than just doing the action. If you begin to work in this way, you begin to develop small action patterns which have a simple basis above and beyond the technical.

You choose a principle: I work with at least three directions in the body at the same time, all of which must have a specific basis. What is valuable in our training today is that we work with various principles more than with set exercises. These are principles which we ourselves have invented and which we develop until they are transformed into something new, something we feel is professionally exciting. If someone watches our training today, they could very well be confused, because it is so individual that it can often be difficult to see the different principles. Difference – multiplicity in space – is fascinating. But if one is able to follow one of the actors for a longer period of time, one will discover that the work contains set principles and systemic work on what at first glance seems to be a kind of free expression.

Can you summarize some of the most elementary training principles?

Training is often lonely. Even though we often work at the same time, we are working alone.

All actions must have precise directions. We use the space. You orientate yourself in space in relationship to the wall, or to the ceiling, towards the floor or towards a particular part of yourself, etc. The points must be clear. Let the feet draw large, clear figures on the floor. The hands must also leave clear lines in the air.

It helped me a great deal when I understood how essential the position of the head is in an exercise. Does it follow the direction of the exercise? Does it break that direction? There are many possibilities for variations. You can often transform all of your set training by working in a new way with the head. Many balance problems can also be solved by holding the head in a new way.

This kind of simple technical difficulty or task can open up whole new areas for work and the outer picture of what you are doing will be changed.

If one doesn't lift the arms above the head, then the head becomes one of the body's external 'graphic' points. It is one of the accents in the lines which the body can draw. The head will habitually follow the eyes. One can, of course, work in opposition to this, but that is another story. The point in the space to which we direct our eyes is very important. We have a tendency to look down towards the floor, to make the world around us as small and closed as possible. The eyes can lift the head, pull the head after them. Look outward. This will also influence the size of your actions. The arms and the legs – the whole body – end up in relationship to a larger space.

You can also use the eyes to find new rhythms: if you direct the eyes towards one part of the space and then release them as late as possible, as if you are on the way to a new direction.

Look the space in the eyes. Use as much time as necessary to perceive but don't meditate. It takes a fraction of a second, and one must use that time. Control the space with the eyes. The space surrounds you completely. You survey all of it. Cheat the space with the eyes. The space believes that you are going to look at a particular part of it, but at the last moment you surprise it and look somewhere else. A place that didn't think it was going to be looked at. It's not a question of playing, just seeing. You can 'place' the eyes in various parts of the body. Use the chest, the hips, the knees. Anywhere you like. You can even use two pairs of eyes. One pair in the knees and one in the elbows. But first begin by using them where they are, in the head.

Use the whole space, including that part of the space which is behind you, which you don't see. Every action is made up of several movements, several phases. Show each one of them. Change direction and speed in the space. Find the extreme limit of the balance field. The end of a movement must be controlled: it is the beginning of a new movement. Change rhythm. Copy the rhythms of various animals. Copy the rhythms of various actions. Follow the rhythm, don't play.

Every action contains at least two directions. There must always be a force which is working against the obvious, automatic, daily action sequence. Rather than moving the whole body at once, you can begin from the shoulders. This pulls you around, the torso follows, but – the hips resist. They prefer to turn in another direction. It is only when the hips and torso have worked against each to the maximum point and you almost have to stop, because they are equally strong, that you 'release' the hips and let them unwillingly follow. You can do this quickly or slowly, and the tension can be extended a great deal or just a little. And you don't need to 'show' it. You're just turning on the spot. There's nothing special about it. But seen from the outside, your action becomes more visible than if you merely turned.

When you fall, you try to hold yourself up. The most important thing is to find the point in the body which can work against the direction of the fall. The legs bend and you fall forwards – but the hips and the torso can use all their strength to avoid following – they want to go up.

If someone tries to push you away, you struggle to stay where you are. All action ought to have a built-in opposite direction. You are pushed down to the dark and lifted up to the light at the same time. What we are talking about here is elementary physical know-how: 'rules' which make the exercises lighter and clearer.

These 'rules' have parallels in daily life. It's very seldom that you do just one thing at a time. You go over to visit a good friend, you look forward to it. At the same time, you'd also like to stay home and watch a film on television. The sight of a person you love changes your radiation, your electricity, the nature of your presence on stage, if you really 'see' that other person with all of your senses. This change is important but it doesn't make the actor active. The actor becomes active because of the need to touch the other person on the cheek with the back of the hand. Even if the action is not finally done, because there is no dramaturgical place for it, the desire to do the action has an effect on his physical presence as perceived by the spectator.

I use verbs – action words – which presume an object outside the active: to pull, to push, to hold on to, to resist against. One of the reasons why some actors can seem chaotic and unorganized in their work is because they are not familiar enough with the power of opposition. You must always find a mass outside yourself, something that pulls or pushes you, something you want to push, something you want to cut through.

Nearly everyone has tried to push a car to get it started, tried to pull something with a rope, tried to go into water up to one's neck, tried to walk slowly in sand so soft one's feet sink, tried to cut cheese, tried to run against the wind. In all of these daily actions, our strength and weight have one direction. The resistance is outside us. The actor must be able to create the illusion of action with or against varying weights and resistances. Not to use it for the purpose of illustration, as in classical, anecdotal pantomime. But both mime and pantomime use the rules governing this double-action, this muscular contradiction in the execution of action. It is easier for the actor to render his daily actions on the stage alive if he has first learned and then absorbed or expanded this technique.

I use elementary pantomime exercises to explain this problem in practice. Start by trying to illustrate. It looks easy, but it's difficult: use your forearm as a sword. Cut through the air. The air is a mass which gives varying resistance. Reach backwards with one arm and pull something – it won't help to tense the arm muscles in the way that a real action would necessitate, in the way a real weight would demand that you move. This tension must be shown by another part of the body. But at first, you will still have to use just as much strength as in the real action. Later, it can change into something which is almost invisible and which doesn't demand a lot of strength.

Do you differentiate between energy in space and energy in time?

Yes, but there is always the question as to whether or not this differentiation is a direct part of your technique and consciousness, at least if we are talking about training and the actor's actions. I think that this is a differentiation which has a very specific meaning, when you are observing from the outside, as a director, and are using the actor as material. Of course, it also has a specific meaning for the actor who is working on how to transfer any fast action and its energy to a slow and almost invisible action with the same energy, with the same inner power. It is a kind of tension which holds on to you. Both in training and in direct performance work, we have made a lot of use of the translation of one action form into another form or tempo. For the actor, the action might remain as it originally was in his inner world, but the spectator sees something completely different. Part of this ambiguity might perhaps shine through such an action and the spectator will therefore be able to read it in various ways.

One could say that energy is the building up of a tension field in or around the body. But energy is also a tension field between two people, that is, a relationship. In your training, do you work with tension fields between two people?

This is something we have almost never done. Several years ago, we did do pair work, with very specific acrobatic exercises, where you had to react at the right moment so as not to hurt yourself or your partner. In these forms of martial training, we worked on understanding our partner's rhythm and intentions and on being able to react or to project clear signs. But this was always only in connection with very specific and defined exercises. We later tried to do the same in a more improvised form, but regardless of whether it was an improvisation for a performance or a training improvisation, we were unable to read more in it than general concepts such as love, hate and aggressiveness – that is, concepts unsuitable for the actor, because they are captions. There were no specific details or variations in the actions and reactions. They lacked multiplicity and 'life'.

The tension field we build up between two people is generally done by putting two previously set actions in relationship to each other but since each action has already been set on its own, you use a kind of physical dialogue technique: an action done by one actor provokes a reaction from another actor, a purely question–answer principle. How long you can maintain a tension between two people is of course dependent on what it will be used for, but as a general rule, you will know this only when you get close to the construction of a dramatic situation.

In *My Father's House*, we did an entire scene, the 'conspirator's scene', with the help of several group improvisations. This was in the very first version of the performance. It was a scene we had to remove because it lost all its life. At first, it did work dynamically in the space, and with clear questions and answers, but its basis in each actor was much weaker than what we had built the rest of the performance on. It withered and died and we cut it.

There are many ways of finding material. There are certainly also ways to work directly with another actor in a kind of improvisation, if you set up strong principles which force you to use clean reaction, not to play.

There are action patterns in *Oxyrhincus Evangeliet* which are based on a kind of double improvisation, that is, two-person improvisations. We needed to find certain set action patterns, an action sequence which would always be repeatable, and so we made movement improvisations with the use of props. A chair or a long staff, which both partners held on to at the same time and with which they did everything possible, lifting them, and so on. And then you set a pattern, a choreography: one step to the left, the chair is turned to the right, level with the head, etc. You then took the prop away and repeated the same pattern, as if the chair was there. When you then separate the two people, each of them has a set action pattern with no meaning whatsoever.

The first thing I do in such a situation is to give the action sequence a meaning.

My 'because' will hopefully be so important that the movement's tone or harmony, in the musical sense, that is, the over- and under-tones, will ring through in spite of everything without the movement being changed and without my having expressed the because. Without this content, it would be difficult for me to keep a performance alive. And I wouldn't be interested in it anyway.

An action which has been made in this way, with another person, will almost never be done with the same person in performance, but instead with an actor who has prepared his material with someone else. The meaning action takes on in performance is almost never that which the actor had imagined he was expressing. The meaning is what the spectators experience through what they see and is influenced most of all by the context in which the action is placed. When actors realize this, I can well understand that many become interested in what I call the world of dance or dance terminology as a way of thinking.

I am perhaps atypical in this regard, with respect to my relationship to my work at Odin Teatret at the moment. It's difficult for me to have a relationship to an abstract movement. My thoughts and reaction patterns are far removed from dance, while many of the actors here are interested in dance as a phenomenon, as a combination of movements and actions, more or less abstract movements and actions. Even though the energy and the change of space which they are causing are very specific.

For me, regardless of what the spectator sees, regardless of the use made of my actions by the director, my knowledge of what I am to do at a given moment, without having to think about it beforehand, is dependent on my whys. These whys are outside me, and they are not dependent on my psychological states. They are whys placed out in the space. I walk over there because I want to do such and such. I fall because of such and such. I would never try to express rage, although I can of course establish a series of whys which are the same as in a situation of rage. I would never try to pump myself up to rage. It's possible that I might become angry, be led to anger by certain inner actions which live parallel with the scene. It is most likely here, in this respect, that there is a certain difference in the action–reaction basis which I use as an actor and the more ordinary technique which many of the other actors use.

Is the inner action sequence in a performance a connected chain?

It's difficult today to say how it works because it happens in so many different ways at once. But I once dreamed of being able to create a connected and logical inner sequence for myself for a whole performance, that is, a specific and emotionally logical development which covered the whole course of the performance. I don't think I ever managed this. It would necessitate a complete separation between the performance's outer action, which the spectator sees, the performance's dramaturgy, and whatever it is inside me that causes me to execute the actions. I think this was a dream I tried to make a reality until *My Father's House*.

It has often happened that my placement in the dramaturgy or structure of the performance, apart from *Ornitofilene*, has been that of the outsider. I nearly always end up being the contrast to an action, the reflective part of an action, or a mirror-image. The one the actions happen around, the character who also becomes one of the easier keys for the spectator's understanding of the performance. This has sometimes happened for purely practical reasons, as when we did *My Father's House*. I was editing a film when the work began, so I wasn't present at the first rehearsals. I arrived later, and saw material that I had to establish a relationship to. In *Come! . . .*, it was difficult for me to find a way into the work. I remember that I asked that no matter what happened, no matter what I did or didn't do, that I be allowed to be in the performing space the whole time, preferably somewhere where I wasn't in the way. And so slowly, out of this situation, we built up actions which for the most part consisted of my establishing a relationship to what the others were doing. This so-called improvisation, which was the basis of my action sequence, was an answer to (an understanding or misunderstanding of) what I had experienced of what the others were doing. This became part of the performance, manifest all the way through, with certain slightly twisted or distorted approaches, so as not to be too direct.

If you are driving somewhere in a car by yourself, it might well happen that you sit there and smile, perhaps move your mouth a little bit, you're in a kind of double life, a waking dream. It's as if someone is sitting beside you and you're talking with this person in your waking dream. You move your mouth, you make small body movements, you turn your head one way or another. These are specific actions and you could actually repeat them in the same way as you repeat a physical action pattern.

You can build up a precise action on the basis of the reactions resulting in a little smile, a little nod of the head, a little sound one makes while driving a car, by enlarging these reactions, giving them place and form in space. And at the same time, this is an inner process which is alive, which you do not attempt to stop.

Precision is not an unequivocal word. Some actors think of precision as the conscious and exact execution of a movement and every detail of it. This is certainly acceptable, but for me, it is most of all a question of the precision of the will involved. Will on both the large and the small scales; the will – the necessity behind each movement, or, better, behind each action and in the work situation as a whole.

As the years go by, when you work with this kind of free, imaginative or relived improvisation, it becomes apparent that the material you manage to find is limited. We all have our own individual psychic clichés or ways of reacting. It has sometimes been necessary for me to work with improvisation in the third person. A more intellectually interesting form of work in which you don't try to open up the personal sluices. You can translate very simple (but preferably active) sentences into physical action: 'Brecht picks up his pen. He sharpens it. He writes on the paper.' I say to myself: 'Pen = sword-goosefeather-weapon.' 'To sharpen = to load.' 'To write = to stay in one place-to form.' 'Paper = the whole field of vision, the whole space.' I am thus saying: 'Everything must be seen through a magnifying glass.'

'Brecht picks up his pen': the hand touches the shaft of the pen, at the same time as I bend my knees slightly. The sword is exaggeratedly long, so the right arm makes a high, round movement in order to lift the sword. It is brought forward and held vertically, in front of the nose. When the tip of the goosefeather passes the nose, it tickles. This results in a funny little three-part zig-zag movement of the head, which pulls back and up – the movement is led by the nose.

'He sharpens it': the sword-feather is put into the left hand, which is extended as far as possible, at the same time as it changes into a weapon. So, with my right hand, I make a large 'loading' movement.

'He writes on the paper': the weapon-feather is moved to one side,

Figure 23 Brecht's Ashes, 1982. Brecht and Arturo Ui (Torgeir Wethal and Francis Pardeilhan). A network of tensions creates the fictive body. Brecht is ready to defend himself. Photo: Tony D'Urso.

behind and down, as if it were a long punt-pole dipped in the water (the ink-well) in order to push off. The right hand changes grip, so I take hold of the feather as one would do in order to write. The left leg is stuck (sucked down into a mouse-hole). I move as far as possible towards the left and then from there draw a line as high and as far forward as possible and then down to the right. At the same time, I take a step with the right leg, as large as possible and to the side (the left leg is still stuck). I keep this position with the legs, while the right arm and torso draw a horizontal line to the left. The first 'A' has been written.

I speak in the third person and set an action pattern which has a relatively unimportant basis and which later I can either develop further or leave as it is.

Can you describe further your function in Brecht's Ashes, *where you play Brecht?*

He became the observer in the performance. In the whole performance, he has only one emotional outburst, dramaturgically speaking.

I'm talking about the scene where Margarete Steffin dies. This is a scene in which he has his own action pattern and lets his reactions out. This perhaps also happens in the scene where he tosses his books around the room. These are small fragments which work because he does the opposite in the rest of the performance. He is a pure observer, the 'keeper of the minutes'. In order to perform this non-participatory presence, I had to use small motivations completely different from those which made up the external action sequence of the performance. Withheld actions which resulted in different body tensions. Even though he just stood there, he didn't disappear, he was visible. He was often the central point from which the rest of the performance flowed. For a long time, all of my work consisted of finding these simple body tensions. I couldn't maintain the form of attention which emanates from a particular position, an attention to what is happening in the room, if I hadn't chosen something which causes it. Something which pushes you forward from a particular place in your back, as if someone for some reason was pushing you backwards at your shoulders at the same time as you try to pull away. So I reach a position which is a non-executed action and this position gives me a base from which I maintain a relationship to what is happening in the room. But if I just try to assume that position, then the tensions won't be the same every time or they will lose some of their quality.

And since this was done for most of the performance as an elementary way of making a base for myself, then the small fragments work in a different way when you suddenly interrupt these tensions and react in the space instead. The tensions I use in the performance are so small they are almost invisible, but as soon as I take them away, another form clearly appears. It's a break because it is another way of using energy.

For me, this was a performance motivated for the most part by what was happening in the room at the moment it happened. It was motivated in and of itself, one could say. This is part of how I was worked into the dramaturgy and was part of the performance's more intellectual reality and was something that occupied me right from the beginning. Also because it was one of the few times that we chose texts that we wanted to present as they were. We looked at an enormous amount of textual material until we found the texts we wanted to use and that we wanted to be understood. In other performances, we have always worked far away from text tendering. We have always otherwise used the text as a point of departure and let it speak for itself so that there is also room to say something else.

In *Brecht's Ashes*, it was difficult for me to accept that a small manifestation, a minimal physical activity in space, could work, and that you still existed as an actor, even though this was all you had to work with.

I probably hadn't finished my work in the performance until we had done it 100 or 150 times. I kept on fighting with it and against it. I kept on filling it out, and understanding it, giving it small, perhaps invisible details. In fact, I am almost never ready when we begin to perform and continue to improvise with small details.

There's a scene in *Brecht's Ashes* which is based on fragments and associations from several of Brecht's performances. In this scene, as 'Brecht the director', I give a signal to Tage [Larsen] and Roberta [Carreri] – Mackie Messer and Polly Peachum – to begin an action. Then I turn towards Julia [Varley] – Johanna Dark – who is at the other end of the space and walk towards her to signal to her when she should 'enter' the scene. All I have to do is take a few small steps and all the attention in the scene is focused on Tage and Roberta. These steps were a nightmare. First I just 'walked'. Later, Eugenio intervened and began to work technically on these steps. I got stuck. We let them stay the way they were. At one point, when we were looking for material for another scene, I did an improvisation which contained a passage where I walked from one place to another. We plucked this passage out and used it in the scene where I walk towards Julia. I walk. I'm holding my arms slightly behind me. The thumb and index fingers of both hands are pressed slightly together. The torso is bent slightly forwards. The action is taken from an improvisation and there I know why I am doing it and ought to be satisfied.

But in my work in this performance, I had another goal: to be able to motivate all my actions on the basis of the performance's outer logic. I have always had to have a conscious attitude with respect to the story and my place in it. The context is strong. My signs are small, nearly illegible, but they have to be there. The fragment must be understandable on yet another level – what is this action, slightly reminiscent of a man pulling something behind him? For me, it became 'the director' pulling both the actors' attention and a scene along, so that both can be put together or expanded with another action. This isn't something which the spectator can understand, but neither was it the idea that the spectator should understand. It was just to help me walk in a way that wasn't 'slack'.

At last I was satisfied and so was Eugenio (possibly). It took a year for this 'technical passage' – 'Go down there and give Julia a signal' – to become an action.

How did you work on your role in The Book of Dances?

We have almost never used the term 'role' but rather have created certain characters out of parts of ourselves, out of our needs, which then later appear as roles in the performances. But here it was different. At one moment I realized that I personally never would have called either *The Book of Dances* or *The Million* performances. This was connected to the fact that they were technically constructed. We learned dances – two steps to the left, one step forward – and then, slowly but surely, the score was filled out. I can take the characters from both performances out on to the street and use them in contexts which have not been predetermined because they have taken on their own 'lives'. They cannot in fact be used incorrectly. They have an arsenal of possibilities which derive from their respective natures and from which they can choose.

I undervalued this way of working for a long time. It was as if it could never be genuine or serious enough. But perhaps it is something which becomes genuine and serious in spite of oneself and ends up containing more expression than something which starts in the opposite way, from the slow formation of what is inside you and that is important to express.

We went down to Carpignano and after a while began to work on the dance performance. It was something I had no desire to do. I think this was partly because I had not been training for some time. I had very little to offer. I made three small dance fragments and the part that became the final dance, almost as a kind of dictation. I made a mask. It was a clown-like half mask. When I was making the first version of the mask, I made a mistake and the mask pushed against one of my eyes. I couldn't open this eye more than a couple of millimetres. I didn't correct the mistake. The deformation of the eye became a small but very important aspect of the 'clown that could only frighten people'. The mask was made of plaster and paper. I sweated a lot. The mask always softened up while I was working and since there were a lot of acrobatic elements in the performance, the

Figure 24 The Million, 1979 (Torgeir Wethal). The Priest dances the samba. Photo: Jan Rüsz.

mask got ruined. It could be repaired but after a while I had to make a new one.

We were performing in Padua and were staying with Donato Sartori, a sculptor. He offered to make a leather copy of the mask. It turned out to be a fine mask. I couldn't use it. He had made an interpretation of my dance. The mask contained his impression of what he had seen. It was creepy. But one of the reasons for the 'clown's' 'dark' and slightly frightening expression had been the face which tried to be 'soft' and couldn't. The figure was intriguing because it was ambiguous. Donato made a new mask for me which resembled the original mask. I've used it for several years now, I use it in *Anabasis* as well.

While I was making the mask I remembered an image from *The Hunchback of Notre Dame*, the film with Charles Laughton, where Laughton pushes his head through a window, or someone else pushes Laughton's head through a window, and two eyes are drawn on his head, completely grotesque. A short fragment which doesn't actually have anything to do with my mask and yet it was always in my mind while I was making the mask. At the same time, there was the old dream of the clown who could only make people cry, who elicits only disgust or scorn: the black clown. This is something that appeared slowly, after the mask had been made. The Dwarf didn't exist in the first version. I don't remember when he appeared, whether it was when we first began to work on the street or after we had been doing it for some time. I can't remember who suggested it, whether it was Eugenio or myself or one of the others, or whether it came about because of a character which I had been thinking about for years: Lagerkvist's dwarf, which I think is one of the most incredible characters ever. This character was something I had been thinking about, but not something I had thought of expressing. But, when he appeared as the Dwarf, a great many things from a long period of time melded together, a whole series of needs.

At the beginning, it was a dance which had been put together technically, without any meaning, a combination of forms with various set energy expressions. But the various elements have developed and changed to another quality, with a whole other driving force, and this I am unable to define because it's general – always present. It's almost on a level with rage, but without knowing why one is angry, and it is characteristic of both the Priest and the Dwarf that they are literal and have their own nature, that is, their own inner life. They are not hidden, they do everything the spectator sees, with a great deal of contradiction, contradiction which is both natural and necessary for them.

For me, the Dwarf only exists with the mask. When I put the mask on, it's not me any more, and at that moment I can allow myself to do a lot of things I couldn't otherwise do. It still works the same way, when, every once in a while, I take it out of the closet.

What is your inner motivation for the transition from dwarf to standing?

Strangely enough, he existed without that transition being a problem. In the dance performance, he was first the Dwarf, and then stood up and remained standing. And of course it was a very precise transition with a very precise motivation, but only as in any performance, where you have a reason for doing any action you do. The movement of standing up was a big triumph for him.

In *Anabasis*, he changed all the time, in response to his rather itchy, tickling, teasing inner world. It nearly always happened on cue: you saw something and you reacted. He was a bit different as a Dwarf from when standing, but not so very different.

In good performances, it's improvised, but as time goes by, there's nothing you haven't done before in one combination or another. You have so many movement principles built in that you improvise and react, but using a set form which you choose with lightning speed.

How do you avoid having elements from one character infect another, or how do you avoid creating the same reaction forms in different characters?

There was one period when I made three different characters at the same time: the Priest, the Dwarf and 'Brecht'. But each one of them was made on the basis of a very specific background. If I took the Priest out of the context and the performance he had been made in, and let him take part in a parade or a street performance – his actions would be done as he wanted. That's how headstrong he had become.

And if I were to participate in the same situation with the Dwarf, then completely different movements would emerge. The two characters would never be able to take a step or jump in the same way or with the same energy, quality, or form.

This is because they are based on different, elaborated movement patterns and because the theatrical exploitation of the very different costumes becomes a part of the characters.

After a break of nearly two years, we had to redo parts of *The Book of Dances*. It still 'sat' in the body. I had to do my final dance. The actions came, one after the other, without my even having to think about them. But halfway through, I got stuck. I couldn't remember what I was supposed to do. My colleagues showed me one strange jump after another but I couldn't figure out what they were trying to tell me. I started over again. When I came to the difficult part, I remembered. It came back 'by itself' because now the point of departure was correct.

I used a cane in the dance. And I had been holding it incorrectly and the actions became impossible. What the others had shown me as a jump was in fact something I had done by concentrating on the outer side of my right hand, at the end of the little finger. All the power of the sats was

Figure 25 The Book of Dances, 1978 (Torgeir Wethal). Photo: Tony D'Urso.

concentrated at this point. It was this point which pulled me up in the air and directed me. I didn't know how the jump actually looked but it was surely almost exactly the same every time I did it. The first time I tried to repeat the dance, I was holding the stick incorrectly: my hand was turned inwards, the joint was held stiffly.

But when you start on a new performance, the problem you run into is that you can easily carry along parts of what you have done in previous performances. It's safe territory. Things that you know work after having used them for four or five years. You are first ready for something new when you've got the previous performance out of your body.

We all have habits and clichés which shine through in spite of our experience and the new things we try to do. Even though we are almost completely masked in *Oxyrhincus Evangeliet*, some people would nevertheless be able to recognize each of us after a few seconds. There's something in your movement pattern which – no matter how hard you try to break it – is repeated. And yet you must work away from a remembered technique. You keep on until you find a new track, which you then follow. Not because it absolutely must be different, but because you want to go further. But if you want to go further, you have to find new points of incidence to give you enough resistance so that the way towards a new performance leads to new experiences.

7

DRAMATURGY

PERFORMANCE TEXT

A theatre performance is a flow of energy between the actors and the
spectators given form in a particular way in accordance with a particular
goal.

The performance text is the wave of meaning elements which make up
the theatre performance. What is particular about this 'text' is that it exists
only when it is seen by the spectators. Unlike a book, a film, or a painting,
it cannot be separated from its own production. The 'performance text' is a
series of expressive elements, which are present at the same time, just as all
the expressive elements of a painting are present at the same time – in
contrast to written drama, which can only be acquired by being gone
through from beginning to end. The spectators can see and experience
many elements at the same time and are free to choose where to direct
their attention. The performance is a polyphony of the actors' actions, use
of text, changes in the lights, changes in the space, which are not necessarily subject to a common point of view.

The spectators are 'led' through the performance's inner life or logic.
This occurs not only with respect to the performance's action (the plot, the
story), which could be called the performance's linear dimension (horizontal progression), but also with respect to the performance's simultaneous
or spatial dimension (vertical progression). The performance's dynamic is
a balance between these poles and the spectator's attention is stretched
between a time dimension and a space dimension.

One could say that on one level the actor performs 'acting people' and
this is perhaps what the spectator 'sees', but on another level the actor does
something which has nothing to do with either drama itself or its characters: the actor creates a network of tensions between himself or herself and
the space and in relationship to the spectators.

Let us take as an example a scene with five actors. The focus shifts
between them. The technique which one actor uses to bring himself or
herself in or out of focus or to create focus for another actor may perhaps
be a distortion of balance or a kind of movement which attracts or deflects

124

attention. The actor plays 'the role' but creates also something which is part of the theatre situation itself: movement-forms in space which create the context for what the spectator experiences as the 'performance text'.

The term 'dramaturgy' derives from the Greek, *drama-ergon*, and refers to the inner or invisible energy of an action. An action is a work, an activity. The dramaturgy of a performance is the way an action is told or shown and becomes functional as dramatic energy.

The actor's dramaturgy is that particular and individual way in which the action, the 'character', the prop is brought alive. It is the way the actor uses the text and the subtext, the tone colours of the words, the way sounds and movements are created, the space filled with presence, directions, and different kinds of energy. And it is the way in which the spectator's attention is caught and held as the actor enters into a dialogue relationship with the spectator's daily logic.

The spectator's presence is worked into the performance structure by following one of two different principles. According to one of these principles, the performance is defined by a particular ideological or political point of view or a definite, well-known story. The spectator's fascination is based on recognition of the accepted and in such a case there is a high degree of traditional or ideological coding.

Another type of performance is based on the concept that meaning is not particularly set. The performance can have a built-in ambiguity and the spectator must actively create his or her own meaning and find and choose between many different possibilities. This performance type is not unequivocal in its language and coding and contains several different points of view and experience possibilities. At the same time, it is more the nature of this experience which is important (the degree of intensity, the 'otherness' of the experience as compared to daily life) rather than one particular content or meaning.

In this kind of theatre, the spectator is not only worked into the tension structure of the text. The dramaturgical role of the spectator is physically expressed through the way he or she is placed in the performance space.

In *Oxyrhincus Evangeliet*, such a placement causes the spectators both to be and to feel that they are an active part of the dramaturgy. The spectators become a part of the performance text (the way the story is told and brought alive in the space).

The space is a defined whole. A red room: the walls, ceiling and benches are covered with red fabric. The spectators are brought into the space a few at a time and led up to a curtain, which is then pulled to one side. One feels as if one is entering a secret space, reserved for the initiated. People whisper to each other and find a place to sit on the benches. It's almost like being in church where one is not entirely sure how one should behave. Should one take one's shoes off? Is talking permitted? In front of the benches, a red curtain is hanging, just like the curtain in a traditional theatre space. So far the space is classically divided, with a stage in front of the public. Candles are hanging from the ceiling and are lit: the feeling of being in church is strengthened. One can hear voices whispering behind the curtain. Are the actors walking around back there? One is in any case aware that there are certain figures on the other side of the curtain. The lights go out, so that the space is lit only by the candles. One hears footsteps and understands that the performance has begun. Suddenly, the red curtain falls. Behind it is a large dark space. One sees a group of people. Is it the actors? They are sitting in rows, just like oneself. Slowly one realizes that one is looking at the other half of the audience, sitting across from one like a mirror-image. The effect is comical (Figure 13, p. 69).

The space suddenly changes from a traditional theatre space to a space where the spectators are sitting across from each other. The curtain is lying in a gangway between the two sides where the spectators sit and it is slowly pulled out, making a sound like water running.

A clock strikes and afterwards one hears it ticking. Someone appears in the gangway. Later in the performance, lights come on behind where one is sitting and the actors can be seen moving behind the other spectators. At no point in the performance is it possible to see what is happening outside the space. But many sounds come from outside the space: songs, breathing, the sound of knives being sharpened, the sound of people running.

The space becomes a part of the story. Or better: the space has an independent dramatic quality, on a par with other dramatic elements, but this dramatic quality exists only because of the spectators' presence. The spectators may feel as if they are surrounded, and this can lead to claustrophobia: what would happen if one didn't want to see any more of the performance, what if one needed to go to the lavatory? How does one get out? One can feel frightened, confused, uncertain. One can feel as if one is a part of the space, as if one has been made a part of the space's secrets, as if one is in on the secrets or excluded from them.

The space has become independent. And the spectator is also in another situation, outside of usual or daily space.

As the performance begins, the clock strikes twelve. And when the performance ends, the clock strikes eleven. Time is obviously going backwards.

The space is not a specific space, not a specific place. It's almost a kind of 'journey' outside time and space. Maybe one is inside a heart, or inside the soul.

The type of theatre represented by *Oxyrhincus Evangeliet* is a complex theatre where the relationship between the tellers and the spectators is not unequivocal. There is no definite conclusion or end to the story. It is a kind of dramaturgy which reminds one of a musical composition. There is no one main character, but several equal characters. Actions are neither psychologically nor causally motivated. There is a musical polyphony: the various voices both have their own value and are part of a greater whole. The composition is not based on linearity but on reflections, counterpoints, repetitions, the ambiguous and paradoxical nature of the actions in relationship to the performance's theme: the relationship between revolt and treason, independence and subjugation, as expressed in the relationship between the Father and the Prodigal Son.

At the same time, the performance has to do with rejection of power and social law. It is up to the spectator whether or not this occurrence has a changing meaning in relationship to the world outside. The experience of simultaneity results in a new way of perceiving daily life which is never exactly the same. The experience of a particular speed means that time (one's own time) can be perceived from a new and other dimension.

8

THE DANCING TIME-SPACE 1983–8

Oxyrhincus Evangeliet and *Judith*

In 1984, twenty years after the theatre was founded, Odin Teatret changed its structure. The institution became Nordisk Teaterlaboratorium, made up of a number of smaller groups, of which Odin Teatret was the oldest.

One of the other parts of Nordisk Teaterlaboratorium is Farfa, started by Iben Nagel Rasmussen. Farfa has made *Wounded by the Wind*, *Marriage with God*, *The Land of Nod* and the training demonstration/performance *Moon and Darkness*. The Canada Project, led by Richard Fowler, has produced *Wait for the Dawn*, based on Camus' *The Stranger*, and also conducts theatre projects with minority groups, among them the mentally handicapped. And finally there is ISTA, which has to date held six congresses and seminars with such themes as the actor's expressivity, the female role, and the relationship between the actor's and the spectator's identities.

The transition to this new organizational structure is emphasized by the theatre's new logo, based on Niels Bohr's coat of arms. It consists of the yin-yang symbol combined with the motto *Contraria sunt complementa* ['Opposites are complementary'].

The design is the Chinese symbol for Tao and expresses the balance between accumulating energy and direction-orientated energy. The design re-creates graphically the same S-shape found in the bodies of various Asian dancers (in Indian terminology called *tribhangi*, tree arches, because of the S-shape in the whole body), as well as in the movement of a wave.

This is a short introduction to a discussion of the two central Odin Teatret performances in this phase of the group's history, *Oxyrhincus Evangeliet* and *Judith*. Both can be characterized as performances which turn inwards, towards the landscape of dreams. The outer movements are stationary but open up a larger landscape of longing and suffering in the world of dreams and shadows.

THE ACTOR IN THE PERFORMANCE

Oxyrhincus Evangeliet was performed 214 times in 1985-7, and was filmed by Torgeir Wethal. The performance has to do with a 'gospel' and its composition is based on the Catholic mass, just as the space reminds one of a church, with a gangway dividing the audience and an altar at each end (Figure 13).

The framework for this performance derives to a certain extent from Mario Vargas Llosa's book, *The War at the End of the World*. Llosa's story takes place in Bahia, the north-eastern corner of Brazil, in the 1890s. Under the leadership of the 'great adviser', the 'returned Messiah', a motley group of people occupy the town of Canudos. There are poor peasants, escaped slaves and lawless *cangaceiros*. The revolutionaries build a 'holy city' in accordance with 'God's' true laws. The city grows steadily and calmly and attracts more and more people, inspired by the fervour and meaning which the 'great adviser' radiates. Is it a social revolt or is it religious fanaticism? The book deals with the rise and fall of the town. The military sends several armies against the town but they are rebuffed with cruel zeal, with all the men, women and children fighting for the town and the 'holiness' it represents. The story ends with the town's total destruction.

In *Oxyrhincus Evangeliet*, we are in a holy town peopled by *cangaceiros* with various names: Joan of Arc, the Grand Inquisitor, Antigone, the Prodigal Son and Sabbatai Zevi, the returned Messiah. Golem is also a character in this society, an artificial being, a being without a soul which disobeys every dictate. In the performance, the Golem is at one and the same time an immobile mask or puppet and a breath, a swaying mobility: the one who passes the sword.

Each and every one of these characters has found the 'truth', that principle which they believe in and will defend. And each and every one of them has enclosed this principle in a series of rituals, witness to the presence of the 'holy' and the magical. Sabbatai Zevi performs a series of tricks: he plunges a sword into a large and heavy stone, he sucks water out of the stone, he performs a disappearing act by exiting at one end of the room and popping up at the other end seconds later. Joan of Arc sets fire to herself as a form of theatrical ritual while her red heart flashes sentimentally in the dark and she follows the swaying Holy Grail. The performance is filled with 'cheap', theatrical mysticism and tricks, emphasized by a strange disorientation experienced by the spectators in the space because all levels of the room are used for performing: behind one's back, in front of one on the gangway, behind the curtains. Out from behind the curtains, for example, comes the mystical Golem, the swaying body without a soul.

A singing, dancing, Hassidic Jewish tailor arrives in this society of holy 'confidence men'. The wanderer, looking for the Messiah and believing

129

that he finds Him everywhere. One could also say that the holy town is a figment of the tailor's imagination, evoked as a kind of nightmare.

In any case, Zusha Mal'ak (the wanderer or angel) stays in the town and witnesses the actions and rituals while he sees to his daily sewing.

He sees how the new Messiah is heralded as a sovereign by his 'soldiers'. He sees a child born and sacrificed to this sovereign, killed and devoured as the Eucharist.

The 'Prodigal Son' called Polynices also returns to this town and subjects himself to the new sovereign. He is received and forced to deny his sister Antigone and, as a form of penance, lets himself be crucified. At the same time, the new Messiah and sovereign does a 'resurrection number' as a black angel. The Prodigal Son is united with his sister, but they are separated once more and he is guillotined, with the Grand Inquisitor as executioner.

Antigone grieves for her dead brother and wraps his body in a cloth, but she is threatened by the Grand Inquisitor who stabs her shadow, and her brother's corpse is taken away from her. Nevertheless, she attacks the law, represented by the altar-piece. She draws her own sword and attacks, but is knocked to the ground by other swords which fall from the altar-piece, directly in front of her. She is dragged away and buried alive. Only her head is visible while she sings and expresses her continuing revolt against the immobile, blood-dripping power which considers her from the balcony as if her revolt was a theatre training. Meanwhile, the observers, in a kind of inversion of the Eucharist, drool and spit blood into the Holy Grail.

During the course of the performance, the tailor has cut and made a little human figure out of paper. Seated across from this figure, the tailor now celebrates the Sabbath and asks, 'Now tell me, Rabbi, when is the Messiah going to come?' But of course the rabbi doesn't answer and Zusha Mal'ak becomes more and more confused because the rabbi neither sees nor understands what is happening around them.

This is a kind of sketch of the 'action' or the dramatic logic, which also contains several other stories: Antigone, who in the Greek drama defies King Creon and buries her brother Polynices and is therefore buried alive as punishment; Oedipus, who unknowingly murdered his father and returned to his home-town and became its new sovereign; Borges' novel, *The Dead Man*, where a young bandit takes the old leader's power and his mistress, only to be killed himself; or the biblical story of the father who sacrifices his son for the sake of mankind.

There are stories from medieval chronicles. The Holy Grail appears, and the magic sword Excalibur, which King Arthur alone could draw from the stone and thereby demonstrate that he was the rightful king. From medieval mysticism comes the 'alchemical spirit' or the 'holy voice' in the talking stone. There are Gnostic and cabbalist texts and liturgical songs. The languages used in the performance, spoken and sung by the actors, are the dead languages of Coptic and Koine (found in apocryphal texts).

The performance is full of rituals which represent 'God' or the 'truth' but these holy 'rituals' are obviously empty and counterfeit. It's about magic which has already been reduced to simple tricks. Zusha Mal'ak, believing that these tricks represent 'sparks' and the return of the Messiah, is disappointed over and over again. But he continues to hope, continues to believe in the value of what he is searching for, and, in a certain way, finds himself in this land of appearances and false roles.

ELSE MARIE LAUKVIK

How do you perceive the beginning of Oxyrhincus Evangeliet? *What is your perception of your character, Zusha Mal'ak?*

Zusha enters the space. For me, it is night-time in his tailor's shop. He is somewhere in that borderland between waking and dreaming. He has worked all day and he's tired. Things slowly come alive for him and he is wandering, searching for a new state and a new space. He calls upon God and applauds, and new spirits appear. For him, the world is full of miracles because he is a believer. It's like he hears birds singing. He applauds them. He hears breathing and suddenly the clock strikes. His prayers have been heard. There is an answer. He explains that he is Zusha and goes over to the wall and kneels in front of the altar, to which swords are attached, but he doesn't see the swords. He realizes that something is happening. There is a sound, murmuring. His eyes fill with tears, his knees begin to shake. He turns around because he can hear a child crying. He is suddenly out on a long wandering. He's in a wood, where he is chopping firewood. Work is also a ritual. He hears sounds. Someone is with him. The white figures appear. He plays with them.

In the improvisation I did, he was the grandson of a tailor. One day he revolted. He tied a thread to the door and ran out of the house. He wrapped the thread around a tree, then around another tree, and yet another. He laughed the whole time. He danced between the trees. That was my first improvisation.

The other characters appear and he is astonished. He sees the Grand Inquisitor crawl along the bridge, dragging a heavy stone behind him. He thinks it's the Messiah. He thinks it's a kind of pilgrim carrying a heavy burden (as Jesus carried the cross), with a whip wrapped around his head as a glory. It's the high priest who condemned Jesus to death.

They hear a shout, 'The Lord is coming', and he understands that he has made a mistake. Another Messiah is coming. He is almost in ecstasy and is certain that now the Messiah is really coming.

When we started to work, Eugenio gave me the costumes, the hat and the prayer shawl, which had been bought in Israel. At first I thought that Torgeir was to play the Jew. But Eugenio asked me to put on the costume. I was to find a jacket and I was to play a Hassidic Jew.

I had actually wanted to be a 'wood nymph' and had bought a long blonde wig. So I took the wig and made it into prayer curls. The next day I was to show Eugenio the character, show him how it moved. I began to improvise and what I did actually became the first scene. I tried something I had never done before. I spoke at the same time as I acted. It was like reawakening a character. I told Eugenio who the character was, what he did and experienced. We recorded this on a tape and so it was easy to reconstruct afterwards. It is often difficult to remember the sequence of the actions in an improvisation, but I was able to learn this one very quickly. We did three improvisations with the character, in various situations. They were used and later put into context with the others' improvisations.

Zusha Mal'ak is a Hassidic Jew with a cabbalist background. In my interpretation of the character, it is he who conjures up the universe the spectators see. It is both happening and not happening. It is his 'vision', something he experiences when the clock strikes at the beginning and end of the performance. He has very little contact with the other characters because they are not real but rather born out of his cabbalist vision. It's like a religious ecstasy experienced by someone who has sung, prayed and danced for hours. While he is waiting for the Messiah, he has a vision, a frightful vision. The important thing for me is that he accepts that people are also evil.

Zusha Mal'ak came to me when I began to improvise. I had a certain historical point of departure because we had been talking about the 1600s, when a certain Rabbi Susha lived. He was very poor, innocent, and a little child-like. He had the innocence, insight and experience of a child, not that of a wise man. A kind of purity, humility. A number of stories have been written about him, although I hadn't read them when we began to work.

I improvised and he became visible: he was felling trees. Suddenly a whole series of images began to flow from my subconscious. It was almost like experiencing a miracle. The character was out in the woods and was cutting timber. At a certain moment, he smelled coffee. Something he had never smelled before. It was very clear to me that he was from the Ukraine. I don't know whether they had coffee in the Ukraine in the 1600s but, in any case, I later read that there were many Jewish settlers there.

A few days later, we did an improvisation which led to sequences of action where a child is sacrificed, murdered. We had been told that each of us was to prepare a sequence. We were to show different ways of killing a child. I had forgotten all about this assignment. I came down to the rehearsal room and realized that now we were supposed to show the sequence we had prepared. So I went to the closet in my dressing-room and grabbed some cloth, some fabric remnants, and some spools of thread.

132

Figure 26 'I am Zusha Mal'ak, the tailor.' Mal'ak means 'angel' but it may also refer to Mehallek, 'the wanderer'. It seems as though the rabbi doesn't want to listen. Zusha insists: 'Don't you see that everything's going wrong? Now tell me, Rabbi, when is the Messiah going to come? What will happen when he comes?'

Hassidism is a mystic movement which began in the Ukraine and spread from there between 1760 and 1810. It still exists today in the form of Hassidic communities. It is a kind of popularization of the cabbala, with emphasis placed on brotherhood, song, dance, ecstacy and joyous exclamation.

According to Hassidic belief, it is each person's responsibility to fulfil himself or herself by treating everything as holy and thereby releasing the 'holy sparks' found in everyone. Each individual's unique character is manifest through his or her ability to fulfil a particular destiny, by being oneself, as one is, what one alone can be, and executing one's actions fully in the here and now.

Oxyrhincus Evangeliet, 1985 (Else Marie Laukvik). Photo: Jan Rüsz.

I didn't have much time, so I rolled all these things in some more fabric remnants, and tied a rope around it all to make a bundle in which a child could have been wrapped.

I also used a pair of scissors in the improvisation. I cut the bundle with the scissors to kill the child, and suddenly all the spools of thread fell out. My colleagues burst out laughing because it was so unexpected. What was supposed to represent a child turned out to be a bunch of sewing articles. And all this became the prelude to the scene in the performance, which doesn't have anything to do with a child, where I cut a packet of brown paper and pull a prayer shawl out of it.

133

At the end of *Oxyrhincus Evangeliet*, Zusha Mal'ak is about to dance and says a line of text directly to the audience. The way this text is said is determined by the fact that Zusha is happy, but as we began to perform the piece, I started to feel that this was a mistake. Many of the characters in the performance changed and certain things ended up being out of proportion. Some of the characters became more dynamic, more extreme. So this text needed to be said in a completely different way. It became almost an accusation directed to the audience: 'You are witnesses. You let this happen. You don't do anything.' After this, I turn to the rabbi, who is sitting across from me (the paper figure), and dance the last dance. A kind of protest wells up in me and, in a way, I express my own opinion.

TORGEIR WETHAL

How did the work with Oxyrhincus Evangeliet *and* Sabbatai Zevi *develop?*

All of the work with *Oxyrhincus Evangeliet* was relatively atypical. My situation was that it had been a long time since I had done anything new. I didn't want to be a counterpoint – a kind of dramaturgical nucleus. I wanted to be a part of the whole, someone who had the freedom to go in all directions. I was very interested to see what would happen. What Eugenio would come up with. I was waiting for something, I wanted something. But Eugenio said, 'I'll use what I get.'

Earlier, we had done an internal project, working on Borges' novel *The Dead Man*. We used images and fragments from this work when we began on *Oxyrhincus Evangeliet*, as well as a character, a kind of non-god, which had been started by an actor who was no longer in the group. This character had several relatively inhuman traits and was very central to Eugenio's ideas about the performance. I was to take over this character and almost by accident, once again, I became a dramaturgical nucleus. It was hard. We began with many different points of departure, without a main, connecting theme. What Eugenio had suggested didn't work at all for me. It was difficult for me. I had no desire whatsoever to create material here and there all over the place, in a disconnected way. I needed the opposite.

It's always irritating for the actor, all the hindrances put in his way, or put right on to him in the form of unwieldy costumes, in an impractical performing space. And yet it's necessary. If the director doesn't do it, you have to do it yourself. They are difficulties you have to fight with and break down. It's always what you are able to do in spite of these concrete hindrances that takes you further. In this context, Eugenio had an idea about the god which no longer had any human characteristics. A completely stilted and constricted character which was to be given form with the help of costumes and props. But none of these things lit any fires for me. I had trouble accepting the artificial hands but only really protested when a voice machine turned up. The kind of instrument one uses when one's larynx has been destroyed. That really was too much.

So I began to work with a voice which was similar to the mechanical voice, and with an elementary movement structure in space, in relationship to the emerging dramaturgical necessity. Small details slowly began to emerge by means of various kinds of improvisations. I used a kind of improvisation which was spread over three or four days: one step at a time or one little action at a time. And then I stopped my inner movie and set what I had found, gave a form to what I had found or changed it a bit, and then made another step. After some hours' work I had a whole set improvisation which I could repeat to the smallest detail and which had a connected inner life. At the same time, the performance began to take on its own life. And from then on I began to construct my relationship to the performance and began to understand my own character's function, began to understand what the others were doing.

The things that happen during a rehearsal period may seem to be accidental, but in fact are not. I use sun-glasses in the performance. This came about because the lights in the rehearsal room began to bother me, and to protect my eyes I put on sun-glasses when I wasn't actually in a scene. They became part of the character. But only because the *cangaceiro* Eugenio was thinking about did in fact wear sun-glasses. I had never seen a picture of him, had never thought that he might have worn sun-glasses.

So once the performance was finished, you could say, as Eugenio said at some conference, that this was a performance born out of hatred for the generals with black glasses.

Slowly but surely, on the basis of these small details, a character emerged. A character which, for me, lies somewhere between the Priest and the Dwarf, on the one hand, and my other characters in the other performances, on the other hand. A character with its own life, its own personality, its own basis in itself. Sabbatai Zevi as a point of departure or a source of material led me nowhere.

I think that the performance first became 'mine' when I began to become engaged in everything that was happening in it by becoming attentive, at least as much as in *Brecht's Ashes*, by having an attitude towards each scene and by intervening and saying what I thought. It slowly became something I needed to be in. My participation in the performance was built up on the basis of very few things. That was the hardest thing to accept. That part of the character which approaches an independent life has, once in a while, a desire to do something more, to express itself in other ways. I think this character (as well as 'Brecht') is one of the coldest, most matter-of-fact things I have ever done.

There are two or three small fragments in the performance where the action can be changed minimally without its influencing anything in

Figure 27 Sabbatai Zevi (1626–76) was influenced by the cabbala and, by means of exercises and meditation, gained a false impression of his own power. During the Cossack massacre of the Jews in the Ukraine and Poland in 1648, he proclaimed that he had been chosen to free the Jewish people. In 1665, he declared himself the returned Messiah and gathered followers all over Europe and the Middle East. In 1666, he was imprisoned in Istanbul and was given a choice between conversion to Islam and execution. He renounced Judaism but many of his followers continued to worship him as the Messiah. This worship led to the violation of Jewish norms and sexual laws, the ritual of eating of forbidden foods, ritual adultery and scorn for the Torah.
    Oxyrhincus Evangeliet, 1985 (Torgeir Wethal and Tage Larsen). Sabbatai Zevi and the Grand Inquisitor. Photo: Jan Rüsz.

particular, without its disturbing or bothering the others, and where I manage to get out of my cage for a moment. That was the hardest thing, to keep on creating his limits, his resistance, he couldn't do this or that because it was – seen from the outside, the way I perceived him – physically impossible. He can't stretch his arms out quickly, he can't move quickly at all. His speed and movement were limited, almost stunted.

I think one of the reasons why it has continued to be a relatively cold performance for me is the concentration required. It's necessary to be very exact in order to hold the performance. We have made 'mistakes' when performing all our performances, 'mistakes' seldom noticed by the spectators, because as a performer, you can move in and correct the mistake, make the whole thing look as if it was supposed to happen that way. In *Oxyrhincus Evangeliet* this is impossible, because the actors are unable to communicate with each other. We can't see each other, we can't hear each other, you hardly know where the other actors are. It has gradually become almost a reflex, but you nevertheless have to focus all your concentration on it. And this has actually helped me. You could say that everything in this performance is artificial, but it is an artificiality which has changed its nature and become one of the richest parts of the performance.

In Japanese theatre, it is said that there are actors who create absence through their presence. Is this not in fact what you are talking about here?

I don't think so. But such a statement can be interpreted in many ways. Absence can also mean living in a situation which is completely different from what the spectator sees at the very moment the performance is taking place. It can also mean, and this perhaps fascinates me even more, that the actor can act and work in spite of himself, through the context he is placed in. There is a moment when you reach a kind of security and inner stillness which you can take into the work with you. When this happens, it is no longer necessary to show that you can but that you are. But then we are

137

actually talking about the opposite, about presence as energy and quality of tension in oneself.

How was it possible for Eduardo de Filippo, an Italian actor and author, to stand off to the left, almost offstage, for half an hour, with his back to the audience, without doing anything, and yet the audience looked only at him and forgot about the action that was happening on the rest of the stage at the same time? This is a secret no one can tell you and you can't try to learn it either. I don't know if this is something I'll ever be able to do as an actor but I am more and more interested in finding out how one reaches the greatest action without doing anything.

I can create material with minimal variations, as happens in *Oxyrhincus Evangeliet*, but actually only because I try to find out how it works.

There's a moment in the performance, after the scene in which Antigone and Polynices are covered with a sheet on the floor and I am hanging as if crucified. This scene is interrupted and everything changes in the darkness. It's something you hardly see and it's one of the few places in the performance where there is a kind of power discharge.

I look up, put my hands together, lower them, turn my head to the right, lower it. Small actions with no independent meaning that I can play with. If you saw them in a close-up, they could have four different meanings, depending on what order I did them in, whether I move my eyes, lift the head and look at the action down on the floor, or whether I tilt my head in order to see, whether I focus with my eyes from the beginning, also physically, or not. Different choices give completely different results. There are also fragments which are choreography or outer form without any direct meaning for me. This never happened in previous performances. But in these fragments, I allow myself to be fascinated by the movement itself, the order and the pattern. This would have been impossible some years ago and at variance with my perception of my profession. This is certainly another form of 'absence', where your actions work in spite of you.

There is a sequence in Oxyrhincus Evangeliet *which we could call 'the sacrifice of the child'. I would like you, Torgeir and Else Marie, to describe this sequence as you experience it, the basis and motivation for your actions, in order to illustrate your different techniques in the performance situation.*

Seen 'from the outside' by the spectator, this scene can be briefly described as follows.

Zusha Mal'ak has lost his prayer shawl. Confused, he bangs with his fists on the curtain through which Sabbatai Zevi has just disappeared. The clock strikes at the same moment as Sabbatai Zevi reappears, at the end of the gangway, by the stone. His face is still veiled. Zusha goes towards him and lays his head on the stone. Zevi kneels and caresses Zusha with the puppet hands.

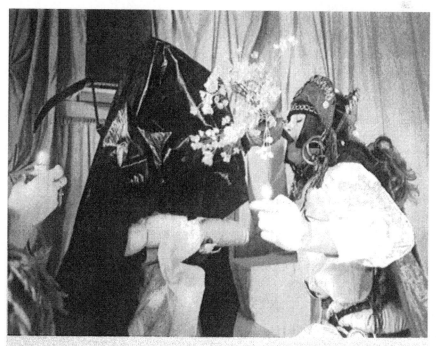

Figures 28 and 29 Antigone sacrifices the child, which is killed by Sabbatai Zevi to Zusha Mal'ak's horror. The Grand Inquisitor and Joan of Arc take part in the sacrifice and eat the child's eyes. *Oxyrhincus Evangeliet*, 1985 (Torgeir Wethal, Else Marie Laukvik, Julia Varley, Roberta Carreri, Tage Larsen). Photos: Jan Rüsz.

Antigone's song is heard at the other end of the gangway. She is sitting on the floor and pushes a child wrapped in white cloth out from under her skirts. Beside her, below the gangway, the Grand Inquisitor and Joan of Arc, holding candles in their hands, attentively observe the birth of the child.

Antigone stands and walks, singing, down towards Sabbatai Zevi. She presents the child, lifts it up over her head, almost in ecstasy, holds the child over Zusha's head and places it in Zevi's outstretched arms. Zusha becomes afraid as Zevi takes the child with a rapid movement. Antigone dances backwards, turns and falls to the floor.

The Grand Inquisitor and Joan of Arc take up positions beside Sabbatai Zevi. All sing. Sabbatai Zevi takes the knife with the flower that the Grand Inquisitor has laid on the child. He slowly lifts it over his head, then suddenly plunges it into the child's face. At the same time, the song increases in volume and intensity. Zusha, crying, runs to Antigone, kneels by her side, takes hold of her and shakes her to bring her out of her ecstasy. Zevi cuts the child in the eyes with the knife and passes the 'bread', stuck on the knife point, to the Grand Inquisitor and Joan of Arc.

Zusha's crying and singing suddenly stop, he looks around, stunned, as if it had all been a nightmare, stands and speaks out into the space. And he lifts up his coat-tails and dances like a winged black angel. Who was it? Whom did he meet? Finally, he understands: 'Sabbatai Zevi'. Zevi reacts with a jerky movement. Zusha runs towards him, kneels in front of him once again and collapses as though he has been struck.

Torgeir, will you describe the sequence?

I exit at one end of the gangway after the sequence where Zusha Mal'ak cuts the paper. I run around the back in order to enter on time at the other end. Along the way, I have to put on my sun-glasses and when I'm wearing them I can see even less than before. I enter with my back first, stop, and distort my balance to the left. At the same time, I point with one hand and 'freeze' the position. I try to point with my hand at the same time as the clock strikes. The position has a 'tension-filled life'. My face is turned towards the Torah. At a certain moment I realized that that little pointing movement was understood by the spectators as a kind of pointing-out of the Torah, a kind of signal to the Torah: 'Go away'. This became his 'attitude', which can mean that Sabbatai Zevi is the false Messiah.

If I manage to reach this position as the clock strikes, most of the spectators do not see me because they are watching Zusha's action at the other end (his confusion at the disappearance of the prayer shawl), so the 'trick' in the scene works, the moment of surprise. Sabbatai Zevi has exited at one end and is suddenly standing at the other end.

The next sequence is based on a kind of improvisation, where you improvise a step at a time, a mini-action at a time, all of which is then set and repeated before you go further.

I turn around to face Zusha Mal'ak, to make a movement with my hand: 'Come here'. In the improvisation, I was planting something and it began to rain. I show the rain with my hand.

The movement also comes from a 'transcription'. The hand movement is 'the rain'. Rain is coming out of my fingers. The hand movement gradually changes character, influenced by the dramaturgical context. I wave with my fingers and then stop the movement, turn my hand and make some pinching movements. Even though Zusha is 5 metres away, it is as though Zevi is pinching Zusha as he approaches. It's a little crude, a little vulgar, a little slobbery, as if to see – feel – what kind of person is coming. Then I go back to the original rain movement, but at a slightly different angle. It looks as if Zevi is showing his ring. It's a twisted version of a 'Come and kiss the ring' movement. It's a kind of *double-entendre* action, expressing my perception of the character at that moment. Then I draw my other hand from left to right, across my lap. This was originally a 'sow the grain' movement.

Then comes another movement from the same improvisation. It's a final image, a position, like a painting. It is the large, coming danger: an 'eagle' position.

Then Antigone's song begins and two small things happen. They are details left over from an improvisation without having gone through a dramaturgical filter because from the very beginning I felt that they were right even though they are absolutely inexplicable. I lift one arm and pluck a fruit and hold it. With the other hand, I pluck a flower. I felt that these two small arm movements went well with the song at that moment, so they've been kept just as they originally were. There is no actual logic that connects Antigone's song and these actions, but they fit together.

The spectators hardly see it because their attention is most likely directed towards Antigone at the moment she begins to sing. This is how it is with many things in this performance. We perform as if we are seen the whole time but many of our actions are not seen.

From this outer point, where I am holding my hands up and 'hold the fruit and the flower', I then take the small wooden hands out of my belt and lift the arms a little bit, from the elbow. It looks like an impulse that would lead to an attack but it turns into a slow embrace of Zusha Mal'ak.

I stand behind Zusha and protect him, perhaps against the song. But here as well there is a *double entendre* in the action: I am protecting him against something in society, but perhaps only to seduce him further. This is the only direct meeting between the two characters in the whole performance.

From my side, the action contains literal protection. It derives from the composition of an image. Else Marie was lying on the stone, almost like a sacrificial lamb, but in a very difficult position. So my position was adjusted in order to help her, to hold her up. It has since been changed into a position which is easier for me to hold but it has kept some of its meaning. The sacrificial lamb is laid lovingly on the stone.

Antigone then stands, at the other end of the gangway. I can just barely glimpse this through my veil, as a changing light.

Then comes a strange reaction which originally came about because I had to make certain tensions in my wrists in order to be able to stand slowly and silently. I get up from the sitting position with the help of these tensions in my wrists. This became a movement in which I turn the palms of the wooden hands outwards and place my wrists together into a V-shape. This movement became a little push away, a reaction against the child and the woman, and led to what I was to do next, and I already knew what it was. It became a 'get away from me' reaction and I move into the background. So it's a pure break, physically and logically, which can be understood in many ways. This 'Don't come near me – get away from me' reaction was a shadow-play or feint, because in the middle of a turning movement made by Antigone, the tension changes and I stretch my hands out. I open up and simply express 'Will be happy to take the child'. I remain standing with my hands stretched out over Zusha Mal'ak. All of my upper body and my arms are stretched forward and one leg is extended behind me.

So the child is placed in my arms and Antigone withdraws. Then comes an exciting little moment. All I actually have to do is stand and move backwards slightly, holding the child. Which I do. But the moment when I move backwards is crucial. Because of the veil, I see very poorly, and the duration of Antigone's song can vary. The relationship between Antigone's song and my physical score is not always quite exact. At a specific point in the song, she falls. I can feel that moment. It's important that I step backward a quarter of a second before she falls. I step back and she falls, as if she has been hit on the cheek, because I tug on the umbilical cord. I don't know how it happened, but I have to pull before she falls. It's essential. The movement itself may well be a pure construction, but at a certain moment it also became filled with this logic.

So I move backwards, to the wall, with a number of flat, almost sliding steps, which is almost impossible to do in the high-heeled boots I'm wearing. The others have begun to sing. I carry the child to its baptism. Walk to the baptismal font, proud as a father. I present the child and the Grand Inquisitor places his knife, to which a flower is attached, on it. I softly take the knife and lift it, ready to stab the child. It's a very literal action. It's not difficult but I am nevertheless careful as I stab. It is a sacrifice. I take the knife and spear an eye, which I give to the Grand Inquisitor; and spear the other eye, which I give to Joan of Arc. The song increases in volume and intensity. The duration of the sequence varies a little, depending on how long it takes to spear the eyes. I raise the knife again, as if to stab one more time, but instead of stabbing, I stamp hard on the floor, to stop Zusha's crying, to interrupt the sequence. I try to stamp and continue the upwards action with the knife at the same time. Usually, the stamp would make the arm movement stop, but here, the hand's soft movement continues up over my head. Just a little, virtually invisible break with cliché.

Then Zusha Mal'ak says his line, which ends with, 'Who is it? Sabbatai Zevi?' Now comes a reaction, the result of my position, ready to stab. Originally, the hand was raised as a threat: 'If you expose us, I'll stab you', directed towards Zusha Mal'ak. There is a little change in the position of my leg because of the sats, the leg is lifted a little bit. It developed into something which for me became a horse kick, became a horse's hoof kicked against the wall of a stall. It's something that happened by accident and which I then kept. The smell of the word 'horse', of penned-up wildness. But only in the right leg.

This is once again a way of playing with clichés. The stabbing isn't repeated after all. Instead, the knife is laid softly and carefully upon the child. The bone-hard and the soft are an aspect of this character. He has something both 'funny and frightening' about him. I frighten and caress with almost the same movement.

Zusha Mal'ak runs towards me. I blow in his face. It's not evil, almost like when children at play hurt animals. I take the small wooden hands out of the belt and strike them lightly against the black veil. This is actually to make it easier for Julia [Varley] and Tage [Larsen] to get hold of the ends of the veil, but it also means 'Come again'.

As the lights go down, I cough, almost naturalistically. I slowly get up and lean back smoothly and fluidly. Physically this is very difficult to do and I tremble a bit. This is because of the stiffness which is always there, like a ruler in my neck, as if I'm not used to moving, as if the head and the body are badly connected so that the head can't move on its own. Sometimes I move as if my head is frozen to my spine. It's a way of holding on to the movement. It reminds me of my old drawing teacher, who had a stiff neck. He could only move his head if the rest of the body moved as well.

Else Marie, will you also describe the sequence?

Zusha's prayer shawl has been stolen and he turns towards the black-clothed character and says, 'Who are you?' He thinks it's maybe the Messiah. He moves slowly, almost sneakily, over towards the black-clothed character. At the moment he reaches him, the black-clothed character orders him to lie down on the stone. Zusha thinks he's about to be executed. He kneels and puts his head on the stone, ready to be sacrificed on the sacrificial stone. It is a complete subjugation. At the same moment, he hears a voice in the distance, singing a very beautiful song, and he understands that he has not been forgotten. The black-clad character helps him up from the stone and holds him, protects and caresses him while he sits on the stone. It reminded me of Michelangelo's Pietá.

Someone comes to save him. He reacts with joy and has a new revelation: a child is born. The white-clad character carries the child forward and presents it. The child is passed over his head and, frightened, he discovers that the black-clad character is holding the child. He begins to freeze and understands that the black-clad character is dangerous. He crouches like a foetus on the stone. At that moment, he is Isaac, about to be sacrificed to God by Abraham. He feels that he is in danger and is one with the child. He is frightened by the black-clad character's actions because he hasn't yet understood whether this character is real or not. But then he sees the knife and sees it stuck into the child. He experiences this as a brutal child-murder (like when Herod declared that all boys under the age of 2 were to be killed). And he cries, as Rachel cried for her children (the cry at Rama).

He hurries down to the white-clad character, who has fallen on the floor, to bring her back to life: 'Why have you brought these children into the world if you let them be sacrificed, if you commit them to this brutal destiny?'. He experiences it doubly. When the knife is stuck into the child, it's like it's being stuck into Antigone at the same time. Even though he doesn't know the white-clad character, he is crying for all those who have been killed or sacrificed. Then he hears a foot stamp and wakes up. It's a sign or signal that brings him out of the situation.

He has a new revelation and looks up with a happy smile. Like the Jews who didn't let themselves be broken, because they believed they were God's chosen people. He knows that there is meaning in the madness. He realizes that someone is following him. He takes hold of his coat-tails and lifts them up, as the Jews do as a sign to Heaven before they dance. He holds the coat-tails apart, but then gets a new feeling, which makes him let go of first one coat-tail and then the other. He realizes that the black-clad character is the Messiah of evil: Sabbatai Zevi. He runs towards Zevi as if to protest against him. Zevi blows in his face and he falls as if he has been struck.

My inner images in this scene are in fact the same as my interpretation. I react according to the inner pictures and associations or interpretations I get along the way.

TRAINING AND PERFORMANCE IN RELATION TO *JUDITH*

Antigone, in *Oxyrhincus Evangeliet*, is buried alive but the scenic effect makes it seem that her head has been cut off. One sees only her naked face on the floor. Here, in *Judith*, it is a male who loses his head to a woman,

144

Judith. The severed head is on stage from the very beginning of the performance, albeit wrapped in cloth.

The story of Judith comes from the apocryphal *Book of Judith*. The Babylonian army general Holofernes has besieged the city of Bethulia and cut off the city's water supply. Judith reproaches the old leaders for considering surrender and promises to free the city by her own exploits. The young widow (rich and beautiful) prays to God for help. She goes to Holofernes' camp and offers to show him a way into the city. She is received by the general who invites her to a feast. She seduces him, or allows herself to be seduced by him. He drinks until he is confused and drunk and Judith takes his sword and cuts off his head. With the head in a food basket, she slips out of the camp and returns to the city. As the rumour of Holofernes' death spreads, the Assyrian army flees. Judith is cheered for her accomplishment and is led away to a dance in her honour.

The production has a very simple scenic architecture. The audience sits as if in a cinema with straight rows. The only light source is a spotlight on the floor just in front of the first row of seats. The actress herself turns on the spotlight at the start of the performance and its effect is regulated only by her distance from the lamp. When she is very near it, her dress catches the light. And when she is further away from it, shadows are thrown, creating a double of her on the large, white, silk-like backdrop. All the way through the performance there is taped background music which the actress talks to, sings along with, and which sometimes echoes her voice. This is the first time that Odin Teatret makes use of both that kind of 'classical' spatial arrangement and that kind of background music.

The actress is already standing onstage (wearing a deep red housecoat) as the audience enters. Behind her close to the backdrop, there stands a small Japanese dwarf tree: a bonsai.

After a short prologue, she sits down and it is as if she's relaxing after having completed her tasks. She could just as well be in her home, in the hospital or at the beach.

She moves very slowly in the deck chair, as if asleep. One hears very subdued Oriental music. She leans over the side of the chair, almost falling out of it. Now, physically out of balance, she begins to speak. Like a field general, she points out into the space and says, 'Go and occupy.' One hand slides up in front of her face and eyes as if she cannot look at the horror caused by the occupation. Her hand continues up over her eyes. Suddenly she exposes the whites of her eyes, appearing demented. Then she stands and her head jerks down and her long braid dangles like a rope. She loosens her braided hair and with a hairbrush she points into the space, a lightning fast movement that marks a cross as if trying to emphasize what is to follow. The hand with the brush slides slowly past her face. The shadow on the backdrop looks as if a knife is drawn across her throat. She lets the brush glide through her hair and says, 'She took a hold of his hair and

145

because she twice struck with all her might, she cut off his head and removed it from its body.'

Now the tempo shifts drastically from slow, almost soft movements. She grabs a fan from her skirt and it quickly opens as she jumps up from the chair. Her long hair falls down and around the fan which she holds open in front of her face. Stooping she fans harder and faster, as if she were being choked or shocked by what has just happened.

The music has become very violent. The shadow on the backdrop has gained almost too much life: the flailing hair looks like the sea in a storm. Exhausted, she sinks on to the deck chair. The music stops. She leans back in the chair and sings a duet (with her own voice on tape). She stands and starts to loosen the belt on her housecoat and it is as if she is forced forward and on to her knees. She sits on the floor like a child that has been caught doing something wrong, and knocks on an imaginary door. To force herself out of this nightmare, she hits herself on the head and chest, then leans slowly backwards, ending spread-eagled on her back. On the backdrop, it now looks as if the dwarf tree is growing out of her lap and between the shadows of her knees. One sees a landscape: the little bonsai tree, which is traditionally thwarted in its growth by the binding and cutting of its roots, suddenly becomes a huge tree in this mountainous landscape.

Music by Dvořák. She notices the bundle on the floor, pulls it to herself and begins to take off the cloth wrapping, as if the bundle were a gift from God. She hesitates. She puts one end of the cloth into her mouth, sticking a finger down her throat, then allows her hand to glide down between her breasts: it is also an erotic gift.

She walks forwards towards the spotlight darkening the stage. She turns and the light creates a red circle on the housecoat. She jumps over the head removing its cloth covering at the same time. Its face is hidden behind a black veil. It has a long black wig. The music shifts to Bach's 'Passacaglia'. The next sequence is a dance in which a series of different positions are repeated. Frightened, she covers her eyes with her arms and pulls back, holds a baby in her arms, falls and caresses something. While she repeats these images and shifts between them, she comes closer and closer to the exposed head on the floor. Her face is distorted, her mouth open in a silent scream. Her eyes metamorphose. Sometimes they stare and are severely focused, other times they become distant and turn inward. The change in the eyes in this way indicates a jump between two realities.

She removes the wig from the severed head as if scalping it. Singing she lays the wig over her own face. With a sudden movement she throws off the wig and then slowly removes the housecoat. The delicate slip she is wearing underneath the housecoat shines with the same quality as the backdrop.

She seductively whispers and removes two hair-combs from the basket. They first form a fan, then become a veil. She spits into one hand and brings the two combs together to form a glass from which she drinks. The

Figure 30 Judith, 1987 (Roberta Carreri). A sea in revolt. Photo: Torben Huss.

combs become the wings of a butterfly. It flutters and flies about, landing on her slip, sitting on her shoulder. She catches the butterfly and rips off its wings, which she puts under her own arms as if to change herself into a butterfly, a bird, maybe an angel. But she is a warped angel who cannot fly and hobbles forward instead.

The combs become claws which she cautiously licks. The music stops. She makes a crown out of the finger-sized hair-combs and places it on the severed head. She turns to the shadow as if to a mirror and fixes her hair – like a princess. The combs become the claws of a bird of prey which she lifts up, ready to attack the head on the floor. But she doesn't attack, she changes the claws into a kind of peep-hole. She looks through the peep-hole and we focus on her eye. Once again she licks the claws. She rubs her hands together in expectation, rests her head on them, and with increasing tension she places the claws on her hips where they become crab-like animals. These animals slowly crawl down over her breasts and stomach, continuing downwards until they abruptly attack and bite into her crotch.

She approaches the severed head and with great expectation removes the veil and ties it around her own face. The head rests exposed on the floor in front of her – its eyes are closed and it has a suffering expression on its face. A white wooden sculpture with red hair and beard, it resembles a portrait of Christ, but it also reminds one of the condemned man in *My Father's House* when she rolls up the veil and ties it around the eyes. She takes out two long hat-pins, places them in her hair and lies down to sing a love-song to the severed head.

Church bells. She stands, holding the head, which is still blindfolded: a bride and groom. The atmosphere changes abruptly because of the music: threatening, brutal bells and war drums. She walks forward with glistening eyes, exhibits the head, holding it up. She falls, turns the head towards herself; sitting with it in front of her, she mimes taking off her clothes, trembling. She lifts the two hat-pins, which are now like two pointed awls. With wild delight she pierces the face before her with the two small awls, first one awl into one eye and then the second awl into the mouth. She shows the face to the spectators. The two small awls sit in the face like quivering arrows. She removes the veil with her teeth and exhibits the whole face – look, what a man (*Ecce homo*).

A clock strikes. She wakes from the intoxication of the dream or ritual and gathers the different props together. She brushes her hair while she relates the rest of the story: how Judith managed to slip by the soldiers and how she was greeted when she reached home again. She puts the red housecoat on again, takes a white water pitcher from the basket and waters the little tree. Tango music. She begins to dance, holding the pitcher in one hand, in a wild and desultory, almost liberating, way. She stops at the same moment as the music. Her slip continues to swing and wraps itself around her. She stands totally still, holding the pitcher in her hand. Water pours out of the pitcher and splashes on the floor. She realizes what she has done and mops up the water.

The course of the action in the performance is a stream of consciousness which is outside the daily dimensions of time and space. Like a day-dream, one long image in time, maybe a flashback or a dialogue with a shadow which is reborn through her actions – like her memory. It is a personal ritual sacrifice that opens borders, obliterates restraints: the Occupation.

The ritual ends in a possibly insignificant action: Judith waters the small dwarf tree, the tiny stunted tree which is prevented from growing because it has been bound. Although removed from its natural environment, it lives on, and must be watered. It must have a chance to overcome its fate and its immobility.

This is an image of the life of the actor. The actor's actions are not life itself but shadows which are given vitality and materialized on stage. Memories and dreams become visible and exist in the present. The actress does not only tell a story or simply analyse the dramatic conflict, but dances with it and within it. At one moment she is Judith, thinking back to what has happened; the next moment she is the subject of what has happened and uses the severed head as the object of her love and an irresistible erotic attraction; the next moment she herself is the object of what is happening with the props, which seem to have a life of their own and direct her responses. She is possessed by Holofernes; he is also a part of herself.

She both pushes the process towards the inevitable and allows herself to be put into the role of the victim. This fate must be accepted in spite of its possible consequences.

ROBERTA CARRERI

How do rehearsal/training and performance fit together for you?

They have a natural connection which has changed over the years. I can describe it very concretely by using as an example *Judith*. But let me first explain exactly what training has been for me. This is important in order to be able to understand how it has changed.

Training is the time and space in which the actor works both to build up presence and to break down mechanical or automatic reaction patterns. The actor's ability to be present can be the result of talent or it can be built up, it is something that can grow and be strengthened.

You must be present in order to do acrobatic exercise. You can't cheat by thinking about something else, that's how accidents occur. You are forced to concentrate on what you are doing. Some of the exercises can be done in slow motion in order to train the body to feel how the point of balance slowly shifts from one point to another. A somersault could be defined as a slow shifting of the point of balance, millimetre by millimetre.

When a somersault is done this way, there comes a moment when the back is in a certain position, when it is very difficult to control the movement. It is difficult to avoid losing control of the weight which would break the continuity of the movement.

Slow motion is important because it forces you to find the connection between each part of your body and your centre of gravity. Slow motion is an example of what we call a 'principle' in training. You decide some of the rules of the game and then you respect them, always. In slow motion you decide to respect/accept the rules of slow rhythm. In slow motion you withhold your energy and use it to hold the 'dead weight' back as well. Through this process you create your own opposition.

Another thing that has been important for me is work with the quality of presence. A very basic element, which is both elementary and dramatic, is the changing between different qualities of energy in movement, such as fast and slow, straight and round, strong and soft, open and closed. Dramatic tension is then created on the physical level. This tension has no particular meaning, but is experienced by the audience all the same.

I have worked a great deal with re-forming energy, suddenly holding it back and then letting it go.

How did the work with Judith *begin?*

In 1981, when Eugenio returned from ISTA in Volterra, Italy, he presented us with a new exercise. We were to sit on the floor and move one joint at a time: wrist, shoulder, elbow, neck, the eyes. We called it the segmenting exercise. It became a key to a new direction in my work. The first eight years of my work at Odin Teatret were concentrated on how to send energy out into the space with large movements, on trying to fill the space with energy. This had become quite automatic. I would work without using my brain. My body knew how to work by itself. The training carried *me. I* was not directing *it*. My body flowed with the stream of energy that it had been my goal to dive into for many years. Precisely for this reason, I needed a new direction. I had to force myself not to move. So I sat down in a chair. It became the springboard for an examination of new possibilities, a fantastic source for an ocean of new directions.

I worked at moving only one joint at a time. Right down to the smallest details like the eyes: first seeing only 5 metres in front of you, then 10 metres, and then 100. The exercise became a part of my daily training. The advantage of this exercise was that I constantly had to force myself to control my body. It is essentially an exercise in concentration and in the beginning it becomes enormously tiring; not physically tiring, but mentally tiring.

The cheapest chair I could find that could also be folded up, a necessary consideration if I was to be able to bring it along on tour, was a deck chair, like the ones used on the beach.

When I work with an exercise for a long time, I begin to make images. The body's movements create internal images, and I see landscapes in front of me. I experience body positions I have never been in before. Positions which are unnatural and non-habitual for my body. I always try to over-extend myself in the most extreme positions. Sometimes I end up in a position that is daily, but I've got into it from a totally unusual direction. The movements and positions all resembled recognizable daily movements and positions and yet were also abstract. I dissect and fragment the movements.

Some of the first images that came up were of the beach. Which beach? Who am I? What am I doing? During this period I also worked with music by Satie and this music carried me to a beach in Venice. I had a feeling that it was around the end of the last century.

The Lido in Venice! Who am I? A refined woman, because I move very slowly and quietly. I was alone on the beach. It wasn't summer, I was there because I was sick. I thought of James Joyce's daughter Lucia Joyce. He once lived in Trieste, not far from Venice, and I imagined that it was his daughter on the beach. In fact, Lucia Joyce was a little mad.

At that time, refined women had their hair arranged in a particular way, but I imagined that a woman who was a little mad would have her hair down, like the way madwomen are portrayed in Japanese theatre tradition. I had always had my hair in a braid during training, but now I let it down and worked with it as if it were one more segment of my body. It had its own life which was of course also influenced by inertia and gravity. But if I slowly leaned forward, I could let it flow over the back of the chair in different ways. And if I leaned forward as far as I could, then my hair would fall to the floor. So, I was a young woman, a little mad, waiting on a beach. That image finally carried me to a totally new character: Penelope, who waited for Odysseus on a beach.

These images came on their own, but I didn't reject them. Out of the physical behaviour pattern a new world was created. I entered this new world. I was also reading Joyce during this period and in his *Ulysses* we find Molly Bloom. So I learned Molly Bloom's monologue in order to have some text to work with and also in order to put some meat on the bones of the 'ghost', the character that was slowly taking form in my training. The behaviour and the movements I had were 'inspired' in this way. Of course, you can work with the segmenting exercise and be just as dead as with any other form of training. It is in itself neither a key nor a guarantee that you will enter a special kind of presence. But after working on the chair for a while, an energy with a certain quality of presence arises from within these images. It was not just a puppet-like response. The pattern began to repeat itself like a rhythmical progression.

Around this time I happened to go to the cinema and saw the American film *Apocalypse Now*. In the beginning of the film, there is a sequence which shows a jungle in a rain of napalm. These pictures affected me very strongly. The jungle is set on fire to music by the Doors: 'The End'.

The landscape I now see is no longer a beach where perhaps a crab crawls by and I stretch out my legs, or where I see the shadow of a man I'm waiting for and I get up out of the chair.

Now I see the jungle, in flames, and so my eyes begin to react differently. I begin to work with my eyes by focusing on these very dramatic images. Before, the images were very close by; now, on the other hand, I am looking out to the horizon. In a way, I simultaneously expanded the landscape and went deeper into it.

I did not begin working with these jungle images in order to obtain a particular effect with the eyes, but rather simply because I had seen this film and because it had made such an enormous impression upon me. But, at the same time, I was conscious of the fact that the audience would thereby experience more life in my eyes. So training is always a balance between the conscious and the coincidental.

After a while, the character became 'the white woman'.

In 1983, I saw a Butoh performance for the first time. I was unbelievably touched by the performance and later talked with the actress, Natsu Nakajima. I attended a three-day seminar led by her. She worked with a very intense physical training which seemed to have nothing to do with the performance I had experienced. This of course made me curious and quite interested in learning more.

In 1986, I went to Japan to work with her for a month. At this point in time, my life was in the midst of a series of personal changes. My child was about to begin school in Denmark, and I would be prevented from touring with Odin Teatret for eight or nine months a year, as we always had done. I thought, 'Maybe I should make a solo performance?' At the same time, I deeply desired to have a child with Torgeir, whom I live with. I could not decide what to do. It tormented me, I got sick, but I went to Japan anyway, with a longing for a child which wasn't yet born – the unborn prince.

In Butoh one dances one's sorrow or happiness. The Japanese dancer I trained with had just lost her master, who had taught her everything and who had served as her reference point for twenty years. She would dance his death. Her only student, a woman dancer, had just lost her brother, a suicide, and she wanted to make a performance about his death. I therefore felt it only natural that the only way through my longing or sorrow was to dance the unborn prince, who was not dead but had never lived.

I would not tell Natsu about the background for my work, but when I had to say something about my theme, I said: a woman expecting a child. We began to call the woman Mary because Natsu thought of Jesus' mother.

We created a choreography which for me dealt with the unborn prince while Natsu thought it was about Mary.

This became the material which I showed to Eugenio and my other colleagues, when I returned to Holstebro. And after a few months Eugenio said that we could make it into a performance.

We had to find a story. We thought of another Mary, Mary Magdalene. There was in fact a lot of material about her. After Jesus died, she fled from Jerusalem. She was possibly carrying his child. Here again was the unborn prince. All in all, she appeared to have been a very special person, both before and after her meeting with Jesus.

At the same time, I continued to work further with some of the Butoh principles. Eugenio asked me to take a scene from an earlier production and redo it according to the rules I had learned in Japan.

Can you define the rules found in Butoh which create its particular physical language?

In classical Japanese theatre, like Noh and Kabuki, there are very precise rules governing physical behaviour and choreography.

These forms are repeated generation after generation. Butoh does not have the same kind of codification. Butoh is a theatre form that came about after the Second World War, when a number of Japanese dancers learned American-style 'modern dance'.

After the war, when Japan was for the first time defeated and then occupied by a foreign civilization, theatre life was quite open to Western influence. But after a few years, the artists themselves began to struggle to find a Japanese identity. Butoh, therefore, arose from the tensions between a Western movement pattern and the need to rediscover Japanese roots.

What is special here is that the dancer doesn't represent a character in the first person, but rather a 'ghost' or the shadow of a character. You work a great deal with matter: you are a stone, fog, earth, water, air. Your body is like earth. At one time, the whole body was often smeared with white clay. But the white clay was difficult to work with. It cracked and peeled. And now the white paint from classical Japanese theatre is used instead, still to cover the whole body.

The strangest technique of all for me to learn was how to work with the eyes. I had learned how to focus the eyes through an earlier meeting with Asian theatre. In Indian and Balinese dance, the focusing of the eyes is very significant. It is said that even though the Balinese dancers wear masks and their eyes cannot be seen, their ability to focus the eyes is the deciding factor for the audience's experience of the masks.

But the situation here was just the opposite. I had to think of my eyes as two black holes, like 'the eyes of the dead'. You see everything, and you see nothing. I was told not to look with my eyes but rather with the so-called 'third eye' in the middle of the forehead. Something changed. With earlier training, when I worked in a space with focused eyes, I always knew

Figures 31 and 32 Judith, 1987 (Roberta Carreri). Notice the energy of the eyes in the two pictures. Photos: Torben Huss.

what it looked like from the outside. I was able to see myself as an observer might. Without focusing, this was no longer possible.

Certain specific muscles are used when focusing the eyes. Focusing can also be adjusted. You can condemn another person with the eyes, you can threaten with a glance, and your eyes can become burning coals which send off sparks. People who are in love have a special light in their eyes. But if you tense the eye muscles, everything falls into a fog. It's just like being near-sighted without glasses. Contours and colours flow together. The focal point is gone. In a way, you disappear into your own world, and this can be seen from the outside.

At that time, I dreamed of finding a way for the actor to be able to produce something that resembled a close-up in a film. With a film close-up you can easily enlarge an eye so that the audience sees nothing else. In the theatre the audience always sees the whole scenic image.

In the four or five years that I have been working with non-movement in the chair, I have always tried to work with minute changes that could nevertheless be observed. In fact, it is possible for an audience to feel the smallest change in tension just as if it were being shown on a huge cinema screen.

Back in 1980 I had worked with another Japanese actress, a Nihon-Buyo dancer, Katsuko Azuma. She taught me a lion's dance, fragments of which became a part of *The Million*. In order to perform that dance, certain specific muscles had to be tensed. I later recognized the same kind of muscular tension in Butoh dance. I learned these tensions by learning the positions and the choreography. The back of the neck is always stretched out while the chin is pointed downward, as if a steel wire was attached to the occiput bone and pulled upward while the other end of the wire pulled downward from the end of the spine. In order to be able to dance Kabuki it is absolutely necessary to find that tension. And it was a totally abnormal tension for me because I have a very weak back.

This position gave my body a complete new feeling. I began to feel the inside of my body as Katsuko Azuma had described it: 'a ball of steel covered with velvet'. It's a kind of strength or power in action which I made up my mind to learn. It's a kind of kinetics with a dynamic stillness. I tried to work with this kinetics in connection with the segmenting exercises, trying to make movements which were never automatic but always dynamic. It was exciting to find a training that suddenly had meaning. For six years I had trained out of obligation; that is, I had to train if I wanted to be at Odin Teatret. Training had always been a form of ritual for me, a way of getting stronger, more supple. But my meeting with the Japanese actor helped me finally to give my training a real meaning. I learned that training was the space, the time, in which an actor works within a circle of radiation. Azuma explained this phenomenon by describing the difference between a young Noh dancer and an old master who go through exactly the same movements and the same dance. The difference lies in the radiation of energy: the young dancer's radiation only reaches the first row of seats, while the master's encompasses even the furthest seats. You can keep pushing the borders of your radiation outward, little by little. What works is not making your actions larger but making your internal energy stronger – to reach even further outward by moving even less. This became the goal of my training and its most fascinating aspect.

I also worked with other training principles, of course, but in this case I could feel something special happening. It touched a string in me much as performing does when it functions perfectly. Often in performance situations I feel a vibrating string inside me and I could now consciously touch that string in training.

I remember a rehearsal late in 1979 when we were working on *Brecht's Ashes*. I was working in the room with some of my colleagues. Suddenly, for the first time, I could turn on the switch and be present in a rehearsal situation just as if it had been a performance. I could touch that string and immediately be in the 'now', in the action and burning in it.

Eugenio had to stop us, of course, because it was a rehearsal and we needed to repeat things. It felt unbelievable because I did not know where the switch was, just that it had been turned on. It was a little like having jumped from one half of the brain to the other. Like jumping into another form of reality, one that is even more real, more real than your average, daily reality. In daily reality you are used to playing different roles, but in this 'other' reality you are absolutely – only – what you do. Training teaches you to grab on to that reality and be concentrated.

Back to your work with Mary Magdalene; how did it develop?

Eugenio gave me a book with paintings of Mary Magdalene in many different situations. I took some of these pictures and laid them in a row and learned them by rote. I taught myself the physical positions and worked on making transitions between them. I then had a complete progression in picture form. I sang as I went through the progression in order to give my body a certain type of strength. This was a way to gather material based on five or six situations: Mary at the cross, Mary in ecstasy, Mary carrying the jar of oil to wash Jesus' feet.

At the same time, Eugenio began to think that I needed a relationship with another character in order to create a dramatic situation. There needed be someone for whom I acted, someone in relation to whom I did things. And based on his analysis of the material he had seen he felt that this someone should be close to the floor. He thought of Salome, and later of Judith. This was exciting because it gave me the opportunity to create a balance between the two who for me represented the profane and the holy.

I had always worked with at least two characters within the same role. I am Judith in this production, but also Salome and Mary Magdalene.

Many months went by. Eugenio read many different works about Judith and through them we were able to define her multiplicity. One can understand her as a holy woman who executes a ritual and acts in God's name. But one can also see her as a cold and calculating woman who in fact falls in love with Holofernes and then kills him because she can't resist him. So it was as if the profane and the holy melted together and therefore, after a while, I no longer had as much need for either Salome or Mary Magdalene.

Gradually a series of characters melt together and become one character even though many of the other characters' different characteristics have been preserved.

> For many years my face had no use
> But now I have a face that can be loved
> a face that can be happy
> I have seen the world's most beautiful eyes
> They were bright, they looked like a smile
> I have made them more
> lively and naked
> I turn back to them
> I run
> My body runs faster than my thoughts
> and nothing, nothing
> can overtake me
> I must witness my own death
> in order to know that I still live

> (Prologue in *Judith*)

9

THE TRAVELLERS OF SPEED

THEATRE AS METAPHOR

Most of European theatre in the last hundred years has limited itself to a particular perception of nature or reality, consistent with a Newtonian perception of reality. There are of course exceptions, such as Pirandello, Genet, Artaud and, not least, that theatre tradition which, as an extension of the work done by Grotowski, began to research or explore theatre as an energy system between actors and spectators. Here we move over to another reality perception, influenced by Einstein and Bohr. When Bohr spoke of the consequences of quantum leaps and the theory of complementarity, he used theatre as a metaphor. He said that we are both actors in and spectators of that reality which in fact can be compared to theatre.

Quantum physics implies a departure from the concept that objects can exist independently of our perception. Nature and its laws cannot be described objectively. It's a question of an image or a rendering of a reality which is not identical with that reality. The observer or spectator is a co-creator of the image which is formed.

We dream of rediscovering 'unspoiled' nature. But nature is changed by human observation. The same thing occurs with 'human nature'. The dream of spontaneous, authentic and original behaviour is an illusion. When the thought is first thought, it's no longer something unspoiled, a change has already taken place: a cultural change.

Experience has taught us that there are certain natural laws which are valid: the law of gravity, the law of centripetal force, the law of cause and effect. Time and space are of measurable size in this reality's theatre but the precondition for these measurements being correct is that we do not take the observer's speed into account.

Einstein's special theory of relativity (1905) shows that the terms time and space are relative and depend on the speed of the observer. 'What would happen if we caught a ray of light and rode on it?' he asks. How would the world then look? Time would stop and distances in space would disappear. What would be left? A swinging in the now. A wave of here.

158

The elasticity of time points at an area which is not limited by space and time but exclusively by 'personal speed'. As Eugenio Barba says:

There are people who live in a nation, in a culture. And there are people who live in their own bodies. They are travelers who cross the Country of Speed, a space and time which have nothing to do with the landscape and the season of the place they happen to be traveling through. One can stay in the same place for months and years and still be 'a traveler of speed,' journeying through regions and cultures thousands of years and thousands of kilometers distant, in unison with the thoughts and reactions of men far removed from oneself because of skin color or history. Speed is a personal dimension which cannot be measured with scientific criteria, although science and progress themselves have roots in this unmeasurable dimension.

(Barba, 1986a: 11)

QUANTUM LEAPS

Bohr's term 'quantum leap' is an attempt to describe something which cannot be described with the usual terms of the classical world-view. The quantum leap describes a 'leap' made by the electrons between various possible orbits around an atom. The jump is a transformation of energy which can be predicted and analysed. If one wishes to measure the change of energy, the electron disappears and can be studied in neither space nor time. And if one sets the positions of the electron, then one cannot describe the transition from orbit to orbit and hence the energy transformation. The electron is either placed in space or is manifest as speed but, at the same time, the electron is both a wave and a particle.

This is a way of saying that a differentiation between mass and energy is invalid, as, by extension, is one of the basic assumptions of classical physics. The concept of the 'quantum leap' refers to the lack of continuity in nature and Bohr accepts this discontinuity and recognizes that quantum mechanics is a limited description of nature.

This has consequences for the understanding of human perception and of what is called the after-effect dimension, or the causal laws of nature. The laws of nature can only be formally described with a certain degree of probability because it is not possible to make a sharp differentiation between mass and energy. The lack of a distinction between mass and energy is in opposition to one of the Western world's fundamental, dualistic thought-structures: the differentiation between the spirit and matter, between the material and the immaterial, between nature and metaphysics (God), between subject and object. The description of nature and the relationship or balance between man and nature become a kind of energy system where, as has been said, one cannot differentiate between actor and spectator.

In order to create as satisfying an image of nature as possible, Bohr uses a complementary form of description where energy is described both as a wave movement and a particle movement.

The concept of complementarity includes the idea of contexts and entities which are created by different aspects of reality, that is, connected or discontinuous continuities. It is a term which is found in both Eastern and Western thought and which also relates to elementary experience from daily life: to the connection between the two sexes, the contrapuntal behaviour or relationship between conflicting emotions.

The relationship between spectator and character is complementary. It is based on a difference and yet a commonality exists. All are participants in and spectators of one unity: the reality of theatre. The spectators' points of view are creating the performance and the performance is a direction of the spectators' attention through the actors' actions, the light, the space, etc. The performance becomes as a form an empty ritual, which has to be filled with personal meaning for the spectators and for the actors.

If the scenic behaviour is perceived as a reconstruction and not an illustration of daily behaviour the actor can move both within and outside the role. The actor can let himself or herself be carried by the action, can draw the action out, can differentiate himself or herself from the action, comment on it, attack it, deny it, follow new associations, jump to new stories or roles. The narrative can be interrupted by changes in point of view, atomization of known reality, and new montage. The actor makes these jumps visible by means of body technique (physical and mental technique).

Schechner (1985) uses the term 'restored behaviour' to describe the behaviour in every form of performance. This is to say that performance behaviour is considered to be different from daily behaviour. It is behaviour with its own construction and logic. This restored behaviour can be worked with in the same way that an editor works with strips of film. The montage or the context makes the meaning. This perception means that an action can be moved from one context to another and thereby change meaning in a kind of dramatic quantum leap.

THEATRE AS RITUAL

A differentiation is usually made between ritual and theatre by saying that ritual leads to a change in the participants in or practitioners of the ritual. These rituals can integrate the participants in another form of social commonality or can mark the transition from one state to another (confirmation, marriage, etc.).

'Theatre', on the other hand, is generally considered to be an action characterized by a sympathetic insight or transport to a fictive universe or a new dimension, a new space relative to the daily, but where the actors and the spectators are brought back to the point of departure without any change.

It is Schechner's view that this differentiation is incorrect. He maintains that many theatre forms in the twentieth century have approached the transforming power and dynamic of ritual and have tried to include the gripping and transforming elements of ritual, especially with respect to the actor's work. These actors change with their roles. Chaplin's discovery of his tramp character changed his life. He discovered it accidentally and spent the rest of his life finding out who it was. Some actors, like James Dean or John Wayne, identify themselves completely with their roles and grow with them. Other actors have had to fight to escape their roles, like Sean Connery, who had to work hard and long to break with his role as James Bond, with which, for the public and the film industry, he had become identical.

Other actors develop their characters so that these become a part of their language and the performance a part of a cultural unity: a way of living, communicating, speaking and establishing relationships. Repetition of the actor's work, training and performance reality leads to a transformation and permits a development in spite of well-defined rules, norms and habits.

The work of shamans is an example of how the repetition of actions, even though they are fictive, can transform reality. Lévi-Strauss tells about Quesalidt, who wanted to expose the shaman's medical practice as quackery. In order to do this, he stayed with some shamans and one day asked one of them to integrate him into the group. He was trained in actor technique, magic and singing, and learned a series of tricks which he gradually mastered to such a degree that he not only revealed the other shamans as quacks but also earned himself a reputation as a skilful shaman. As the years went by, he began to believe in his own ability to heal, even though he knew it was all based on tricks. He imagined that the sick became well because they believed in him and that they believed in him because he was skilled in executing his art and knew it deeply. He ended by believing that these tricks were a manifestation of his own authentic power. He didn't become a great shaman because he cured his patients, he cured his patients because he had become a great shaman. He turned into what he had sought to expose (Schechner, 1985).

If one wanted to make a parallel between this experience and the actor's craft, one could say that the actor becomes a 'master' through the training of a particular form of behaviour and that, at a certain point, this training becomes an identity. Or the craft becomes an individual 'language' which surpasses technique. One can also see such a development at Odin Teatret. Barba speaks about a training activity, a series of physical activities with built-in rules, which, over a period of years, changes into a particular way of thinking. One doesn't become a great actor/director because one wants

161

to entertain one's spectators. One entertains one's spectators because one has become a great actor/director.

There are certain rituals which result in an integration to a higher status, a transformation which is a step forward. It can also happen that 'integration rites' become 'disintegration rites', which, in part, make it possible for the individual to isolate himself or herself and to keep outside of tradition, society, status. There are rites which make it possible for one to remain a stranger.

Something similar happens with the actor through training. At the beginning, training is an initiation into the theatre, into the profession. It integrates the actor into a particular collection of values, principles and movement forms: the group's culture. It prepares the actor for performance, breaks down daily behaviour forms and builds new ones.

In these cases, the training continues to be important, even though the actor no longer needs to be integrated into a tradition, group, or method. The reason for the training changes.

The actor reaches something which is personal and which exists apart from the performance, the director and the spectators.

Iben Nagel Rasmussen says: 'This is one of the reasons I have not stopped training. It is one of the most important things I have. It develops and becomes something other and more than training. It becomes my language and my independence. Otherwise, the theatre remains the director's theatre. . . . I am convinced that there is a language which belongs to the actor and which can communicate directly, without going through the director.'

The theatre process as a way of living can be summarized in a series of phases, as follows.

Training is work with physical and psychic expression possibilities, a dilation of the body's energy through the elimination of the body's blocks. A language is developed: a second nature which gives form to the actor's presence and breaks down mechanical behaviour.

Improvisation is an exploration of energy, an exploration of a fictive landscape and actions, as an extension of, or perhaps because of, the training principles.

Montage and preparation of material (the dramatic text, music, lights, the actor's score) are set and repeated until the whole performance is fixed and can be presented to the spectators.

Warm-up before the performance (for the actors and perhaps the spectators) prepares for the theatre's reality.

When the performance begins, a kind of border is crossed which delineates the difference between two forms of reality. Sometimes this border is clearly marked, other times it is just felt by both the actors and the spectators. Something has happened, something has changed. The performance's intensity or flow is the result of the way in which its dramatic rhythm is created through transformations of the space.

The performance is both the energy which is created in the room in the here and now, and the repetition of a fixed sequence. Or one could say that what has been set and prepared is brought alive and done as if for the first time. 'The performance wave' is the energy flow between the spectators and the actors, who bring 'dead' things, such as props, costumes, light, space and shadows, alive.

Just as there is a beginning point, where the performance begins, so the performance also has an end point, where the actors and the spectators return to the neutral.

This 'coming out of' the performance, this cool-down, can be made a part of the performance, or it can happen without structure. The differentiation between the actors and the spectators can also be sustained, if the actors suddenly disappear and the spectators are left to end the performance. One could say that this is a protraction of the cool-down which is left up to each individual.

With the repetition of the performance, a 'performance text' is created, which perhaps slowly changes, as happens with Odin Teatret's performances, performed for several years. The individual performance leads further towards the next performance. Perhaps certain theories are expounded, experience is collected and worked on, new ways and means become possible, or the same thing is repeated. For some, the mask stiffens, remains, for others, it's a question of constant change. The theatre becomes part of a cultural context, for both the actors and the spectators.

And a continuation and preparation for a new generation of actors and spectators take place by means of text, images, training and education.

10

THE SCREAM OF THE BUTTERFLY

Once upon a time there were butterflies who had heard about flame. They went to see what it was like. The first butterfly came near the flame. The second skimmed it with its wing. The third flew over it. The fourth threw himself into it and burned. His friends watched his body disappear as it became one with the flame. The fourth butterfly had really known what a flame is like; but he could no longer talk about it.

(Barba, article, 1967: 50)

ELSE MARIE LAUKVIK

How do you get ready for a performance?

I love the empty room. I remember the première of *Ornitofilene*. I was so nervous that I couldn't wait until 8.00 p.m., so I was already there at 4.30. And I sat there and crocheted for an hour, to help the time pass. I've always been the first one in the room. When I come into a completely empty theatre room, I experience a delightful peace, a stillness and a fascination. Vibrations, the potential in the empty room. All the possibilities one can imagine. It's a peacefulness which calms me. I find an empty space. My experience with the creative process as director and actor is that the ideas I get for the creation of characters or changes to be made in a scene or something that needs to be done, come to me when I exist in that kind of empty space.

I lie down and rest. I'm completely alone, not distracted by the others. When I am alone in an empty room, I am cleansed, daily noise is cleansed out of me and I forget myself. This has become a natural need for me. In some theatre forms, the actors use maybe four hours to put their makeup on. You need to reach an inner stillness, I think, an inner peace, an inner relaxation, in order to gain the greatest possible control over what you're about to do.

It's not meditation. I don't do anything other than my daily work.

164

Come to the room, prepare the performance, put the props in place, and this takes me a long time. In *Oxyrhincus Evangeliet*, there are many props that have to be set. The costumes have to be checked, cleaned, everything has to work. The floor must be swept, it must be clean. I need a long time to assure myself that I have everything under control so that I can relax. And I gain strength while I am doing this. This is an experience I have tried to pass on when I work with other actors. The way we treat the props, the props will treat us. They're not just something you throw away when you're finished using them. They have their own life. This is something which is very important, and which is lacking, I think, in much traditional theatre.

I cover Zusha Mal'ak's props with a piece of white silk after the performance. This isn't something I've done with other props but I do it because I know he does it, or rather, that Hassidic holy men do it. The holy things must be covered and protected, just like the Torah is covered.

The same goes for the costume. It also has its own life. If I am to show some of Zusha Mal'ak's movements, I have to have either the shoes or the hat on. Otherwise I can't do it. Without them I would feel completely naked. I have to have a connection between the character and myself.

One of the actor's secrets is the preparation or warm-up before the performance. This means everything to me. I create a whole ritual of movements and actions. And even the order of these actions has meaning for me and determines whether or not it is possible to maintain a constant quality in the performances. It's almost like having guests over: you plan a particular atmosphere, you clean the house, you make some food, serve something good to drink, perhaps put some music on. You create a particular atmosphere by means of particular rituals. I warm up at the same time as I move around, wash the floor or do whatever I have to do. It's especially necessary for me to warm up my voice, not immediately before the performance, perhaps several hours before. Perhaps the room has bad acoustics, so the first time I perform in a particular room, I always use my voice a lot because I want to be completely at ease with the sound in the space.

The connection between the character and myself perhaps comes more quickly with experience. But a certain amount of time is still necessary to find this connection. With Zusha Mal'ak, I don't need so much time, but I use more time to prepare everything backstage. Three to four hours. I use ten to twenty minutes of this time to relax. A totally inactive period, when I sleep or relax in order to find an inner stillness and get rid of private thoughts and problems. If changes have been made in the performance, or if there have been difficulties, I memorize the difficult places – think them through in detail. Which means that I can do these parts of the performance later without having to think about them. Preparation time varies. At the beginning of a performance period, it's longer; at the end, it's shorter.

I focus on the difficult parts of the performance. It can be difficult when many different things have to be done at the same time. There's a scene in *Oxyrhincus Evangeliet*, for example, where I have to cut the paper four or five times – and very exactly, or else I cut into the prayer shawl. At the same time, I have to be careful not to be blinded by a lamp which is shining in my eyes, so I have to keep changing the angle of my head in order to be able to see. When I get up, I have to go past a lamp without bumping into it and without forgetting to sing.

Doing all these things at the same time is difficult, so I memorize how I have to place the packet, in which direction I have to cut, the order of it all.

It's often the technical things that are memorized, a pause that has to be shortened, a particular move or motivation. I never memorize feelings. They are the result of a process. What is important is to have a clear entrance angle to this process and, above all, a stillness, a state of wholeness and complete emptiness.

If the point of departure is the feelings, I think that you end up being limited – also in connection with the improvisations – and imprecise signs and actions result.

The way the performance begins can be difficult. *Ferai* was very difficult because I had to start at a very high level. The king had died and I began the performance with a lament. It was difficult because I had to be at the outer limit of an emotional state. I had to build it up long before the performance began. I had to be in that state at least ten minutes before I started. So I had to go through the performance inside myself, as a way of warming up, in order to be able to do those cries in an honest way.

I use a different technique in *Oxyrhincus Evangeliet*. Here I begin in a state of joy and have to attract attention and create concentration for what is about to happen. My preparation here consists more of creating a good atmosphere and a comfortable situation for myself. I do this by singing some of Zusha's songs.

In *The Million*, I went right out into a physically demanding situation on the stilts. There I was in an attack situation with respect to the spectators, and I said to myself, 'You must not fall.'

I use various techniques and they must be suitable to the atmosphere of the room. The atmosphere can determine how one steals the spectators' attention. If, for one reason or another, we're a bit late, it can be fateful and the whole thing can collapse because the spectators become impatient and a little bit aggressive and you have to fight with them. Having to wait too long to get started can destroy the atmosphere. You have to have a system that will protect you against anything that can happen. Once you've started, many things happen on their own, the motor is running.

Can you change the motivations for movements and actions?

I've always liked having certain small fragments which I can vary a little bit and change from one to another. There are other fragments which are exactly set with respect to time, movement and motivation.

It's possible to perform the same sequence technically, according to the score, according to the movements, in exactly the same way from night to night, and still change motivation. I do this for the simple reason that perhaps after a certain amount of time, I need to change, I need to make it a little more exciting. If I feel that I need to make a little change, so that I can make minimal changes in nuance, I can let my vision of a new situation shine through at the same time as I respect my action. If I don't agree with the director, I use cunning and sneak something in that I want to do, even though it wasn't necessarily what the director wanted.

This isn't something you can do when you are a beginner, but with experience, you learn how to show two attitudes at the same time.

I did this in *Come!* . . . I played the woman in white, the civilized woman, the representative of culture-colonization. But it wasn't completely right. So I tried to combine both the executioner and the sacrifice aspects. To describe the executioner as nothing more than a cruel person would not have been right, because he often suffers as much as the sacrifice. The spectators who see scenes which have this ambiguity are often not sure exactly what they've seen. Such scenes are often the ones that make the greatest impression. It is this multiplicity which makes the theatre special.

I don't think about the spectators at all when I'm performing. I don't want to express particular things, but I need to do these things. Even this can also be difficult for me and to a certain extent I do them in spite of myself. At the same time, I can certainly consider the performance as a gift to certain people. I give myself and invite, so to speak, certain people into my private, secret space.

I am not there as a private person. What I do in the performance creates another character, brought alive in such a way that it can continue, even if I lose consciousness for a few seconds, which in fact has happened in performance without anyone noticing.

Torgeir's placement in the dramaturgy is in the centre, as a spectator or observer. He observes the events which circulate around this point. If he is this labyrinth of actions, do you represent the bird aspect, the vertical aspect, the butterfly aspect? There are many examples of the way you 'ascend'. In Ornitofilene, *you hang yourself and your father doesn't dare to; in* Ferai, *you sacrifice yourself; in* The Million, *you're on stilts and fall at the end. Are you Icarus and burn up because you ascend too high?*

I have a little score with my hands in *My Father's House*, where I make a butterfly. It's actually from an improvisation from before *Ferai*. Where I 'cut' into my heart, take it out, look at it, and while it's beating in my hands it grows wings and I let it fly away as a bird. It's quite a violent image, but beautiful.

You could say that the punishment for going beyond the limit is that you burn up. In this sense, I have perhaps often gone to an extreme limit and, like Icarus, gone beyond all barriers, which is why the fall has also sometimes been hard.

In *Come!* . . ., I dance into ecstasy at the end of the performance and have almost no control over myself. It has perhaps been my strength that I have lived certain feelings right to their limits and yet still kept the control over and awareness of what I am doing.

There are many performances where I have gone to the limit of another level of consciousness, where you no longer consider yourself, something animal or primitive comes into it. As happened in the burial scene in *Ornitofilene*, where I go from the deepest sorrow to hysterical laughter. Reality becomes comical in the middle of sorrow. There one certainly approaches the flame.

The balance between the emotional scenes and the more understandable or intellectual scenes is important. It often happens that the emotional scene is like a blow, almost a shock which 'opens' the spectators' receptivity and ability to understand. The actor's ability to fascinate the spectator depends on the ability to be able to open and close himself or herself continuously. The actor musn't give everything at once; must oscillate between hiding himself or herself and attacking the public. What the actor hides creates curiosity. The good actor steals the spectators' attention so that they forget themselves for a moment. The bad actor perhaps makes small holes in the description, so that the spectator can predict what the actor is going to do and thereby anticipate the action. The result is boring. The actor must be a second faster than the spectator and the action. Then the whole thing becomes organic: another life. And the spectator gets no chance to relax or be bored. The actor must learn to steal the attention by filling out with something which neither the director nor the author know anything about. It is an extra dimension which is the actor's secret. Not because the actor is 'private'. You don't become an actor because you have many personal conflicts but you do perhaps use the conflicts in another way. You stage them or transform them into an artistic language. It's always a question of transcription. You perform a situation to its limit but you have built in a distance at the same time. You can't create in crisis because there will be no distancing from the feelings.

How do you come out of a performance? Do you have a kind of cool-down after a performance?

No one gives me time to cool down. The only performance where I used a slow cool-down was *The Book of Dances*. I enjoyed it. The last scene was a long one, all I had to do was play a pair of small cymbals. So I came out of the performance and watched it, I enjoyed myself. I felt like one of the spectators. In the other performances, there wasn't time for this, since I've nearly always been in the last scene. After the performance, we often have to get out of the theatre as quickly as possible because the room has to be closed, we're on tour. This is tormenting, because you need a cool-down, because you need to come out of the role. We go out to eat after the performance because we're hungry, we haven't eaten for six or seven hours. There is of course a natural 'cool-down'. Certain chemical processes take place in the body and brain, the adrenalin level drops, and it is replaced by tiredness after the use of energy.

If some actors stay in their roles, it's because they haven't been completely satisfied by the performance. They need to play themselves out but it hasn't happened, so they continue. If you've had complete satisfaction with what you've had to do in the performance, then you're finished with it. No question of wanting to continue. Just like a marathon runner doesn't keep on running when he's reached his goal.

What does a performance mean for you?

A performance is almost a complement to my private life. My life isn't particularly precise, but when it comes to the performance I am incredibly disciplined.

When we do a performance, it is the cardinal point and main person in my life. It takes precedence over everything else. It's almost a compulsion. It's terrible if I'm unsatisfied with a performance. I almost don't dare look anyone in the eyes. And the performance can haunt me like a ghost. A bad performance can torment me for a long time afterwards, like a guilty conscience. I am possessed by the thought that it must work. I am completely subordinate to the performance. But not to the character or role as such.

If the performance goes well, then there's a kind of liberation. I have almost a kind of love-hate relationship with the performance. You can't do it harm, because it's a part of you. If it's a bad performance, then you feel even worse, so it can become a vicious circle.

It is very painful for me to show myself. When I perform an emotional scene, I blank myself out and show my inner life. It's a big risk for me, an exposure I don't enjoy. You can't know how you'll be received or accepted. You throw yourself out into deep water.

Perhaps it's due to a basic uncertainty in myself. I remember a beggar I

169

met in Hong Kong. I thought, 'Why should it be me and not him who has the right to live? Should we change roles?'

The pattern goes all the way back to childhood. I was born during the war, under very difficult circumstances. The world around me was frightening, but also compelling.

I loved to sit and look out into space and dream. Or sit and listen to the radio. I would sit glued to the radio, all alone. It was an adventure for me. But I was usually thrown out, we weren't allowed to be inside. We were five children and my mother needed some peace and quiet. I didn't like to run outside, there were many children on the streets, and they frightened me a bit.

I was very young when I was bitten by the theatre. When I was 3 or 4, I saw *Snow White* at the theatre. All I can remember is a scene with moving waves on the stage. I was wildly enthusiastic. I secretly staged various stories. It was my private world. It was all hidden. I was a little embarrassed about my interests, my needs. But I created my own secret space. I read out loud, recited, sang and danced. I was always waiting for a chance to be alone.

When I was 5 or 6, I saw a theatre performance which made a tremendous impression on me. I remember a scene where the sun went down and there was a red light on a girl doing acrobatics. On the way home my sister said, 'There's that girl who was in the performance.' I was sick with envy and wanted to touch her.

My dream of doing theatre was born at that moment. It was the visual aspect, the acrobatic movement, that fascinated me. And the theatre space itself fascinated me.

I remember once being on holiday with my family. I was 13. We were to spend the night and the only place we could find was an old theatre. I was in seventh heaven, just standing on the empty stage and touching the heavy, red, impressive stage curtains.

I never dared talk about wanting to be in the theatre, until I was an adult and decided to try to get in to the National Theatre School. When I told my mother this, her reaction was laughter.

I tried to get in twice, but failed. Unfortunately, I was very shy. I didn't dare telephone an actor and say that I wanted to read with him. So I arrived at the auditions with no preparation.

It was a terrible baptism of fire to perform for spectators but so doing legitimized my need for the 'closed room' and gained a certain social acceptance. We were accepted as actors by the world around us and at the same time, I justified my need to day-dream.

It was at Odin Teatret that I first found a certain sense of belonging. But here as well I must justify my presence. I can be terribly afraid before a performance, where I'm going to have to surpass myself and present something new.

And you never know if you're going to be able to do it. Eugenio has always teased me about my negativism: 'I can't do it.' Before every performance, I'm afraid that I won't measure up to the task, even after twenty years in the profession.

Is this a kind of resistance?

Eugenio sometimes calls me 'the hag against the current'. So maybe it is. Theatre has often been a kind of obligation for me. It has obliged me to discipline myself, to repeat things. I've taken leave a couple of times, but I've always come back to test my belonging and to find new sides of myself. And because there are strong, invisible bonds which tie me to Odin Teatret. It's here I've invested my energy for many years. My roots are here.

Have you felt stage-fright?

We were once performing *The Million*. It was just before I took my second sabbatical. And I was feeling a combination of overstress, nerves and exhaustion. Stress on every possible level. I was simply attacked by anguish. My legs shook and I fell. I think that was the worst experience I've ever had. I suddenly got a case of stage-fright. My colleagues helped me get up and I had to pull myself together. I somehow managed to continue. I don't know if the spectators realized what had happened. Maybe they thought that the fall was part of the performance. I had fallen before. At the première of *The Million*, one of my aluminium stilts broke. I took the first few steps and then noticed that the stilt wasn't holding me up any longer. So I had to limp over to the orchestra. I tried in every way possible to signal to my colleagues that the stilt was broken and that I couldn't continue my number. I sank down, slowly but surely, right in front of the orchestra. But I kept a cool head. I flung the stilts up in the air and waved my umbrella around to make it all a little comical. The other actors didn't realize what had happened, they thought I had merely fallen. They didn't know the stilt was broken. I can remember that Eugenio was standing right beside my box, his face was as white as a corpse. I sat on my box and saw that Eugenio was wearing a belt. I grabbed it from him and used it to tie my skirt up. So the next scene, where I gave birth to the little puppet, was done without stilts. Yet it wasn't a humiliating experience, it was simply dramatic, an accident which I managed to get through as well as I could. And I found out that it was possible to do the scene on foot, without the spectators understanding that that wasn't the idea.

Luckily, I've managed to perform for many years without stage-fright. But now I've begun to experience it, in the last little while. And I think it's because I don't feel very strong at the moment. I need to rest, I'm over-stressed, and so I get stage-fright. When you perform, you can't save yourself, you have to run the full course and take responsibility for your actions, give yourself totally to your work rather than compromise.

Have any changes occurred over the years?

There are some things which never change. They are patterns in your personality. Other things have changed. I have less need to express my ego. I feel more reconciled to life. I don't have the same conflicts. I don't have the same need to say, 'Here I am, accept me.' My artistic 'I' has been satisfied in the meantime. I have nothing I have to prove, apart from something that has to do with singing and music and which is cooking away inside me (a little 'Schubert' asking to be let out). The need to prove something has become the need to explore.

I've forgotten all about Zusha Mal'ak for the moment. I've decided that he can be useful for me. Because there's still something unexplored, something that has to do with music and singing, something which is an exciting part of him. Otherwise I would have let him go altogether. I'm not personally involved with my characters and haven't grown up with them.

I think what has changed me most was suddenly discovering that I was able to direct a performance. It was a surprise because I had never in my life had ambitions to direct. It was a new dimension in my perception of myself. [Else Marie directed seven performances for Theatre Marquez in 1981–90.]

The most important thing for me in the doing of theatre, in performing, is that you thrive at the moment you are doing it, that you are happy with the action you are doing in the moment. The process is the most important thing, not the result. You must work without thinking that people will have to like what you are doing, you must work because of a need that has grown from within. It's not because the actor has a big ego that must be satisfied. You don't get on stage to get applause. We've never experienced it because, apart from the *The Million*, we've never stayed to receive applause. Of course, it warms you when someone comes to you and says that such and such a character is one of the most meaningful things they have seen at Odin Teatret, but my greatest pleasure has been the times when I myself have perhaps been able to create my own character or give form to my own idea and see it become something. I've done this a few times. It's just like being pregnant with a new thought or idea, you can see it be born and come alive. It's exciting.

I personally don't like suddenly having to live up to an image. This is something you see so much of in the theatre world. You have suddenly done something really good and have to live up to it, like playing a role. You can become afraid of no longer being able to satisfy any more. It's as though people always want something and this I refuse. I want to be myself. If I'm a little introverted, then that's my right. I won't go around and play up to something and be the person who says the right thing all the time or be a good example of group theatre where everything in the garden is lovely.

As an actor, do you need to plan certain challenges for yourself so as not to get stuck in particular behaviour norms?

We need to develop ourselves, but it's not something that Eugenio gets involved in. And the performances change in nature, from hard to soft. For me, Zusha Mal'ak is an 'easy' character to play, in contrast to what I did in *Come!* . . ., which was a much more difficult character. Of course, this influences my personality. You can't always choose what is going to be needed, even though it ought to be possible. I still have a long way to go. I don't know if *Oxyrhincus Evangeliet* is the last time I will ever perform or whether I'm going to continue for another twenty years. I've had many such periods, where I've sunk down and then started afresh again. When I came back to the group after each of the years I had away, I couldn't do anything, I had to build myself up again. It's never bothered me. to start over from zero. It's a challenge. I've got nothing against fighting a bit. If everything goes smoothly all the time, it gets boring.

I've been working with my voice for the last few years, while we've been travelling. I can tell that something is happening. Whether or not it develops into something is completely up to the circumstances, what kind of possibilities I get. But there's a need there, something lurking inside. I don't know whether or not it will get time to flower.

[In 1990 Else Marie Laukvik made a solo-performance with the musician Frans Winther: *Memoria*.]

How do you perceive the picture of the three actors [Figure 33]*?*

It is perhaps a picture of the actor's eternal destiny. There's something heavy sitting on their shoulders. At the end of a two- or three-hour parade, when you have walked so far and given as much as you can, you're dead, you're used up. Something has been burned clean, as Grotowski expressed it: the actor burns up, sacrifices herself. This is perhaps a little extreme, but yet it is a consequence for many artists.

The actor owns a world of intimate secrets. She must open the door to this world no matter how much it costs. And run the risk of being humiliated: by the director, by the spectators, or by the narrow-minded, misunderstanding, bourgeois surroundings. It makes me think of the last scene in *The Book of Dances*, where Torgeir throws himself to the ground many times, so that he loses his mask and is completely defenceless. Is there any other role for the actor in society today? What difference is there between Odin Teatret actors and actors in the traditional theatre? I don't know. In many ways, I have lived a protected life. Am I living in a ghetto?

At Odin Teatret, I have sometimes felt locked in, but I know that the world outside this world has nothing better to offer.

IBEN NAGEL RASMUSSEN

What significance does teaching have in your work?

Teaching has in fact taught me a lot. It's been an important part of my work. Even though it can be a lot of trouble and takes a lot of energy. Sometimes, that energy just disappears in the sand. When the large Farfa group was dissolved, I said to myself, 'That's it, no more.' But now I have a student again. It's important to peel off all the mistakes you've made, and pass on what you feel to be essential. Teaching gives you an opportunity to see if your principles are objective, if they have value for anyone other than yourself.

I have developed along with the students I've worked with. Their feedback pushes me forward, surprises me, forces me to articulate myself. I don't teach them what I know I can do, they get me to teach them what I didn't know I could do. It hasn't been my ambition to do theatre research, I've done it because I couldn't do otherwise.

The theatre is a small and limited world but within that world it is possible to rediscover an entire life-process. That's why as a teacher it's important for me to work with the same people, not for a few days but for several years. To live with them. Our relationship becomes my world, my earth. Something more than 'theatre'. The strategy you use for working the earth is different from the one you use to build cities or castles. When I watch my students, I don't get frightened by the absurdity of what they are attempting, because I know that there are many different ways, that the ways are innumerable. The only criterion I use to judge whether or not a given way is a good way to work is if it has perspective and heart.

Eugenio says that the theatre is not a building but the people who do it. Who are Odin Teatret's heirs? Do they exist? Or, fifty years from now, will there be a 'Barbara' [in Italian, a *barbara* is a barbarian; it is also the name of Brecht's daughter, who censored *Brecht's Ashes*] who censors the past and holds on to the rights to a form because of its name, or will it be

Figure 33 Crossing the desert landscape. The actors sit and rest after the performance on old, dead trees in a desolate area. They seem to be waiting for something. Perhaps they are exhausted. The picture tells a story of loneliness. Each character is looking in a different direction. They are affected by the desolate landscape. Though partly out of role and no longer performing, they are still actors. The actor's work is not limited to the performance and is not dependent on the spectator's presence.
Anabasis, Peru, 1978 (Tom Fjordefalk, Iben Nagel Rasmussen, Else Marie Laukvik). Photo: Tony D'Urso.

possible for other people in another time to read our story and misunderstand in a fruitful way?

There was a time some years ago when nearly everyone at Odin Teatret
thought that we didn't need more actors, that the group was big enough.
For me, the question of whether or not the group was big enough was
irrelevant. I felt that it was necessary to pass on what we had learned, to
know that the process didn't stop with us. I adopted students, as my own
responsibility and at my own expense. Other actors later followed my
example and also adopted students. Slowly a new generation was formed at
Odin Teatret. New areas to be cared for and made fruitful. A new period
of hope and fear began. At one point, it looked as though it wasn't going to
be possible for life to push its way through, that nothing would come up out
of the earth. There was a period which many of our spectators judged as
black, without perspective, under the sign of death. But it wasn't an
ending, it was a season, not age but winter.

When that period began we were still working on *Come!* . . ., and I
found that the production contained images of our situation and development. As an actor in the production, I was aware of these images, but they
were not visible as such to the spectators. There's a moment in a scene
towards the end of the production, where I am left alone. I hear a scream
behind me. Who is it? Is it death? I sing a song, it sounds like a lament, like
a burial hymn. But for me, it's also a prayer. I lift my hands to Heaven,
then turn them towards the earth. Pray for the sun to come back, to bring
light and warmth to what is trying to grow under the earth. The words of
the song are important: 'Dark is a way and light is a place'. Dark is a way
but also dark is away, gone.

Then the Death comes close to me, passes by me. Maybe it shows the
way, maybe it disappears. Then I see an open landscape, a field, the land
worked by the pioneers in America, but it's also the 'New World' that all of
us back then in the 1960s thought would be made. And it's also an image of
the situation at Odin Teatret, an image of the new generation which we
were afraid would succumb, and I pray: 'Let everything live.' Then I hear a
hammer-blow: the other actors, on the other side of the room, have begun
to nail a book to a plank. The spectators undoubtedly think of soldiers
nailing a last proclamation on a door or a wooden post, maybe they think
of crucifixion, or of people who turn books, living words, into stiff laws.
When I hear the hammer, I recognize it as an echo from the old days, a
moment when time stood still and the sound of a hammer made my friend
shout out, 'Listen! A carpenter is making a coffin.' In the production, the
sound hits me like a blow, forces me down to my knees. With my face to
the floor, I continue to pray, 'Give the earth power and time enough.' I try
to warm the earth with my hands, I use my hands to try to warm that which
is still locked in the dark, I hear footsteps approaching. Two hands lift my
head and open my mouth. I accept what must come.

Figure 34 Come! . . ., 1978 (Iben Nagel Rasmussen). The shaman dances. Photo: Tony D'Urso.

Spectators have told me that at that moment, my face awakened completely different associations for them. It's as if my face had become a stone, a skull. Of course, I know objectively that the scene is the result of a montage, fragment for fragment, which Eugenio has made with the material from our improvisations. I know that a series of actions has been put together and that this series has very little to do with my own personal associations. One can certainly say that my character in *Come!* . . . is a shaman, a man who is describing a universe created by other men, but if you look closely, you'll discover something else: the shaman is a woman, describing her own destiny.

The two images do not exclude each other, they give life to each other. What the spectator experiences is not the director's world, but it's not the actor's world either. It's the child speaking. We have to clean out our ears, remove the prejudices of yesterday. We must be quiet if we want to understand what the child is saying.

TORGEIR WETHAL

Have there been certain work experiences, certain periods, which have been more important to you than others?

When I think back, I see that I learned or experienced in spurts. Of course, it isn't true, the process of experience is continuous. But a kind of summing up has taken place, an awareness of experience gained in connection with certain particular situations in the past.

For me, the work with the early productions, *Kaspariana* and *Ferai*, was a situation of this kind. Just like the first time I worked as a teacher. This also makes sense, since it is during your first years in the profession that you are most bombarded with impressions and information. And at the same time, you are trying to understand what's happening and to reach what is right. You think that it is possible to find what is right and give yourself and your own expression, your own honesty, great meaning. The work on a production becomes the time when you confront technique and your own needs. But at the same time you understand (and often bang your head against) the fact that every production has its own needs and that they are always different from those of previous productions.

You remember all this after the first years have gone by, as if a slow dilation of your experiences was always occurring, a drop at a time.

One of my weaknesses as a performer, but also one of my strengths, is my relationship to the whole production. It can easily happen that I don't have a particularly strong need to find my own material or to arrive at what the others are doing. The relationship I always have to all of what's happening can sometimes dampen my own need for activity. But this is also a strength because it is partly where I get my material from.

I don't know if it is Eugenio or myself who has always placed me outside the other actors, in contrast to them, and in a particular relationship to the structure of the production and its dramaturgy. When we see something, a phenomenon, we both have a need to find an opposition to it in order to be able to understand it better. I have also often had the feeling that I am the one who must express Eugenio's ideas and images in the production. Maybe the other actors see themselves in exactly the same way.

This has sometimes paralysed me, but it has also been an important resistance, one which I want to keep. Our differences create ambiguity through our meeting.

The productions which gave me the most pleasure to perform, even though they were physically by far the most difficult, were the two non-productions, *The Book of Dances* and *The Million*. These were the two productions in which, in spite of myself, I ended up touching the greatest number of things.

For many of us at Odin Teatret and for many of our spectators, *My Father's House* has a particular memory, a special sound, a special vibration. That production was – in memory – different. Perhaps better than our other productions. The time, the beginning of the 1970s – the time of 'freedom' – had a great influence on how we remember the production. It was also an ensemble with a rare personal strength. But whether all this has anything to do with us, in the production as actors, I actually don't know. The character you are working on at any given moment is always the most important. It's not good if the character you are working on right now is not more important than the one you did last time, if you haven't reached a production as a result, if you haven't had new experiences along the way.

Until now, I have continued working on every production until I feel I have complete control of the whole space. Maybe it's my imagination, but I feel I reach a complete wholeness with what I am doing, almost a kind of invulnerability. It's a strange feeling. In *Oxyrhincus Evangeliet*, it's almost impossible to develop the production any further if Eugenio is not there as a constant mirror. In the 'dark', I myself cannot control, grasp, or see what direction the development is taking.

Have you ever experienced stage-fright?

No, not stage-fright *per se*. What I experience is more a kind of chemical process which begins automatically an hour to an hour and a half before the performance is to start. I am perhaps sitting and drinking coffee with friends and discover that I have begun to sweat. I haven't been thinking about the performance at all, but it has begun, in me. It can also happen that you are not completely involved in the performance when it begins, but it always overtakes you. Not being with the performance, or not wanting to be there, can cause a kind of nervousness. Especially the first times that you present a new production. This is something that I have certainly experienced but it's not something I consider to be negative. The body is giving you a concrete signal. If you hear the 'alarm' in time, you can usually manage to change the situation before the performance begins.

Do you do any particular warm-up before a performance?

I divide my day in two. I do whatever has to be done in the morning and then I take a nap before the performance. If there isn't much time, even ten or twenty minutes will do. When I wake up, then nothing exists but the performance.

I could perform *The Book of Dances* and *Anabasis* without warming up. They belonged to a completely separate social pattern and in performing them I used other parts of my nervous system. I think my habit of napping before a performance came about because after a performance I feel great, I'm wide awake, and always go to bed very late, even though we usually have some kind of work to do in the morning. So it becomes necessary to sleep in the afternoon in order to be rested. It's become a habit which is a little exaggerated but I would feel uncomfortable and unprepared if this possibility was taken away from me.

I almost never do any other kind of preparation. Up to *Ferai*, we had a set period of concentration for at least an hour before the performance. After all the practical things had been prepared, you sat somewhere where you wouldn't be disturbed and went through the whole performance in your head, in detail, both the inner and outer scores. Even though that was many years ago, the need for a 'no-nonsense' time before a performance has remained. You don't have to be serious and walk on tiptoe but I feel most comfortable if we go around and do the things we have to do without chatting about non-essentials. I don't think about the performance, I don't set myself up, it's just a way of being. I think I depend most on a kind of quietness and simple relaxation.

What about cool-down? Is it difficult to come out of a performance?

After the most physically active productions (like *The Million* and *Come! . . .*) and also after *Brecht's Ashes*, but not after *Oxyrhincus Evangeliet*, I have almost demanded the right to have a time to myself after the performance was over. The worst thing that could happen was if someone came and bothered me in the first ten minutes that were mine and mine alone. It's a combination of the fact that you are living on an inner level during the performance and that the physical action pattern develops and often increases in intensity towards the end of a performance. This affects you on many levels. Your adrenalin is going strong and you are physically exhausted. In fact, as far as your consciousness is concerned, you are on another level. I sometimes think, 'What on earth would happen if you didn't come out of this state?' They can be very beautiful moments, like the moments when you have really loved, in all the meanings of the word, but also something else. It is one of those lonely moments filled with inner peace which you can extend or cut off, as you like.

What is your relationship to the spectators? Do you have an imaginary spectator?

No, I don't actually think so. Not while I'm performing. Of course I work towards the spectators throughout the whole process. And at the moment of performing, I work directly with the spectators who are present. That is a sufficient driving force. It is also true that there are a certain few people who influence you more than or in a different way from what spectators normally do.

Oxyrhincus Evangeliet is strange because I can't see, but I still always have a very clear perception of specific spectators.

I think that the so-called 'imaginary spectator' is a term which exists most of all in the director's head. I'm not sure. I don't know how the other actors use the term. I've used it indirectly. In more difficult periods, it can help me if there are certain particular people for whom I have made the production. Not at the actual moment of performing, but people to hold on to, to get me where I have to go, before we begin.

The spectators exist as specific people and they are an active part of the moment of action. If the production is not too unambiguous then they are also almost active creators of what they see, to almost as great an extent as the actors.

What do you as a spectator demand from a production's dramaturgy?

As a spectator, I need a thread I can follow so as not be preoccupied with unimportant things – such as my own lack of understanding. I must quite quickly perceive a connection, a thread and an organic development in the production. The basis, the rules for its development must be established right from the beginning. And the rules must be complied with – otherwise they can't be broken.

My film editing teacher called it the contract which you must make with the spectator. This contract is also a limitation you must always fight against. It obliges you to give structure to the production's external action sequence. This enemy is your best friend.

The contract can be about anything and have an easy or a difficult form. You can say: 'This is just dance. There's nothing here to be understood.' This is sufficient information to help the spectator avoid getting into 'intellectual hot water'. His constant 'Yes, but what does it mean?' disappears and can become 'Look! Now something's happening.' If he knows that what he is seeing isn't supposed to mean anything, he begins to see the meanings. If he knows that there is no connection he must understand, he begins to perceive the whole because simple, learned blocks are removed. It's in the contract. The blocks are not there. This is the simplest draft of a dramaturgical structure that can be made but it's also full of clauses which must be complied with.

When I see a performance, I often have the impression at the beginning that someone is trying to tell me a story, but where does it disappear to? Perhaps the story's literary development is not necessary for the director but its form and development must nevertheless create the context for the emotional logic, which may be what he is most interested in establishing. The production must be a universe and I must be convinced that its rules are right and internally logical, even if I don't understand them. Otherwise, the least important thing, the structure, becomes the most important because it stops me. I get caught up in what I don't understand and lose the ability to experience, to 'seize' what it is actually about.

If you begin with a good literary story – and if your first step is the telling of this story – and if you present it in a realistic, understandable way, then the loom is ready. The main threads are there and you can begin to weave. When you're done, the bearing threads have perhaps become almost invisible, but it is nevertheless these threads which hold the carpet together.

One of the things about Eugenio that often surprises me is his lack of fear of banality and his lack of interest in being original. The simple and banal explanations of what a scene is generally about give space for the performing of details, an opportunity to discover their secrets and organize them.

Was there a definite fracture in the transition from My Father's House *to the street performances?*

For me, this period is associated with uncertainty. We had always been in a little, protected theatre space and then we began to move into various outdoor environments. This meant that you met a lot of people all the time, people that you had no chance whatsoever to get to know. You were alone in a social situation. It was a difficult break to make. But we've actually been through many similar things over the years, with huge transitions from one production to another. This is also one of the reasons that we don't repeat ourselves. One of Eugenio's strengths is his ability to predict a routine and to change the direction of a development. This has earlier created situations in which the whole ensemble was dissolved. Some actors were allowed to come back and others were not, and we began with completely new plans.

Later, with *The Book of Dances, Come! . . .*, and *The Million*, the development was smoother, but there have still been big changes between the productions.

But it's obvious that a great deal happened during the couple of weeks we performed *My Father's House* in Sardinia. We began to go out into the streets and play music. I stayed in the hotel. It was a mixture of fear, of horror, because I didn't have the means, and felt stupid and helpless, and of a conservatism, to which you are led by every form of security; and which I had found with *My Father's House*. Out of this situation, we found a new ocean which we sailed on for many years. The first three or four years of the barters was a good period, a period in which I got a lot back from my theatre work. Not from the barters themselves, as results, but with respect to how they were planned and prepared. The way you came into different situations, how you met the various environments, for a very specific purpose. You arrived in a little town, went into a bar and began to ask around, to see if you could find someone you could talk with to get the contacts made. I'm the world's worst and shyest tourist. I've never begun a conversation in a train compartment. But the barter way of meeting people was something I could use. You are what you are as a function of what you do. In the barter, both partners show a little of what they are.

11

THE SHADOW OF ANTIGONE
The director reflects
Eugenio Barba

Now that the actors have described their inner world, a world with its own rules, its own time and its own space, a world not limited to daily life, let's turn to reflection on the meaning of Odin Teatret and its history. The point of departure is a specific scene in Oxyrhincus Evangeliet, *a scene which developed slowly and took on definite meaning through a creative process. This excerpt is therefore also an example of Barba's way of working as a director, of his improvisation technique.*

EUGENIO BARBA

We are at *Oxyrhincus Evangeliet*. A woman called Antigone has just covered her brother's severed head with her dress. His head has been set out as a warning. The woman is then surprised by a man called Jehuda, the Grand Inquisitor, who draws out of his hat the bunch of flowers which cover the knife he has used to kill other characters in the performance. He holds the flowers over Antigone's neck. But he does not kill her, he does something else. He circles around her, and at that moment the darkness which earlier had blanketed the room is dispelled by the appearance of a golden light, the sun.

Jehuda searches with his knife on the floor: he finds Antigone's shadow, starts to scrape at its edges. He outlines the shadow with the dagger and at the same time seems to be trying to efface it. And so the scene continues, the knife trying to obliterate the shadow, and the shadow inexorably advancing.

I worked for a long time to find all the details for this scene, without knowing why. I asked myself all the while: why am I working so much on this scene, why is this scene so essential for me?

On 8 August 1985, in Holstebro, I was watching television. For nearly the entire evening, the programmes celebrated the anniversary of a historical event: forty years earlier, the atom bomb was dropped on Hiroshima. Among other news items was the report that the pilot of the plane which had dropped the second atom bomb, on Nagasaki, had committed suicide.

183

And then came the customary images, those which by now belong to, I would not say to our imaginary museum, but to our very concrete museum. The images of our individual-collective memory. Seeing these images again, I realized that I needed to look for yet another: in my library, I took down a book which I had bought in Japan, in Hiroshima, in fact, and there I found, amongst other things, the explanation for the scene in *Oxyrhincus Evangeliet* on which I had worked so much. A postcard bought at the Atomic Museum in Hiroshima shows three steps, the entrance to a bank, on which a shadow had been imprinted. A man was climbing these three granite steps when the bomb exploded and the heat of the bomb's fusion stamped his presence into the granite.

Thus I understood why Jehuda persisted in trying to obliterate Antigone's shadow: because it is easy to kill bodies, very easy, but some bodies leave shadows, as if their lives were so loaded with energy that they remained imprinted on history. Even if the people have physically vanished, their shadows remain and darken the beautiful landscape.

There are people who have left deep shadows in the history of our profession: Stanislavski, Artaud, Brecht, Julian Beck. There are many Jehudas who try to scrape their shadows away. But the shadows remain. They remain for those who know how to grasp the meaning of history, for those who want to remember, who do not want to lose the memory.

I mentioned the beautiful landscape and the shadows which darken it. Some people think that theatre derives from literature, and I remember a playwright, Heiner Müller, without doubt one of the most fascinating contemporary writers, who spoke of the sun shining on the beautiful landscape in the time of betrayal, with decaying bodies which were 'nothing but the landscape of their death'.

Why speak of betrayal? What is betrayed? To betray literally means 'to deliver', 'to hand over' someone or something to someone else. But what is delivered into others' hands? One might think that one's own shadow is handed over, like the character who entrusted his shadow to that apparently innocuous old man in Chamisso's novel, *Peter Schlemihl's wundersame Geschichte*.

But what can it mean, to deliver one's own shadow to someone else? It means to extinguish, to surrender, to weaken, or to suffocate those energies which should imprint one's own presence on the stone, on history. It means to refuse, it means being a political man in the sense of attacking what happens in the *polis*, the city, using the weapons which are in the intellectual's hands.

But what are the intellectual's weapons? Once again I asked myself why the figure of Antigone had for a long time, for three or four years, continuously returned to disturb me, like a ghost. First with *The Romance of Oedipus*, which Toni Cots and I made together, and where both in the text and in the actual production Antigone had a principal role. And then in this other production, *Oxyrhincus Evangeliet*. I asked myself: what is Antigone trying to tell me?

There was something disturbing me very much, pitting me against Antigone. 'If you don't agree with Creon's law', I found myself saying to her, 'then don't make your ineffectual gesture, don't pretend to bury your brother with nothing but a handful of dust. You go to Creon every day, see him every day, speak to him every day. So do as Brutus did, take a dagger and kill him, take the power of the *polis* yourself and establish the morality which is important for you, make it respected. But why this symbolic gesture of burial which accomplishes nothing?'

This is, fundamentally, what the blind narrator, the wise man, in *The Romance of Oedipus* says when he presents all the stories of the family of Laius: it is almost with irony that he shakes his head when faced with the ingenuous girl who is trying to change things with her useless gesture.

In *Oxyrhincus Evangeliet*, Antigone appears once again. And I could not understand what lay hidden behind her gesture, what it wanted to say to me personally. I finally understood it when I asked myself what the intellectual's weapon is, what the intellectual could use to fight against the law of the city. I think that the weapon is a handful of dust, a useless and symbolic gesture, which goes against the majority, against pragmatism, against fashion. A useless, inefficient, symbolic gesture, but a gesture which must be made. This is the intellectual's role: *to know that the gesture is useless, symbolic, and to have to make it.*

It is above all a gesture that does not give in to the spirit of the times, a spirit which refuses memory, refuses the past, refuses that which has been, and which believes that all that happened in the 1960s and 1970s is a vanished Atlantis.

A great swordmaster in Japan before the Tokugawa period was recognized by the fact that he was able to strike a blow at his opponent's neck without removing the head. Everyone would think: he missed. Then the opponent would take a step or two, and with the slightest inclination of the torso, his head would fall off.

I believe that for the theatre the experiences of the 1970s, which are no longer in fashion, belong to this kind of mastery. They were a blow dealt to the apparently unitary body of the theatre, and even if many now exult, believing that this body has remained intact, the generations to come will see its head fall. Something else is hidden in this body: another kind of life, in the blood, in the arteries, another vision of our profession, which is not only text, scenic incarnation. Again, it is as the playwright says: 'To be able to accept the decay of the body – because biologically we all crumble – and to try to preserve intact the ghosts of our memory.'

Perhaps, with my companions at Odin Teatret, and with all those who are around us, I succeed in remembering that I must not lose the shadow, the presence, the charge of energy which derives from a single necessity: *to refuse*. I do not accept the present, I want to remain apart, I want to make productions which are of use to me and to my companions, not productions which are requested or imposed. I want to make my reflections, impose my reflections. I will have strength to do so only so long as I succeed in maintaining this refusal.

I know that all those who seek to erase our shadow will not succeed in taking it away. We, and with us Julian Beck, Grotowski, The Bread and Puppet, all group theatre, a certain vision of theatre-making, will remain: their shadow, our shadow.

This is the beauty of this period of time: to see which is the stronger, the steel of those who wish to erase our shadow, or us. This is the real challenge of the ice age in which we find ourselves, the glaciation which is slowly mutating all theatrical and cultural vegetation: to be able to cross the icy landscape, leaving our shadows behind us.

I have no more to say, if not that I contemplate with joy the decade to come: it is the decade in which the group of people who have worked with me for so many years, and myself, will become biologically more than mature. It is the time in which our bodies will begin to become ruins. We will see whether or not we will be able to keep the ghosts of our youth alive in these ruins.

The only hand I hold out, that I would like to be touched and remembered, is towards those people who in ten, twenty, years will say: yes, we saw, we remember, we keep alive the memory of something which happened and which can happen again, differently, but it can happen.

Figure 35 Eugenio Barba, 1972. Photo: Roald Pay.

12

THEATRE AGAINST THE CURRENT: THE THEATRE OF REFUSAL

'Who are you?'

'We are actors.'

'Yes, but who are you?'

These were the questions put to Odin Teatret in 1974 by the people of Carpignano, the town in which they were staying.

It suddenly became clear to the members of this theatre group that their theatre was not just a question of training and performing. Their training was their everyday work, a life and a form of behaviour which were different from those of other people. This differentness was a part of the meeting between the actors and the people who did not belong to a theatre culture.

The fact of being different from others became a central part of Odin Teatret's group culture, expressed with such words as 'reservation', 'ghetto', 'emigrant theatre', or 'exile-theatre'.

The exile existence is a reality for most of the group's members. The group makes it possible for this differentness to be respected as a culture and not judged as madness.

Odin Teatret became a means of communication for its members, a barter. The group became a retroactive and reciprocal process.

Odin Teatret's journeys to 'foreign' lands and to cultures not accustomed to theatre were not made in order to get to know these cultures but to learn that the foreignness in oneself was a creative empty space. And in order to be able to re-create that foreignness. 'The circle of the theatre can be broken. Your theatre can be used as an object of exchange in a reality without theatre, to confront people whom you wish to meet, whose needs are different from yours. You may not be able to start a dialogue, but you can perhaps approach these diverse needs which are otherwise so distant. But you must rediscover a new humility. Be a stranger who dances. People will gather around you because you have accepted that you are not the navel of this living organism, that it is not your audience' (Barba, 1986a: 187).

187

One of the recurrent themes in Odin Teatret's productions is revolt, not popular or collective revolt, but individual revolt. The individual's desire to leave a trace in history, the desire to change the course of history.

In every production, we find the paradoxical individual who sets himself or herself outside, who acts in spite of the ordinary, normal rules, agreements and laws. The individual who has the desire to go against the current, to find new ways, to ask new questions, to make a useless gesture, which must be made.

In order to understand the kind of dramaturgy with which Odin Teatret has worked, it is necessary to understand this 'useless' action. An action which is 'useless' but 'necessary' has neither a definite direction nor an unambiguous tension. One is not looking for a particular result and the action is not perceived from one specific point which determines its meaning. The logic is found somewhere between the useless and the necessary. Why must Antigone, and not her sister Ismene, bury her brother with a handful of dust? Why must Antigone defy the law? And why is life and compromise more important for Ismene?

Odin Teatret's dramaturgy is not linear. It is a labyrinth with neither centre nor periphery, with neither central point of perspective nor unilateral interpretation. The labyrinth structure is a recognition pattern, an entity which is an interpretation in and of itself and which develops as a function of the relationship between the actors and the spectators. To a certain degree, it is left to each individual spectator to find his or her own Ariadne thread from among many possible threads.

But the 'useless' action also has a vertical perspective which rises Icarus-like from out of the labyrinth. Icarus defies the labyrinth and the law of gravity by putting on wings, and he uses them to fly up out of the space. But in his defiant pride he forgets that the sun burns. When he flies too close to the sun, the wings melt and he plunges into the sea.

In a similar way, we see the defiant Antigone be buried alive in *Oxyrhincus Evangeliet*. This punishment comes after she has lifted herself out of history and defied the law.

The revolt has the characteristics of a self-sacrifice. From the daughter in *Ornitofilene* who hangs herself, to Alcestis in *Ferai* who commits suicide with her father's weapon, to Kattrin in *Brecht's Ashes* who warns people against the danger of war and who because of her action is raped and condemned to death, to Antigone in *Oxyrhincus Evangeliet* or Judith, who defies authority and cuts off Holofernes' head.

The act of sacrifice is a recurrent theme, as it also was in Grotowski's theatre. But it is not just a literary theme, it is also the actors' personal theme and emerges from their denial of daily social patterns: individualization as revolt.

Odin Teatret's productions strike a balance between distance and empathy, analysis and emotion. Odin Teatret thus summarizes central

189

aspects of the discussion about the actor's presence, a discussion which has taken place throughout modern theatre history, from Diderot to Stanislavski and Brecht. At Odin Teatret, this does not take place as a philosophical debate on the relationship between being and non-being (pretence). The debate is a praxis, a part of daily life which, most of all, has to do with the training.

The relationship between being and simulating becomes a slow transformation or integration which takes place between the profession and personality. The actor disintegrates with respect to society.

The point of departure is each individual's need to change himself or herself through the theatre. This is why all the productions also deal with Odin Teatret's own history and experiences and with the group's particular conditions of existence as a unit and for its individual members.

This personal and totally specific point of departure means that, on a certain level, the actors can actually represent themselves. They do not, however, represent themselves directly. Rather, a transformation takes place, a translation of personal experience to theatrical action.

In 1969 Eugenio Barba was already formulating this point of departure in his article, 'Waiting for the revolution':

> It is no longer a question of being a missionary or an original artist, but of being realistic. Our profession gives us the possibility of changing ourselves and thereby of changing society. One must not ask: What does the theatre mean for the people? This is a demagogic and unfruitful question. But rather: What does the theatre mean for me? The answer, converted into ruthless actions without compromise, will be revolution in the theatre.
>
> (Barba, 1986a: 26)

Each Odin Teatret production contains an attitude towards (and can be understood as an examination of) the group's being, its meaning as a social relationship, its history and technique.

The productions have a basic dialogue quality. In the first productions, the dialogue was with a text written by an outsider. Later, it became a dialogue with various authors, Dostoyevsky, Brecht and Marco Polo, as well as dialogues with other cultures, such as in *The Million* and *Come!* . . . This dialogue is also expressed in the aesthetic structure, which is often full of oppositions and ambiguities. The composition of the productions approaches polyphony, a weaving together or montage of many different voices and points of view which are perhaps incompatible. These 'voices' are not placed in a traditional, dramatic, conflict relationship and do not have a traditional, dramatic development.

This dialogue aspect is further expressed by an open structure, where the spectator must choose to watch one action from among many actions which are being performed simultaneously. It is impossible for the spectator to see everything. The spectator is thereby obliged to assume an active role as 'watcher', where watching becomes an action which corresponds to the theatrical action.

The barter is a particular example of this dialogue theatre. Here, behind or beyond the theatre, as a relationship between the actors and the spectators, the barter focuses on the differences between two 'cultures' and shows that precisely because of these differences, an exchange is possible without quality or aesthetics becoming an issue. It could be said that one of the consequences of the barter is that it is a demonstration of the spectator's principal and necessary role in the theatre. The spectator's culture is just as important as that of the actor. This does not mean that the implicated cultures are equivalent but rather emphasizes the difference between them.

The consequence of the spectator's active role is that each production establishes its own space, where the spectator has a particular placement determined by the nature of the production. The space plays an active, dramatic role and its architecture, including the spectator's placement in it, is part of the 'action'.

Odin Teatret uses two different but complementary spaces. The closed space is like a bell-jar which ensures the communication between the actors and the spectators, an isolated and local event in the form of a concentrated flow which may not be interrupted. This implies respect both for the work the actors present and for the choice the spectators have made when they enter the closed circle made by the theatre. The opposite pole to the closed space is the open space, the urban space, where the spectators come and go and where the actors also move from area to area during the performance. Communication here is thus based on different premises. The actors' actions seize all the characters, buildings, statues, movements and sounds in the urban space and create a new structure with them. The urban image is transformed into a kind of carnival procession in which all participate. The difference with respect to the closed room is that the spectators have not necessarily chosen the theatre but that the theatre has chosen to be where the spectators are and nowhere else and has chosen to perform for those spectators.

The actor's foundation is his or her presence in time and space. Training is a process of negation, a de-culturation and a deformation of daily behaviour in order to reach another form of energy. As soon as a particular form of behaviour has been learned through training and a particular technical level has been reached, they must be changed. And the training must change direction. The same is true after the work on a particular production and with a particular character. Learned behaviour is deconstructed to make place for something new. The actor must always return to the point of departure – zero – in order to become creative once more. The actor's existential point of departure is an empty space. This applies to the individual productions and it applies to work on the role. There is constant variation.

Training is a wave of energy, a forming of the actor's presence through rhythm and direction in the space, through transformation of the body's weight and mass by means of dilation or interruption. Presence is dilated through the network of tensions created by the actor's imagination. Seen from the outside, training can be perceived as a dance or as the contours of a character. The training becomes material which can be used in a production, directly so as in *The Book of Dances*, or in a montage which expresses a story and a theme.

Odin Teatret is an 'anthropological theatre' which studies the theatre landscape: the landscapes of different cultures and the theatre of different times. But the object of study for this anthropological study is also the group itself. By placing itself in different situations, the theatre group explores its own identity. The daily work – training and the work with performance – changes in a situation where the theatre group becomes the study object of the population of a small town: the object of curiosity and interest.

Odin Teatret has used this strategy. It does not seek to force its knowledge or experience on others but rather is available as an example of the different.

Traditionally, elite culture and high culture are differentiated from popular culture. Odin Teatret was first perceived as an elite and avantgarde theatre without popular appeal. But, in fact, the group later showed itself capable of functioning as a popular theatre without abandoning the principles which applied to its early work.

The group's activities also demonstrate that the differentiation between elite theatre and popular theatre is to a certain extent meaningless and unproductive. In contrast to what has been the usual tradition in anthropology where people were the object of study, Odin Teatret has gone in the opposite direction and has had people to study it. Or, as was the case with the barter, the group has made it possible for two different cultural entities to study and experience each other.

As a theatre group, Odin Teatret is transnational and has no actual national identity. It is transcultural and is not anchored to a particular culture or cultural context (at the same time, Odin Teatret is paradoxically a regional theatre in the town of Holstebro). It is transhistorical, independent of historical conditions and a particular time. In this context, Odin Teatret is a nomad theatre, a journeying theatre, like the wandering performers of other times.

There are many different forms of culture: cultures established in relationship to a particular population and a particular local area and cultures which are connected to a travelling existence, such as gypsy culture. Odin Teatret is the latter kind of mini-society – its identity derives from a particular professionalism and a particular craft which the group has been continuously able to profile in relationship to other cultures and theatre traditions.

Nomadic existence has gradually become a common phenomenon in society, where, in contrast to earlier times, people now move and change jobs many times in their lives. How does one then protect one's identity and cultural engagement in this form of existence? It has become necessary to find completely different conditions for a cultural perception. It is necessary to find another centre, a nucleus of something unchangeable which can be carried with one. Odin Teatret has found such a nucleus in its craft, or, better, in an expansion of theatre craftsmanship.

Odin Teatret as a form of culture is the result of a collision between two different cultures. On the one hand, an active social democratic cultural politics in the town of Holstebro, the basis of which is a cultural pluralism as the prerequisite for a dynamic and developing cultural life in a town otherwise threatened by stagnation; on the other hand, the development of what has been widely called a 'middle-class culture' which grew up in the 1960s: it is an androgynous culture, a liberation culture, a niche culture, and it is a culture which is international in nature.

The hermaphroditic moment is a dissolution of the traditional, historical, sharp differentiation between masculine and feminine. In the case of Odin Teatret, this is seen in the lack of difference in the training and technique of male and female actors. The actors are not limited to performing sex-determined roles. Put in another way, all the actors work with soft as well as hard energy.

A 'liberation' culture is a culture free of traditional, economic and local relationships. It could be described as a floating culture which has to build its own tradition and identity.

The niche cultures are the result of the contrast between the general development of society and the institutional frameworks necessary for that development: the educational sector, the social sector and cultural areas are all places where niches devoted to the production of culture were established in the 1960s and 1970s. What happens in these niches is that an independent life-continuity is established with its own rules, language and principles, which function as a kind of anti-culture to the surrounding society.

Finally, one can speak of an international moment in this culture. This is seen in a number of manifestations and cultural phenomena which have in fact taken place more or less simultaneously over most of the world: the hippy culture, the student revolt, the punk and the squat movement, all contain a refusal of an ordinary, dominating ideology and truth. The absence of a unity culture leads to a point of departure in physical presence.

This is also seen in cultural blending and fragmentation: Indian, African,

Japanese, Chinese and European cultural forms are mixed through eating habits, living habits, dress, art and, not least, travels. This dimension is obvious in Odin Teatret, in its international context, its engagement in the Third Theatre, ISTA, and of course in the training itself and in a production like *The Million*.

The missing points of reference, the centre, the Home, the Father, the Mother, the Nation and Truth, not to mention God and cultural tradition, mean that narration has to a certain extent disintegrated, the progression of narration towards an action-filled climax has been replaced by the empty space, a stationary state. This is not the same as a static space or a stagnant time. Even though no answers are found, questions can certainly be asked. And it is the questions which create the dynamics: their various and distorted natures, their ability to expose new points of view.

To a certain extent, the theatre becomes self-reflective, its own point of reference and its own meaning, which neither can nor must be legitimized relative to something external.

Presence becomes central: the fact that the actor is present as a creative individual, different from the spectator, and the fact that the actor's presence has a suggestive and fascinating power for the spectator, so that the spectator's attention is dilated and maintained. The barter between various 'tribes', the barter in an ISTA between various professional theatre people with different cultural backgrounds, styles, aesthetics and perceptions of the meaning of theatre, is based on this presence. The absent truth is one of the dynamics in *Oxyrhincus Evangeliet*, where history, salvation and revolt are, in a way, disintegrated in the presence of the wandering tailor who finds himself in his work and his dance and includes all others in himself.

Energy is presence, a dynamic presence: to be in reality. Presence always emerges in relationship to its opposite: life in relationship to death. Energy is the tension which results from the relationship between absence and presence.

Exile is absence but an absence which represents 'that which is not': the homeland, as it was before the exile, and which therefore becomes present in absence. A homeland is an unnameable empty space that cannot be described which is nevertheless present in every single description of foreign cities. The journey or the exile therefore makes one's past, one's origin, one's home, visible. The same is apparently true for Barba.

Personally, I think that my motor is my choice to be an emigrant, my indifference to national ties. The only territory into which I sink my roots is the 'country of speed', that tangible and inscrutable dimension which is myself as presence, as a unity of soul-body-spirit, perceptible to others through their five senses.

For me, the theatre is the ephemeral bridge which in 'elected' contexts links me to another: to the actor, to the spectator. It is the interweaving of one solitude with another by means of an activity which obliges a total concentration of my entire physical and mental nature. The theatre is the fortress on the mountain, visible and impregnable, which permits me to be sociable while following the way of refusal.

(Barba, 1988d: 298)

The journey from Italy as a 17-year-old boy and the return to Italy in 1974 are poles which seem to dissolve. Beyond the 'journey' and the 'exile' lies the land of speed which is the body-in-life not bound to time and space but which manifests the absent, the invisible, the memories.

Odin Teatret is outside of time, it makes use of another time and another space. It has to a certain extent become independent of the development of society.

The question is whether this distance and estrangement are not a necessary precondition for the interpretation of 'the times', in order then to be in but not dominated by the times.

To be a 'traveller of speed', like the fool, is to remain outside the ordinary, daily conception of time as progressive and to be independent of the ordinary perception that the course of time must be legitimized and be socially, economically, or politically useful.

The 'traveller of speed' asks questions without expecting answers, acts without expecting a particular result, lets himself or herself be disorientated. It is a dilation of the now, of the moment, a moment which is otherwise unremarkable, a little step towards the future, lightning fast and unremarkably passed. The moment dilates and becomes a whole space, an empty space where anything can happen.

The 'traveller of speed' has no set, defined, central perspective point as a goal (the destruction of the world, death, revolution, happiness, fame) and no definite point of origin as a reference from which development can be perceived as a broadening.

The present is the time of the empty space. One can see forward, one can see backward. One can be in the empty space and experience stillness. One can ask, 'Who am I? Where am I going?' But the empty space must also be filled. The fact that the empty space itself has no direction does not necessarily imply that everything is meaningless or indifferent. On the contrary, one is forced to define oneself – to 'be-come', in one infinity. One is forced to fight to protect history, or, better, to create history. Historical experience is something other than the sum of individual steps. Historical experience is a pattern which is seen from another point of view than that of the wanderer, seen from above, seen from the outside. It is first from this distance that history becomes experience.

Then he sees the stork in the courtyard. And he laughs. And no one has ever laughed as much as he.

195

13

THE SPECTATOR'S PERSONAL THEATRE

ERIK EXE CHRISTOFFERSEN

Right from when I was very young, I felt that I was different, always a little outside. I was a kind of observer of the life of the rest of my family. I was withdrawn, 'mute' and shy. I remember once going downtown with my mother. I was about 5. We were in a store and my mother and the salesgirl were talking about me. They agreed that I had 'lovely' hair. My hair was blond and quite long.

My mother said: 'What a shame he isn't a girl.' I hated her for saying this. I hated being an object of attention. Perhaps because I felt that it wasn't me they were seeing.

I can picture it very clearly. I see a little boy with blond hair. He has no face. His face is a white mask with neither mouth nor eyes. I hated to be the centre of attention. I still do. It's as if I disappear, as if the surroundings are too close.

As a child, I had some 'routines' that made me the centre of attention anyway. I balanced on the edge of cliffs, I crawled high up in trees (perhaps a little too high up) and sat there and hid, I did headstands in the water (perhaps a little too dangerously), I rode on horses and cows. When I was 12, I ran away from home. I lied to my mother and told her that I was just going over to the neighbour's house. In fact, I was going to meet my friend Anders, whom I wasn't supposed to play with. We walked 20 km that winter day, to a farm he knew about, over the fields. We were taking part in our own film.

I often felt as if I didn't belong. I still do. When I see pictures from my childhood, they are usually of 'me' in various roles: Tarzan, Robinson Crusoe, Robin Hood, Hamlet. I think I was eleven when I read Shakespeare's *Hamlet* in the Classics Illustrated series. I was fascinated by that young soldier caught in a game, a production that wasn't his own but where he nevertheless had to play a role. Hamlet is both observer and participant in his uncle's production.

The first time I tried to do theatre was in the school play when I was 13 years old. I hadn't been picked to be in the play; on the contrary, it was

196

Figure 37 Peru, 1988. Still on the way. Photo: Tony D'Urso.

Anders who had been picked. But for some reason or other, he didn't want to be in it, and we agreed that I could have his part. We told the teacher about our agreement and she was very sceptical. She wasn't sure I could keep up with my school work, which wasn't going very well. I was dyslexic. But I insisted. It was fantastic. I was very taken with the director, who was a woman, and with the scenery and with just being there. There were three of us, and we each had our own house on the stage: the tailor, the blacksmith and the mayor. This created a context and certain social relationships that we lived with for long afterwards.

I've often had the feeling of being both an observer of and a participant in my own actions. I observed myself, in a way, when I crawled up in a high tree to hide. So that everybody else would find out I was missing and come and find me. When I was the furthest outside everything that was happening, I felt invisible. This is something I sometimes consciously exploited, if I didn't want to be noticed. Many of my movements were light and stealthy. I was never one to stomp across the floor.

But invisibility can also turn into loneliness and it can become necessary to attract attention to oneself. Everyone has a need to be 'seen' as an individual, different from other individuals. One can be anxious about not being seen. But one can also be anxious about being seen. Are the two things identical?

This is a central question and relates to the actor. The actor creates his or her own image and own identity, through the series of productions and characters – often in spite of that part of his or her personality which would rather remain anonymous. This is the paradox expressed by Hamlet in his famous monologue: 'To be or not to be'. On the one hand, to be: to be visible, delimited and centred. On the other hand, to sleep, to dream, to disappear, to dissolve in the wind, in the water, in the light.

Sometimes one can experience an improvisation as both of these states, or sometimes a performance makes both of these states possible.

I worked for a long time on tight-rope walking, both in order to be something tied to the earth, concentrated and disciplined and, at the same time, to give me the feeling of flying, to be at one and the same time in focus and distanced from other people, outside and yet a part of a commonality.

One of the most basic human needs is to feel that one exists. This is a basic structure which every person 'is concerned with' at the beginning of existence and when 'survival' is threatened.

An uncertain existence or identity can often be so painful that the individual creates a block between the emotional and the conscious. Between the 'body' and the 'head'. This splitting means that one can either be primarily in the 'body' and react almost exclusively intuitively, emotionally, without being able to structure actions logically and rationally, or one can remain primarily in the 'mental', where the impulses to act are consciously controlled (visually or logically-rationally).

It is also possible to oscillate between the two states and to find a mid-point between them: the 'empty space', empty of feeling and meaning. Shakespeare's Hamlet is in this empty space, which, for him, is almost madness. Hamlet oscillates between emotional impulse actions and rational considerations but he can't rid himself of the experience of the empty space.

The actor is in a paradoxical state, somewhere between 'being and non-being'. As an artist, the actor must be 'seen'. He or she has chosen to betray daily life and to do the unexpected action, has chosen the journey of discovery and has therefore broken with daily time and space, has chosen to make his or her inner current of imagination, dreams and energy visible: to be in-form.

The result is an art form where he or she 'is'. Presence is essential for the actor, but not necessarily uniquely so. Presence also helps the actor realize what it means 'not to be'. For most people, 'to be' is natural and daily but this is not the case for the actor, for whom it is a daily fight, especially because the art is connected to the 'being' and therefore disappears with 'not being'.

The actor leaves nothing behind. When the actor disappears, nothing more than a memory, certain experiences, are left.

The actor's motor or driving force is the empty space which must be filled. But this means that the actor must accept this empty space, no matter how painful it might be. It is first through this empty space that stillness, peace and readiness are found. The experience of nothingness is the precondition for everything.

The actor repeats the birth process. Through the continuous use of technique and training, he or she must re-create the ability to be present. Action has a space dimension and a time dimension and thus is different from most other art forms. Action dilates or diminishes the space.

Through work with rhythm and tempo, time becomes the actor's time and can be intensified or delayed until it becomes almost immobile yet dynamic. The actor changes time into a dramatic process and the space becomes a fictive universe.

The actor's 'dilated' body transforms space and time into personal categories. The two categories which in daily life are experienced as differentiated and quantifiable are woven together and become more or less connected.

So the actor is a rootless traveller. The actor flies towards unknown zones and is not bound to time and space, not anchored to the material, but has an indomitable desire to fly and to grow to the limitless, to be one with water and air. The actor executes actions which express emotional discharges but does not disappear into the emotions. The actor can consider himself or herself in the wildest emotional situations and outbursts.

This is the actor as spectator. Let me return here to the story of the stork. The man's journey around the lake, his difficulties, his mistakes, his tasks and his luck are the actor's wandering. The stork is what the spectator sees. In a wider context, the stork is the pattern which creates the spectator's memory.

This book, *The Actor's Way*, is my history of Odin Teatret. It is my 'stork' which is in the reader's hands. For obvious reasons, I can't show the reader a real, live stork but just a text which attempts to re-create the stork.

The premisses for my 'stork' are a desire and a need to know something both about the man's tribulations and about the stork.

For several years, I have attempted to combine practical, creative theatre work with research. In the former context, I am perhaps running the risk of being criticized for being a bad actor; in the latter, I am perhaps an unscientific researcher.

Nevertheless, I believe that the two activities are so close to each other that it is not only possible to arrive to a third activity, where practical work is combined with theoretical insight, it is also necessary to attempt to do so in order to move the theatre in new directions.

With respect to Odin Teatret, I am a spectator. When I describe Odin Teatret, I am also writing about something that I am a part of. Every Odin Teatret production inscribes the spectator into it and the theatre does not exist before the spectator sees and is part of the production. Odin Teatret has a wonderful, imaginative nature. It is certainly taking place in a particular space at a particular time, but where? It's not just what the actors are doing and of course neither is it only the spectators' presence, but the tension between these groups, the difference made visible in the actors' differentness *vis-à-vis* the spectator. The spectators change their behaviour just as the actors do. The personal 'I' becomes 'spectator' and each performance creates its own spectators at the same time as the spectators create the performance.

One can certainly also experience that a performance is not able to draw the spectators in. The spectators may become bored, fall asleep, or leave. But if the production works, it involves them in another reality, an unreal reality, a fictive universe which is immaterial and which can only become something if and as the spectators actually are transformed in this induction process, become absorbed, not totally, but partly. The balance between becoming involved in a kind of induction and maintaining a distance is characteristic of the spectators' situation: they are both themselves and at the same time part of another reality, a reality which takes form in their body and awareness.

This meeting can leave traces or it can disappear into oblivion. Over a period of years, a particular production or series of productions can become a pattern: a stork.

The production itself cannot be passed on but must be re-created as a text and staged as a pattern.

Any account of the theatre and the individual theatre productions also reflects back on the narrator, who has been a spectator and a co-creator of the production.

Only through a combination of induction into and consciously distanced involvement with the scenic action is it possible for the spectator to grasp the unreal, the invisible and the immaterial in a theatre process, the subtext, the unsaid, the hidden dynamics.

A change has taken place because of my work with Odin Teatret. As a spectator, I have become inscribed into the theatre. Each production has done this in its own way.

In 1972, I saw *My Father's House* for the first time. The condemned man with the blindfold over his eyes, the woman with sparkling, shining eyes and a daisy between her toes, or the two mad musicians, started vibrations inside me.

I still remember the atmosphere and the characters which set these vibrations going.

In 1982, I went on tour with Odin Teatret. Not to see the performances, but to look after Roberta Carreri's and Francis Pardeilhan's daughter Alice, who was 4 months old. I had only recently met Roberta and made this agreement with her. In return for looking after Alice, I was to be allowed to go to Holstebro and follow the group's work for several days. We stayed in an older, slightly battered-looking building at the back of a courtyard. Fifth floor, down a long corridor, a small room.

Roberta had to hurry off to the theatre. I had a cold and was a bit sluggish. In the little room there was a chair and a bed, a flowered carpet and naked light bulbs in the ceiling. I sat down. Alice began to scream. I picked her up, I walked around with her, she became quiet, I laid her down, she began to scream again. She had an incredible scream. It suddenly reminded me of *My Father's House*. The atmosphere, the characters, danced in the room. I was a part of Odin Teatret – it was in me. And yet I was something else as well. I wasn't an actor at Odin Teatret but a spectator. And as a spectator, I began to create the theatre.

I studied the daily work and the actors' wandering and I began to look for the pattern that this wandering might yield. A part of this wandering, traces, experiences, became visible through my conversations with the actors. It's their way, but through my attempt to find a pattern, it also became mine. I began to see myself as a story-teller, expressing himself with four different voices which together make up a pattern.

One night in 1987, under the star-laden sky in Greece, I dreamed about a butterfly, tattooed on an actor's back. It was a very clear image and I began to pursue it.

I remembered the image of the fluttering butterfly in *My Father's House*. Else Marie told me that her stilt character in *The Million* began as a butterfly character. There was a butterfly in *Judith*, a butterfly which has its

201

wings ripped off. I came across the story of the four butterflies and the fire in Eugenio's 1967 article on Kathakali theatre. It reminded me of Artaud's actor-martyr who signals from the pyre and of Grotowski's holy actor, whose outer body burns up so that the innermost impulses can emerge.

The butterfly is the actor who sacrifices himself or who is executed, just like the blindfolded, condemned man in *My Father's House* which I recognized in *Judith* in the image of Holofernes' head. At a certain moment, I heard Jim Morrison sing about the scream of the butterfly in the Doors' song 'The End'.

Roberta later told me how she had let a film, where this very song was the soundtrack to images of the jungle set aflame by American napalm bombs, influence her eyes in her work with *Judith*. Later in the performance, she stabs Holofernes in the eyes because she cannot resist him.

At one point, I called this book 'The Scream of the Butterfly'. One of Hieronymus Bosch's paintings, *The Wanderer*, made me change my mind. The fool has the butterfly's slightly frail and fluttering nature at the same time as he is balancing on the edge of the precipice. He turns this way and that, up and down, according to the prevailing order, but he inverts things, changes subject and function and creates disorientation in time and space.

September 1988, after the première of Odin Teatret's *Talabot*. The spectators are given a picture: the butterfly and the fool have combined to make an angel, floating over the world, which is a burnt-out ruin.

I had already written about the production before I saw it. With *Talabot*, Odin Teatret is once again out on the open sea. The production is like a boat, floating with the waves' often unexpected rhythm. The boat is sailing through different times and across geographical space. It's a journey which connects the living to the dead and immediate reality to the unreal world beyond the material world.

The point of departure is the year 1948, the year Antonin Artaud, the author of *The Theatre of Cruelty* (*Le théâtre et son double*), died, and the year the anthropologist Kirsten Hastrup was born.

The central character in the production is the travelling anthropologist, whose name here is 'Kirsten Hastrup', and just like Marco Polo, she is a spectator of the various cultures she meets on her travels. As spectators in the theatre, we also experience her as co-creator and co-composer of the cultures she becomes involved in.

The beginning of the performance: the character of 'Kirsten Hastrup' receives the spectators, who sit on benches arranged in a boat shape (Figure 13). She lowers a gangplank and reveals a museum display case where an Eskimo puppet is exhibited in bluish light. Later in the performance this puppet is called Minik. Minik is the name of the Eskimo child brought to New York with his father in 1897 by the Polar explorer Robert Peary, 'the discoverer of the North Pole'. The Eskimos were to be studied

202

Figure 38 Talabot, 1988 (Iben Nagel Rasmussen). Trickster or the Angel of history. Photo: Tony D'Urso.

by anthropologists. The father died because of the unfamiliar climate. Minik was later shocked to discover that his father's skeleton had been displayed in the museum and he understood that the burial he had attended had been a fraud, just as it was later discovered, and as Minik claimed, that Robert Peary was also a fraud and had never reached the North Pole.

The spectators are confronted with Minik as the exhibited life. But the situation contains a kind of double vision.

The image is a mirror. Minik saw not only his father but also himself, as someone who didn't belong to the society of frauds he was surrounded by. And he asked: 'Why did my father die?'

So Minik becomes a representative of and a point of identification for the 'hidden' in the spectator, the part which is in 'exile'.

I myself remember the feeling of being exhibited and remember hearing my mother say, 'What a shame he isn't a girl.'

Figure 39 Theatre Akadenwa, 1987 (Erik Exe Christoffersen). The dance on the water. Photo: Jens Tönnesen.

SELECT BIBLIOGRAPHY

This bibliography is divided into six sections: (1) books by Eugenio Barba (cited in the text by surname and date only); (2) articles by him; (3) interviews with him; (4) books and articles about Odin Teatret; (5) books and articles about the productions; (6) other works, not by Barba, cited in the text.

1 BOOKS BY EUGENIO BARBA

(1965) *Alla ricerca del teatro perduto*, Padua: Marsilio.
(1979) *The Floating Islands*, Holstebro: Drama.
(1980) *Modsætningernes spil*, Copenhagen: Berg.
(1981) *Il Brecht dell'Odin*, Milan: Ubulibri.
(1982) *Cendres de Brecht*, Paris: Cahiers de l'Herne 35, 2.
(1983) *Bemerkungen zum Schweigen der Schrift*, Cologne: Verlag der Teater-assoziation.
(1985) *The Dilated Body. The Gospel according to Oxyrhincus*, Rome: Zeami Libri.
(1986a) *Beyond the Floating Islands*, New York: Performing Arts Journal.
(1986b) *'Brechts Aske 2'* and *'Oxyrhincus Evangeliet'*, in *Thebens Syv Porte*, ed. Exe Christoffersen, Aarhus: Aarhus Universitets Forlag.
(1989) *De flydende øer*, Copenhagen: Borgen.
(1990) With Tony D'Urso, *Voyages with Odin Teatret*, Brindisi: Editrice Alfeo.
(1991) With Nicola Savarese, *The Secret Art of the Performer*, London: Routledge.

2 ARTICLES BY EUGENIO BARBA

(1962) 'Expériences du Théâtre-Laboratoire 13 rzedów', *Théâtre-Laboratoire 13 rzedów*, (Opole).
(1963) 'Efterkrigstidens teater i Polen', *Vinduet* 3, (Oslo: Gyldendal).
(1964a) 'Det Magiske Teater – 13 rækkers teatret i Opole', *Vindrosen* 11, 4 (Copenhagen: Gyldendal).
(1964b) 'Teater i bakeveje', *Samtiden* 8 (Oslo: Aschehoug).
(1965a) 'Theatre Laboratory 13 rzedów and ritual theater', *Tulane Drama Review* 9, 3 (New Orleans).
(1965b) 'Mod et sakralt og profant teater' and 'Teatrets nye testamente', *Teatrets Teori og Teknikk* 1 (Oslo: Bonytt).
(1967) 'The Kathakali Theater', *Tulane Drama Review*, 11, 4 (New York).

(1968a) 'Dr Faustus: Textual Montage' and 'Actor's Training', in Jerzy Grotowski, *Towards a Poor Theatre*, ed. Eugenio Barba, Holstebro: Odin Teatrets Forlag.

(1986b) 'Harlekin og hans to herrer', 'Meyerhold – Dappertutto' and 'Kjetteren Vakhtangov', *Teatrets Teori og Teknikk* 6 (Holstebro: Odin Teatrets Forlag).

(1970) 'Vsevolod Meyerhold', *Teatrets Teori og Teknikk* 12 (Holstebro: Odin Teatrets Forlag).

(1971a) 'Et antropologisk teater: introduktion til Odin Teatret', in Eugenio Barba and Per Moth (eds), *Meddelser fra Dansklærerforeningen*, Copenhagen: Gyldendal.

(1971b) 'Priëm ostrannenja, Verfremdung, Hana', 'Kabuki: en introduktion' and 'Mei Lan-Fan', *Teatrets Teori og Teknikk* 15 (Holstebro: Odin Teatrets Forlag).

(1980) 'Theateranthropologie: über orientalische und abendlogische Schauspielkunst', in Manfred Brauneck (ed.), *Theater im 20. Jahrhundert*, Hamburg: Rowohlt.

(1981a) 'Anthropologie théâtrale en Action', *Theatre International* 1 (London).

(1981b) 'Creating the roles', *Canadian Theatre Review* 31 (Toronto).

(1982a) 'Theateranthropologie', in Rudi Scholz and Peter Schubert (eds), *Körpererfahrung*, Hamburg: Rowohlt.

(1982b) 'The way of opposites', *Canadian Theatre Review* 35 (Toronto).

(1983) 'Theatre Anthropology', *The Drama Review* 94 (New York).

(1985a) 'Odin Teatret, storia e oggi', *Alfabeta* 7, 69 (Milan).

(1985b) 'The dilated body', *New Theatre Quarterly* I, 4 (Cambridge: Cambridge University Press).

(1985c) 'The nature of dramaturgy: describing actions at work', *New Theatre Quarterly*, I, 4 (Cambridge: Cambridge University Press).

(1987a) 'The etymological intellectual', *New Theatre Quarterly* III, 10 (Cambridge: Cambridge University Press).

(1987b) 'Entre texto escrito y espectáculo', *Repertorio* 1 (Universidad Autónoma de Querétaro).

(1987c) 'Tradizione dell'attore e identità delle spettatore', *Hyphos* I, 1 (Lecce: Scena Editore).

(1987d) 'The shadow of Antigone', *The Act* 1, 2 (New York).

(1987e) 'Teatro: memorie e utopie', *Alfabeta* 9, 103 (Milan).

(1987f) 'The actor's energy: male/female versus animus/anima', *New Theatre Quarterly* III, 11 (Cambridge: Cambridge University Press).

(1988a) 'Anthropological theatre', *The Drama Review* 117 (New York).

(1988b) 'About the invisible and visible in theater and about ISTA in particular: Eugenio Barba to Phillip Zarilli', *The Drama Review* 119 (New York).

(1988c) 'Eurasian Theatre', *The Drama Review* 119 (New York).

(1988d)'The way of refusal: the theatre's body-in-life', *New Theatre Quarterly*, IV, 16 (Cambridge: Cambridge University Press).

(1989) 'The fiction of duality', *New Theatre Quarterly*, V, 20 (Cambridge: Cambridge University Press).

(1990a) 'Four Spectators', *The Drama Review* 125 (New York).

(1990b) 'The third bank of the river', *The Act* 2, 1 (New York: Performance Project).

(1992) 'The Third Theatre: a legacy from us to ourselves', *New Theatre Quarterly* VIII, 29 (Cambridge: Cambridge University Press).

3 INTERVIEWS WITH EUGENIO BARBA

(1969) By Bent Hagsted 'A sectarian theatre', *The Drama Review* 45 (New York).

(1976) By David Zane Mairowits, 'Aarhus Festival and beyond', *Plays and Players*

24, 3 (London).
(1977) By Giovanni Lista, 'Théâtre vivant', *Canal* (Paris).
(1978) By Per Moth, 'At udnytte vort handicap, forvandle det', *Rampelyset* 133 (Thisted).
(1979) 'A conversation with Barba', selected documents from Cardiff Laboratory Theatre (Cardiff).
(1981) By Piergiorgio Giacché, 'La scuola de Barba e il teatro di gruppo', *Scena* 9 (Milan).
(1982a) By Patrick Pezin, 'Interview d'Eugenio Barba', *Bouffonneries* 4 (Lectoure).
(1982b) By Franco Ruffini, 'Le paradoxe pedagogique', *Bouffonneries* 4 (Lectoure).
(1984a) By Franco Quadri, 'Colloquio con Eugenio Barba', in *Il teatro degli anni settanta: invenzione di un teatro diverso*, Turin: Einaudi.
(1984b) By Gautam Dasgupta, 'Anthropology and theatre', *Performing Arts Journal* VIII, 3 (New York).
(1985) By Niels Olaf Gudme, 'Det foregår i Helvede', *Tusind Øjne* 81 (Copenhagen).
(1986) By James Brandon, 'Ingmar Bergman's *King Lear*: a discussion with Eugenio Barba', *Asian Theatre Journal* III, 2 (Honolulu).

4 BOOKS AND ARTICLES ABOUT ODIN TEATRET

Aubert, Christiane and Bourbonnaud, Jean-Luc (1970) 'L'Odin Teatret', in *Les voies de la création théâtrale*, Paris: CRNS.
Barba, Eugenio (ed.) (1967) *Vor By . . .*, Holstebro: Odin Teatret.
Barba, Eugenio (ed.) (1973) *Odin Teatret Expériences*, [Odin Teatret's productions 1964–73], Holstebro: Odin Teatrets Forlag.
Berg, Hans Martin (1986) *Treklang, år med Odin Teatret 1968–84*, Copenhagen: Vindrose.
Bourseiller, Antoine (1969) *Viva Barba*, Paris: Le Nouvel Observateur.
Bovin, Mette (1988) 'Provocation Anthropology', *The Drama Review* 117 (New York).
Bredsdorff, Thomas (1986) 'Ved undertekstens grænse (om Barbas Oxyrhincus Evangeliet)', in *Magtspil*, Copenhagen: Gyldendal.
Carlson, H. G. (1971) 'The Odin Theatre in Holstebro', *American Scandinavian Review*, (New York).
Christoffersen, Exe (ed.) (1986) *Thebens Syv Porte*, Aarhus: Aarhus Universitets Forlag.
Christoffersen, Exe (1989a) *Skuespillerens Vandring*, Aarhus: Klim.
Christoffersen, Exe (1989b) 'Tradition og fornyelse', in Eugenio Barba, *De flydende øer*, Copenhagen: Bergen.
Christoffersen, Exe (1992) ' "Waterways". Atlantis: the staged production', *Il colpo dei Barbari. Internationalt Kulturtidsskrift* 9 (Copenhagen).
Czertok, Horacio (1978) 'Al sur del Odin Teatret', *Cultura* 8 (Buenos Aires).
Daetwyler, Jean-Jacques (1980) *L'Odin Teatret et la naissance du Thiers Théâtre*, Berne: Palindrome.
Damkjær, Niels (1985) 'Teatrets Anatomi', *Rampelyset* 168–9 (Graasten).
Dannevig, Siri and Greve, Wenke (1982) 'Et teaterlaboratorium', *Samtiden* 1 (Oslo: Aschehoug).
De Toro, Fernando (1988) 'El Odin Teatret y Latinoamérica', *Latin American Theatre Review*, March (University of Kansas).

D'Urso Tony and Taviani, Ferdinando (1977) 'L'Étranger qui danse', *Album de l'Odin Teatret 1972–77*, Maison de la Culture de Rennes.

Fowler, Richard (1981) 'Denmark: Grotowski and Barba, a Canadian perspective', *Canadian Theatre Review* 32 (Toronto).

Marotti, Ferruccio (1973) ' "Odin Teatret" di Eugenio Barba', in *Tutto il mondo è attore*, Terzoprogramma 2–3, Turin: Eri.

Molinari, Renata (1988) 'La strada della ricerca', in *Il Patalogo Undici*, Milan: Ubulibri.

Pavis, Patrice (1989) 'Dancing with Faust', *The Drama Review* 33, 3 (New York).

Pets, Thomas and Berger, Hans Georg (1980) *Eugenio Barba's Odin Teatret*, Munich: Theatre Festival '80.

Rasmussen, Iben Nagel (1991) 'De stumme fra fortiden', in *Itsi-Bitsi*, Holstebro: Odin Teatrets Forlag.

Restuccia, Alberto (1987) 'La "buena nueva" de Barba', *Jaque* IV, 174 (Montevideo).

Rosenthal, Geneviève (1976) 'Les guerriers de l'Odin Teatret', in *Les Nouvelles Littéraires*, Paris.

Saurel, Renée (1965) 'A la recherche du théâtre perdu', *Les Temps Modernes*, (Paris).

Saurel, Renée (1967) 'Séminaire nordique à Holstebro', *Les Temps Modernes*, 23, 256 (Paris).

Saurel, Renée (1970a) 'De Rom à Holstebro: Un même but, des voies diférentes', *Les Temps Modernes*, 27, 288 (Paris).

Saurel, Renée (1970b) 'Le mythe du théâtre politique en Scandinavie', *Les Temps Modernes* 27, 292 (Paris).

Saurel, Renée (1978) 'ODIN Nave Almirante del Tercer Teatro', *Cultura* 8 (Buenos Aires).

Saurel, Renée (1982) 'Odin Teatret à Choisy, les Tafurs à Gensac', *Les Temps Modernes* 38, 431 (Paris).

Schechner, Richard (1984) 'Third Theatre', an interview with Jerzy Grotowski about Eugenio Barba, *Village Voice*, 1 May (New York).

Taviani, Ferdinando (1975) *Il libro dell'Odin*, Milan.

Taviani, Ferdinando (1980) 'Odin Teatret e Eugenio Barba', in *Enciclopedia del teatro del 1900*, Milan: Feltrinelli.

Taviani, Ferdinando (1986) 'The Odin story', in Eugenio Barba, *Beyond the Floating Islands*, New York: Performing Arts Journal; translated as 'Historien om Odin', in Barba, *De flydende øer*, Copenhagen: Bergen.

Teminke, Raymonde (1976) *Un italien en Danemark, des danois en Italie*, Paris: La Pensée.

Watson, Ian (1988) 'Eastern and western influence on performing training at Eugenio Barba's Odin Teatret', *Asian Theatre Journal* 5, 1 (Honolulu).

Watson, Ian (1989) 'Eugenio Barba: the Latin American connection', *New Theatre Quarterly* V, 17 (Cambridge: Cambridge University Press).

5 BOOKS AND ARTICLES ABOUT THE PRODUCTIONS

Aubert, Christiane and Bourbonnaud, Jean-Luc (1970) 'Kaspariana', in *Les voies de la création théâtrale*, Paris: CNRS.

Banu, Georges (1982) 'Les cendres', *Théâtre Public* 46–7 (Gennevilliers).

Barba, Eugenio (ed.) (1970) *Ornitofilene, Kaspariana, Ferai*, Holstebro: Odin Teatrets Forlag.

Barba, Eugenio (ed.) (1974) 'Breve til "Min Fars Hus"', *Teatrets Teori og Teknikk* 22

BIBLIOGRAPHY

(Holstebro: Odin Teatrets Forlag).

Barfoed, Stig Krabbe (1977) *Theaterturnée in den Dschungel*, Berlin: Die Deutsche Bühne.

Bocchieri, Rosanna (1988) ' "Talabot". Il potere dei morti sui vivi', *Sipario* 483–4 (Milan).

Carreri, Roberta (1991) 'The actor's journey: "Judith" from training to performance', *New Theatre Quarterly* VII, 26 (Cambridge: Cambridge University Press).

(1976) *Come! And the day will be ours: Materiali sullo spectacolo e sul lavoro dell'Odin Teatret*, Pontedera: Centro per la sperimentazione e la ricerca teatrale.

Daetwyler, Jean-Jacques (1974) 'L'Odin en Italie. L'expérience original d'un théâtre danois dans un village du Salento', *Journal du Jura* (Geneva).

Dumur, Guy (1965) 'Cérémonies secrètes', *Le Nouvel Observateur*, 30 June (Paris).

Forser, Tomas (1980) 'Odinteatret förvåner med pjäs om Brecht', *Teatertidningen* 12–13 (Stockholm).

Fumaroli, Marc (1968) 'Eugenio Barba's *Kaspariana*', *The Drama Review* 41 (New York); retitled (1970) 'Something blossoming . . .' (see Fumaroli, 1970).

Fumaroli, Marc (1969) 'Funeral rites: Eugenio Barba's *Ferai*', *The Drama Review* 45 (New York).

Fumaroli, Marc (1970) 'Something blossoming in the state of Denmark', in Eugenio Barba (ed.), *Ornitofilene, Kaspariana, Ferai*, Holstebro: Odin Teatrets Forlag; originally published (1968) in *The Drama Review* (see Fumaroli, 1968).

Gagnon, Odette (1984) '"Cendres de Brecht 2" et "Le Million"', *Jeu* 33 (Montreal: Cahiers de théâtre).

Garcia, Luis Britto (1977) 'El teatro al encuentro del hombre', *Revista de Antropologia* 3 (Caracas).

Hastrup, Kirsten (1992) *Out of Anthropology. The Anthropologist as an Object of Dramatic Representation*, *Cultural Anthropology* 7 (Washington DC).

Holm, Ingvar, Hagnell, Viveka and Rasch, Jane (1977) *Kulturmodel, Holstebro*, Copenhagen: Rhodos; translated as (1985) *A Model for Culture, Holstebro*, Stockholm: Almqvist & Wiksell.

Marotti, Ferruccio (1973) '"Ferai" – La costruzione dello spettacolo', in *Tutto il mondo è attore*, Terzoprogramma 2–3 Turin: Eri.

Meldolesi, Claudio (1982) 'Ceneri di Brecht', *Scena*, March (Milan).

Munoz, García Francisco (1983) 'Cenizas de Brecht 2', *Primer Acto* 197 (Madrid).

O'Beeman, William (1984) 'Brecht's Ashes 2, The Million', *Performing Arts Journal* 23 (New York).

Paladini, Angela (1972) 'Note sul lavoro per "Min Fars Hus"', *Biblioteca Teatrale* 5 (Rome: Bulzoni).

Perrelli, Franco (1972) '"Min Fars Hus" di Eugenio Barba', *Quaderni del Cut* 11 (Bari).

Piccioli, Giannandrea (1982) 'Il teorema dell'Odin', *Quaderni Piacentini* 6.

Quadri, Franco (1980) 'Brecht's Aske', *Panorama*, June (Milan).

Quadri, Franco (1986) 'Come! And the day will be ours', *Panorama*, October (Milan).

Raimondo, Mario (1972) 'Viviamo tutti nella casa del padre', *Sipario* 318 (Rome).

Saurel, Renée (1969) 'Ferai', *Les Temps Modernes* 277–8 (Paris).

Saurel, Renée (1974) 'Min Fars Hus. La maison du père', *Les Temps Modernes* 332 (Paris).

Saurel, Renée (1980) 'Chronique sicilienne avec Odin et le Teatro Libero', *Les Temps Modernes* 36, 411 (Paris).

Seeberg, Peter (1970) *Ferai*, Copenhagen: Arena.

Shoemaker, David (1990) 'Report from Holstebro: Odin Teatrets "Talabot"', *New Theatre Quarterly* VI, 24 (Cambridge: Cambridge University Press.

Strauss, Botho (1970) 'Archaik und Empfindsamkeit zu "Ferai" von Odin Teatret', *Theater Heute* 6 (Hanover).

Swansey, Bruce (1984) 'Odin Teatret en Mexico', *Proceso* 420 (Mexico).

Taviani, Ferdinando (1972) 'Su "Min Fars Hus" – Schede', *Biblioteca Teatrale* 5 (Rome: Bulzoni).

Taviani, Ferdinando (1975) 'Memoria finale', in *Il libro dell'Odin*, Milan: Feltrinelli.

Temkine, Raymonde (1989) 'Talabot dans Aarhus en fête', *Théâtre Public* 85 (Gennevilliers).

Temkine, Raymonde (1989) 'Talabot. Eugenio Barba's voyage', *Acteurs* 73–4 (Paris: Actes Sud).

Volli, Ugo (1986) 'Un vangelo del male', *Teatro Festival* 2 (Parma).

Watson, Ian (1982) 'The Million', *The Drama Review* 107 (New York).

6 OTHER WORKS CITED IN THE TEXT

Artaud, Antonin (1964) *Le Théâtre et son double*, Paris: Gallimard.

Blixen, Karen (1963 [1937]) *Den Afrikanske Farm*, Copenhagen: Gyldendal.

Cieslak, Ryszard (1982) 'Tyve ôrs søgen' (an interview), *Spillerom* 2 (Oslo).

Grotowski, Jerzy (1968) *Towards a Poor Theatre*, ed. Eugenio Barba, Holstebro: Odin Teatrets Forlag.

Grotowski, Jerzy (1973) 'Teatret og riten', *Teatrets Teori og Teknikk* 20 (Holstebro).

Kumiega, Jennifer (1985) *The Theatre of Grotowski*, New York: Methuen.

Schechner, Richard (1985) *Between Theatre and Anthropology*, Philadelphia, Pa: University of Pennsylvania Press.

ODIN TEATRET PRODUCTIONS: 1965–92

PRODUCTIONS DIRECTED BY EUGENIO BARBA

Scenic arrangement by Odin Teatret

Ornitofilene (1965–6)
'The Bird Lovers'
Based on a text by Jens Björneboe
Actors: Anne Trine Grimnes, Else Marie Laukvik, Tor Sannum, Torgeir Wethal
Architect: Ole Daniel Bruun
Performed 51 times in Denmark, Finland, Norway, Sweden

Kaspariana (1967–8)
Based on a scenario by Ole Sarvig
Actors: Jan Erik Bergström, Anne Trine Grimnes, Lars Göran Kjellstedt, Else Marie Laukvik, Iben Nagel Rasmussen, Dan Nielsen, Torgeir Wethal
Architect: Bernt Nyberg
Literary adviser: Christian Ludvigsen
Performed 74 times in Denmark, Italy, Norway, Sweden

Ferai (1969–70)
Based on a text by Peter Seeberg
Actors: Ulla Alasjärvi, Marisa Gilberti, Juha Häkkänen, Sören Larsson, Else Marie Laukvik, Iben Nagel Rasmussen, Carita Rindell, Torgeir Wethal
Literary adviser: Christian Ludvigsen
Performed 220 times in Belgium, Denmark, Finland, France, Holland, Iceland, Italy, Norway, Sweden, Switzerland, West Germany, Yugoslavia

Min Fars Hus (1972–4)
'My Father's House'

Dedicated to Fyodor Dostoyevsky
Actors: Jens Christensen, Ragnar Christiansen, Malou Illmoni, Tage
  Larsen, Else Marie Laukvik, Iben Nagel Rasmussen, Ulrik Skeel,
  Torgeir Wethal
Performed 322 times in Denmark, Finland, France, Italy, Norway, Poland,
  Sweden, Switzerland, West Germany, Yugoslavia

Dansenes Bog (1974–80)
'The Book of Dances'
Actors: Roberta Carreri, Tom Fjordefalk, Elsa Kvamme, Tage Larsen,
  Else Marie Laukvik, Iben Nagel Rasmussen, Odd Strøm, Torgeir
  Wethal
Performed 350 times in Belgium, Denmark, France, Holland, Japan, Italy,
  Norway, Peru, Poland, Spain, Sweden, Venezuela, West Germany,
  Yugoslavia

Come! And the day will be ours (1976–80)
Scenario by Eugenio Barba
Actors: Roberta Carreri, Tom Fjordefalk, Tage Larsen, Else Marie
  Laukvik, Iben Nagel Rasmussen, Torgeir Wethal
Performed 180 times in Belgium, Denmark, France, Holland, Italy,
  Norway, Peru, Poland, Spain, Sweden, Venezuela, West Germany,
  Yugoslavia

Anabasis (1977–84)
'Ascent to the Sea'
Actors: Torben Bjelke, Roberta Carreri, Toni Cots, Tom Fjordefalk, Tage
  Larsen, Else Marie Laukvik, Francis Pardeilhan, Iben Nagel
  Rasmussen, Silvia Ricciardelli, Gustavo Riondet, Ulrik Skeel, Julia
  Varley, Torgeir Wethal
Performed 180 times in Colombia, Denmark, France, French Antilles,
  Italy, Japan, Mexico, Norway, Spain, Sweden, Wales, West Germany

The Million – First Journey (1978–84)
Dedicated to Marco Polo
Actors: Torben Bjelke, Roberta Carreri, Toni Cots, Tom Fjordefalk, Tage
  Larsen, Else Marie Laukvik, Francis Pardeilhan, Gustavo Riondet,
  Ulrik Skeel, Julia Varley, Torgeir Wethal
Performed 223 times in Belgium, Colombia, Denmark, France, French
  Antilles, Israel, Italy, Japan, Mexico, Norway, Poland, Spain, Sweden,
  USA, Wales, West Germany

Brechts Aske (1980–2), *Brechts Aske 2* (1982–4)
'Brecht's Ashes'
Dedicated to Jens Björneboe
Text by Eugenio Barba

The first version (1980) was based on poems by Bertolt Brecht. A year later, the author's heirs refused permission for further use of these texts. The second version returns to Brecht's sources of inspiration: Chinese poetry and medieval ballads, as well as works by his contemporaries, such as Tucholski and Mühsam.

Actors: Roberta Carreri, Toni Cots, Tage Larsen, Francis Pardeilhan, Iben Nagel Rasmussen, Silvia Ricciardelli, Ulrik Skeel, Julia Varley, Torgeir Wethal

Performed 166 times in Colombia, Denmark, France, Israel, Italy, Mexico, Norway, Poland, Spain, Sweden, USA, West Germany

Oxyrhincus Evangeliet (1985-7)
'The Gospel according to Oxyrhincus'
Text by Eugenio Barba
Actors: Roberta Carreri, Tage Larsen, Else Marie Laukvik, Francis Pardeilhan, Julia Varley, Torgeir Wethal
Scenic arrangement: Luca Ruzza and Odin Teatret
Costumes: Lena Bjerregaard
Assistant director: Christoph Falke
Performed 214 times in Argentina, Austria, Denmark, France, Hungary, Italy, Mexico, Norway, Sweden, Uruguay, West Germany, Yugoslavia

Judith (1987-)
Dedicated to Renée Saurel, Natsu and the woman in the Mei Lan-Fan Club.
Text by Eugenio Barba and Roberta Carreri
Actor: Roberta Carreri
Performed about 200 times in Canada, Chile, Cuba, Denmark, France, Great Britain, Ireland, Italy, Norway, Peru, Poland, Spain, Sweden, West Germany, Yugoslavia

Talabot (1988-91)
Dedicated to Christian Ludvigsen and Hans Martin Berg
Text by Eugenio Barba
Actors: César Brie, Jan Ferslev, Richard Fowler, Naira Gonzales, Falk Henrich, Iben Nagel Rasmussen, Isabel Ubeda, Julia Varley, Torgeir Wethal
Autobiographical and anthropological material: Kirsten Hastrup
Costumes: Lena Bjerregaard
Masks: Klaus Tams and Odin Teatret
Adviser: Ferdinando Taviani
Assistant director: César Brie
Performed about 280 times in Austria, Chile, Denmark, France, Italy, Norway, Peru, Sweden, Switzerland, West Germany, Yugoslavia

Rum i kejserens palads (1985–)
'Rooms in the Emperor's Palace'
Actors: Lena Bjerregaard, César Brie, Roberta Carreri, Jan Ferslev, Richard Fowler, Naira Gonzales, Falk Henrich, Iben Nagel Rasmussen, Isabel Ubeda, Julia Varley, Torgeir Wethal
Performed about 25 times in Chile, Denmark, Mexico, Peru.

Traces in the Snow (1989–)
(An actor's professional autobiography)
Actor: Roberta Carreri

Memoria (1990–)
Text/montage by Else Marie Laukvik and Eugenio Barba
Actor: Else Marie Laukvik
Music: Frans Winther
Performed about 74 times

The Castle of Holstebro
Text/montage by Julia Varley and Eugenio Barba
Actor: Julia Varley
Musical arrangement: Jan Ferslev

The Ecco of Silence (1991–)
(A voice-demonstration)
Actor: Julia Varley

Itsi-Bitsi (1991–)
Dedicated to Eik Skalø
Text/montage by Iben Nagel Rasmussen and Eugenio Barba
Actors: Iben Nagel Rasmussen with Kai Bredholt and Jan Ferslev
Musical arrangement: Kai Bredholt and Jan Ferslev

Waterways/Klanbauterpeople (Holstebro, September 1991)
Assistant director: Leo Sykes
Actors: Kai Bredholt, Roberta Carreri, Jan Ferslev, Richard Fowler, Falk Henrich, Hisako Miura, Tina Nielsen, Iben Nagel Rasmussen, Isabel Ubeda, Julia Varley, Torgeir Wethal

PRODUCTIONS UNDER *NORDISK TEATERLABORATORIUM*

Moon and Darkness (1979–) (Farfa)
(A performance about the actor's training)
Director: Eugenio Barba
Actor: Iben Nagel Rasmussen

214

Wounded by the Wind (1983) (Farfa)
Director: Iben Nagel Rasmussen
Actors: Dolly Albertin, Tove Bornhoft, César Brie, Marta Orbis, Daniela
  Piccari, Iben Nagel Rasmussen, Pepe Robledo, Isobel Soto

The Romance of Oedipus (1984–)
Director: Eugenio Barba
Actor: Toni Cots

Marriage With God (1984–90)
Dedicated to J. and S.
Textual montage and direction: Eugenio Barba
Actors: César Brie and Iben Nagel Rasmussen

Wait for the Dawn (1985–) (the Canada Project)
Direction: Richard Fowler
Actor: Richard Fowler

The Land of Nod (1985–90) (Farfa)
Dedicated to Julian Beck
Text and direction: César Brie, Iben Nagel Rasmussen
Actors: César Brie, Iben Nagel Rasmussen

Ulven Denis (1987–) (Odin Teatret's Children's Theatre)
Director: César Brie
Actors: Lena Bjerregaard, Roberta Carreri, Anna Lica, Tina Nielsen,
  Frans Winther
Performed 200 times

Tristan and Isolde (1989 –91) (Odin Teatret's Children's Theatre)
Text and music: Frans Winther
Directors: Tage Larsen, Catherin Poher, Tom Nagel Rasmussen
Actors: Lena Bjerregaard, Max Olsen, Frans Winther
Performed 85 times

FILM AND VIDEO

Physical Training at Odin Teatret
Director: Torgeir Wethal (1972)
The Odin's physical training is shown with a commentary by Eugenio
  Barba. The film shows the evolution of physical training from collec-
  tively learned skills to the actor's individualization of exercises.

Vocal Training at Odin Teatret
Director: Torgeir Wethal (1972)
The film focuses on the Odin's use of text as vocal action. It includes work
  with various body resonators, exercises which engage the voice as an

extension of the body, and vocal improvisations based on a personal stream of associations.

In Search of Theatre (1974)
Director: L. Ripa di Meana
Production: RAI

Theatre as barter (1974)
The film shows Odin Teatret in Carpignano, southern Italy, an isolated community with no previous experience of theatre.

Theatre Meets Ritual
Producer: Kurare
The film shows barters in Kuriepe, a Venezuelan village, and with the Yanomami, an Indian tribe of the Upper Orinoco in Amazonia (1976)

On the Two Banks of the River
Director: Torgeir Wethal
In 1978 Odin Teatret travelled to Peru. The film, which shows how Odin Teatret managed to perform there and make contact with the people in spite of the restrictive conditions, is essentially about the strategy of insubordination by means of theatre.

Ascent to the Sea
Director: Torgeir Wethal
The film follows *Anabasis* in Peru, 1978.

Vestita di Bianco
'Dressed in White'
Director: Torgeir Wethal (1974)
The actress Iben Nagel Rasmussen in her journey passes through a southern Italian village arousing diffident curiosity and fleeting moments of companionship.

Ferai
Director: Marianne Ahrne
A film version of *Ferai* (1969)

The Million
A film version of *The Million* (1979)

Moon and Darkness
Iben Nagel Rasmussen shows and explains her work method from training to performance.

In the Beginning Was the Idea
Director: Torgeir Wethal
A film version of *Oxyrhincus Evangeliet* (1987)

Corporal Mime
Director: Torgeir Wethal
Yves Lebreton demonstrates the training programme evolved by Etienne Decroux.

Training at Grotowski's 'Laboratorium' in Wroclaw
Director: Torgeir Wethal
The physical and plastic exercises developed by Jerzy Grotowski are demonstrated by his actor Ryszard Cieslak.

On the Way through Theatre
Director: Erik Exe Christoffersen
The story of Odin Teatret is told by Eugenio Barba and through glimpses of the different productions (1992).

OTHER COLLABORATORS

Other collaborators at Odin Teatret since 1964 are: Judy Barba, Leif Bech, Hans Martin Berg, Peter Bysted, Mona Christensen, Ragner Christiansen, Bernard Colin, Kim Dagen, Berit S. Duusgaard, Peter Elsass, Jerzy Grotowski, Hanne Birgitte Jensen, Lis Jensen, Dorthe Kærgaard, Søren Kjems, Bente Knudsen, Knud Erik Knudsen, Christian Ludvigsen, Giancarlo Marchesini, Dag Aakeson Moe, Heidi Mogensen, Per Moth, Reidar Nilsson, Karl Olsen, Poul Östergaard, Toril Øyen, Simon Panduro, Grethe Pedersen, Sigrid Post, Carita Rindell, Pushparajah Sinnathamby, Rina Skeel, Agnete Ström, Odd Ström, Ferdinando Taviani, Jan Torp, Katherine Winkelhorn, Walter Ybema.

INDEX